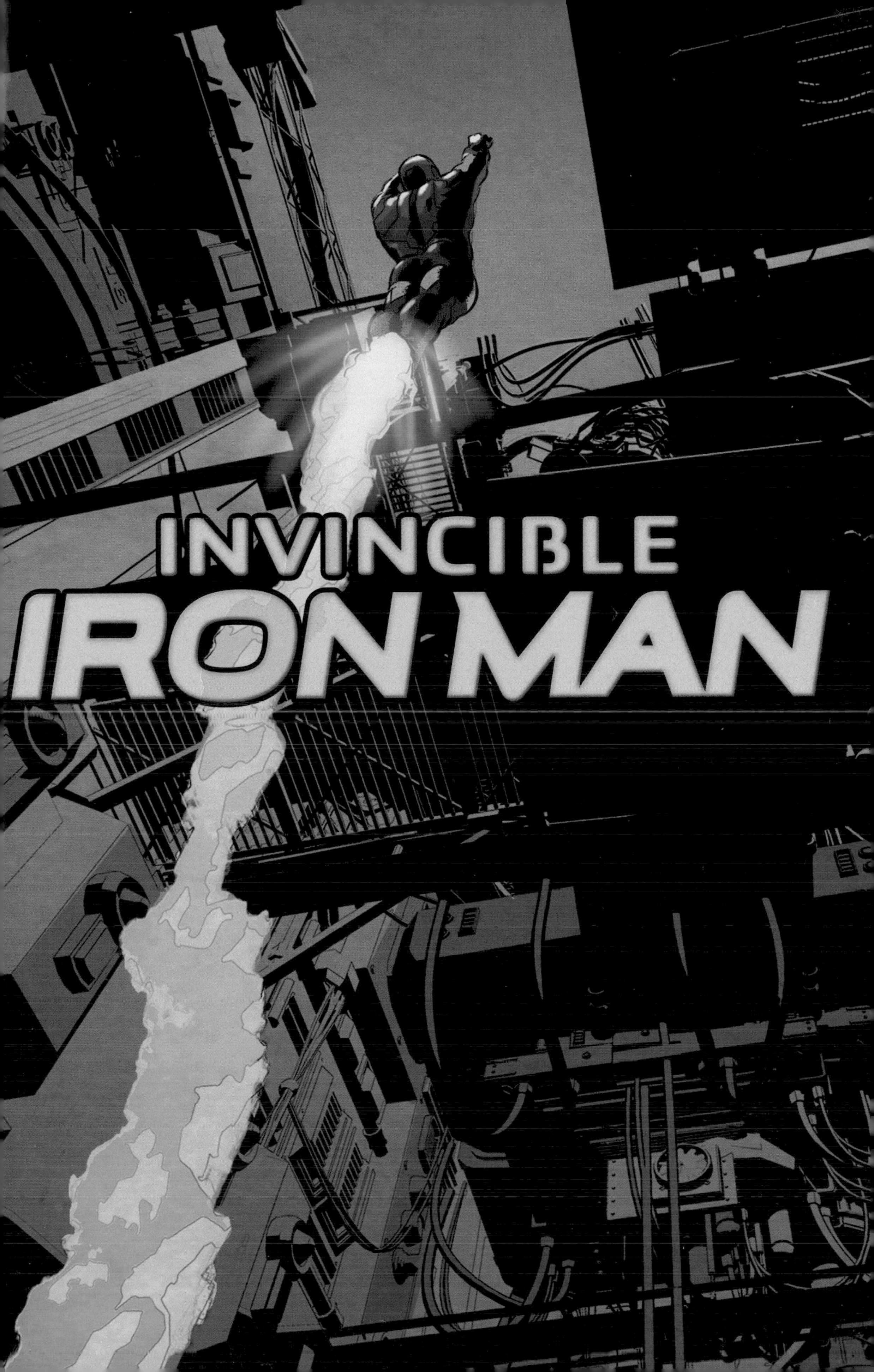
INVINCIBLE
IRON MAN

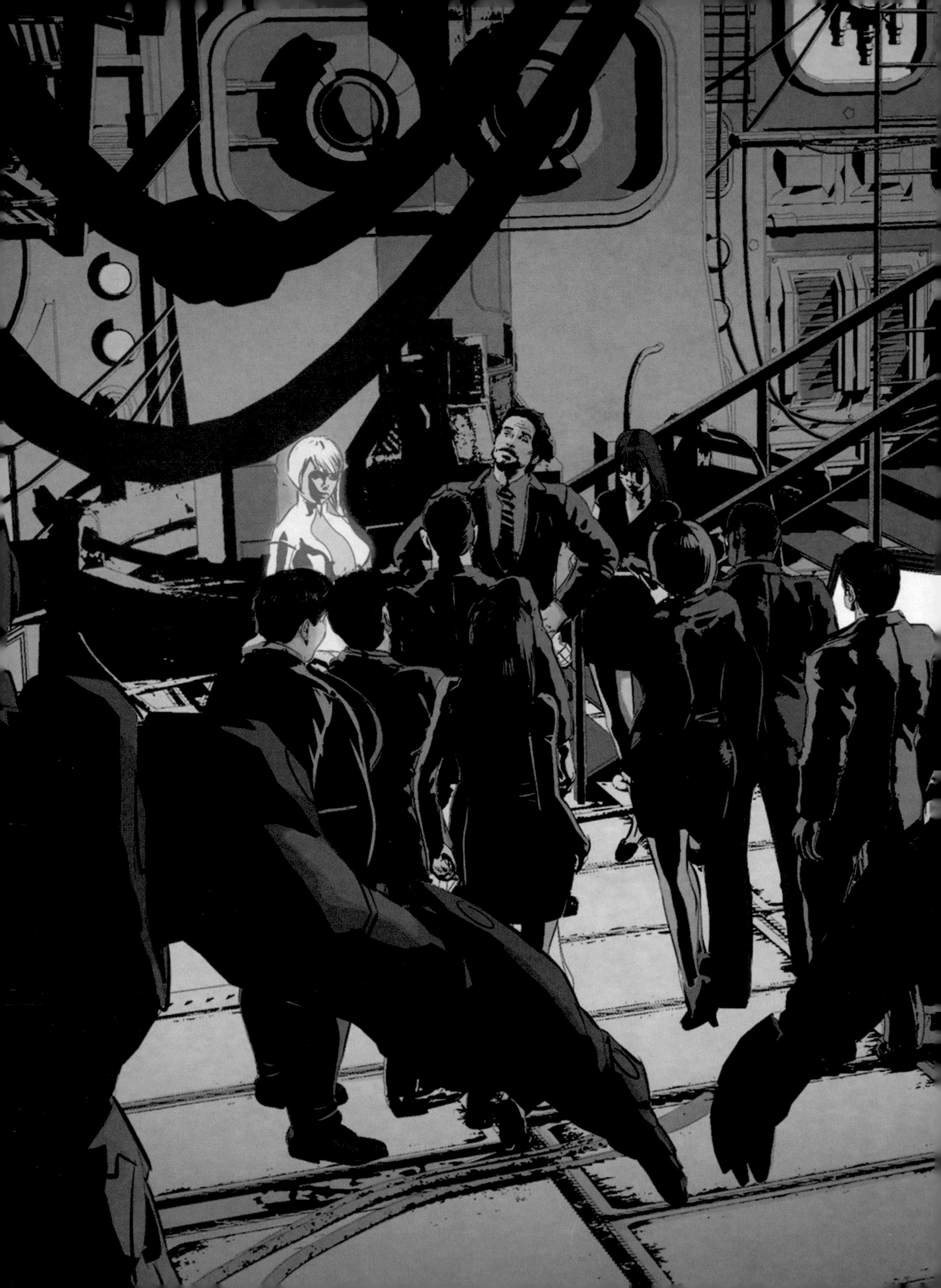

BILLIONAIRE PLAYBOY AND GENIUS INDUSTRIALIST TONY STARK WAS KIDNAPPED DURING A ROUTINE WEAPONS TEST. HIS CAPTORS ATTEMPTED TO FORCE HIM TO BUILD A WEAPON OF MASS DESTRUCTION. INSTEAD HE CREATED A POWERED SUIT OF ARMOR THAT SAVED HIS LIFE. FROM THAT DAY ON, HE USED THE SUIT TO PROTECT THE WORLD AS THE...

INVINCIBLE IRON MAN

CIVIL WAR II

BRIAN MICHAEL BENDIS
WRITER

MIKE DEODATO JR.
ARTIST

FRANK MARTIN
COLOR ARTIST

VC's CLAYTON COWLES
LETTERER

MIKE DEODATO JR. & FRANK MARTIN (#12-13) **AND DALE KEOWN & JASON KEITH** (#14)
COVER ART

ALANNA SMITH
ASSISTANT EDITOR

TOM BREVOORT
EDITOR

IRON MAN CREATED BY STAN LEE, LARRY LIEBER, DON HECK & JACK KIRBY

COLLECTION EDITOR: **JENNIFER GRÜNWALD**
ASSISTANT EDITOR: **CAITLIN O'CONNELL**
ASSOCIATE MANAGING EDITOR: **KATERI WOODY**
EDITOR, SPECIAL PROJECTS: **MARK D. BEAZLEY**
VP PRODUCTION & SPECIAL PROJECTS: **JEFF YOUNGQUIST**
SVP PRINT, SALES & MARKETING: **DAVID GABRIEL**
BOOK DESIGNER: **JAY BOWEN**

EDITOR IN CHIEF: **AXEL ALONSO**
CHIEF CREATIVE OFFICER: **JOE QUESADA**
PUBLISHER: **DAN BUCKLEY**
EXECUTIVE PRODUCER: **ALAN FINE**

INVINCIBLE IRON MAN VOL. 3: CIVIL WAR II. Contains material originally published in magazine form as INVINCIBLE IRON MAN #12-14 and MIGHTY AVENGERS #9-11. First printing 2017. ISBN# 978-1-302-90320-6. Published by MARVEL WORLDWIDE, INC., a subsidiary of MARVEL ENTERTAINMENT, LLC. OFFICE OF PUBLICATION: 135 West 50th Street, New York, NY 10020. Copyright © 2017 MARVEL No similarity between any of the names, characters, persons, and/or institutions in this magazine with those of any living or dead person or institution is intended, and any such similarity which may exist is purely coincidental. Printed in the U.S.A. ALAN FINE, President, Marvel Entertainment; DAN BUCKLEY, President, TV, Publishing & Brand Management; JOE QUESADA, Chief Creative Officer; TOM BREVOORT, SVP of Publishing; DAVID BOGART, SVP of Business Affairs & Operations, Publishing & Partnership; C.B. CEBULSKI, VP of Brand Management & Development, Asia; DAVID GABRIEL, SVP of Sales & Marketing, Publishing; JEFF YOUNGQUIST, VP of Production & Special Projects; DAN CARR, Executive Director of Publishing Technology; ALEX MORALES, Director of Publishing Operations; SUSAN CRESPI, Production Manager; STAN LEE, Chairman Emeritus. For information regarding advertising in Marvel Comics or on Marvel.com, please contact Vit DeBellis, Integrated Sales Manager, at vdebellis@marvel.com. For Marvel subscription inquiries, please call 888-511-5480. Manufactured between 12/9/2016 and 1/23/2017 by LSC COMMUNICATIONS INC., SALEM, VA, USA.

10 9 8 7 6 5 4 3 2 1

FRIDAY'S LOG:

RECENTLY COMPLETED AGENDA ITEMS:

- FAKE YOUR OWN DEATH TO INFILTRATE A JAPANESE TERRORIST CELL.

- KIDNAP THE NEW INHUMAN KNOWN AS ULYSSES WHO CLAIMS HE CAN SEE THE FUTURE AND FIND OUT HOW HE DOES IT.

IN-PROGRESS AGENDA ITEMS:

- APOLOGIZE TO YOUR INVESTORS AND AMARA FOR FAKING YOUR OWN DEATH.

- RESPOND TO PRESS CONCERNS THAT YOU'RE PLANNING TO START A WAR WITH CAPTAIN MARVEL OVER ULYSSES.

- TALK TO SOMEONE ABOUT RHODEY'S DEATH BEFORE YOU DO SOMETHING STUPID (I MEAN IT, TONY).

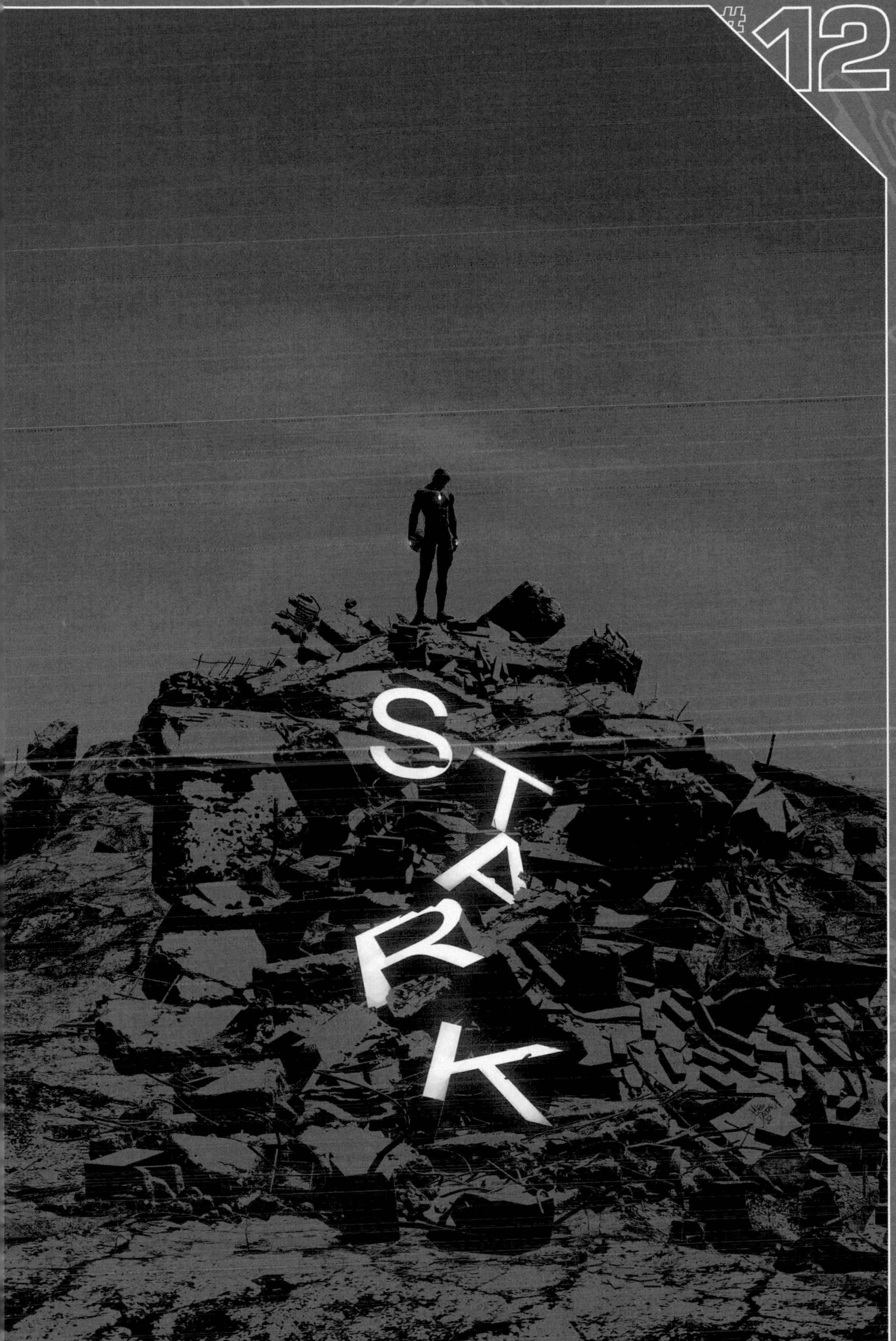
#12
STARK

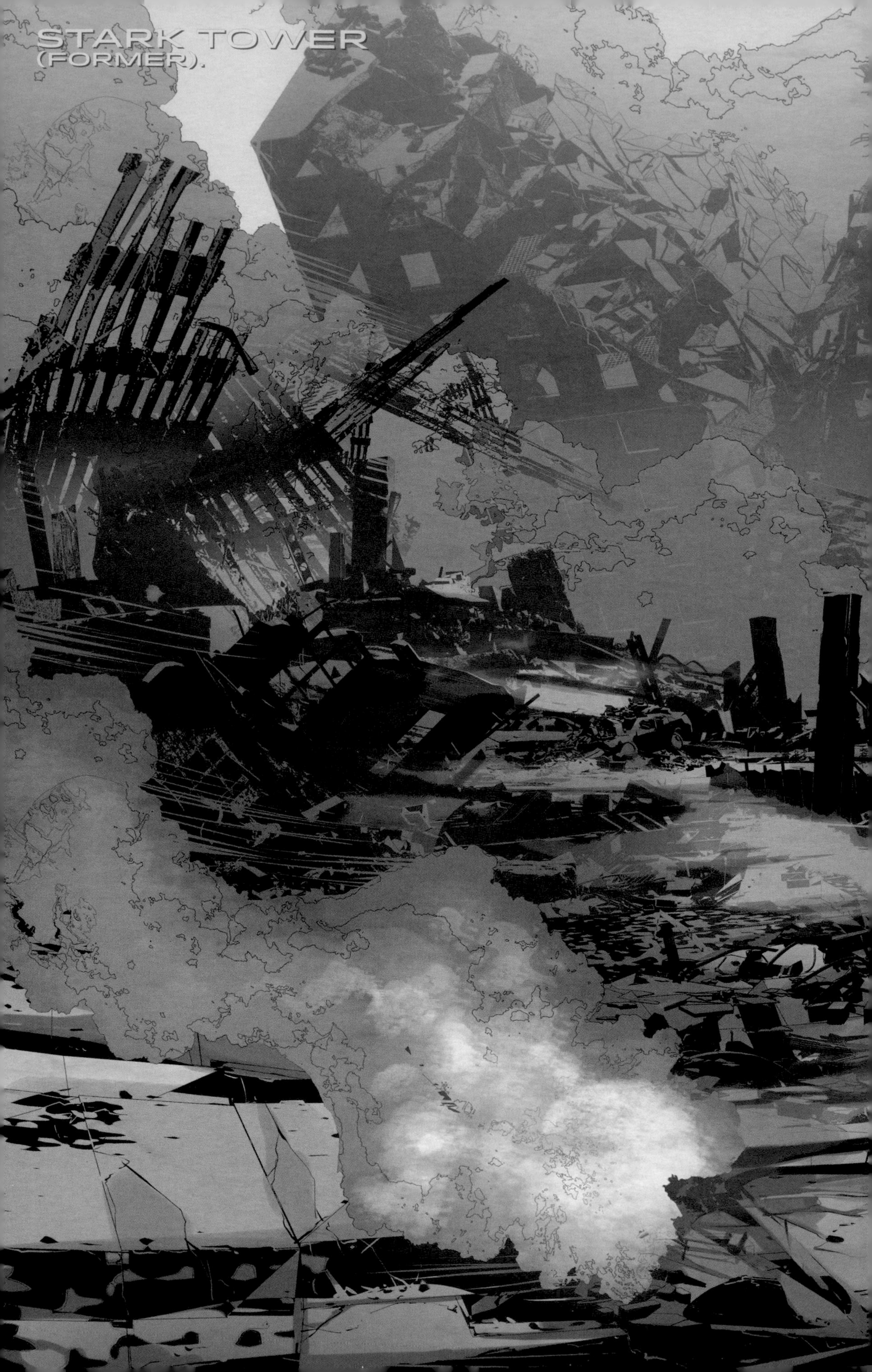
STARK TOWER
(FORMER).

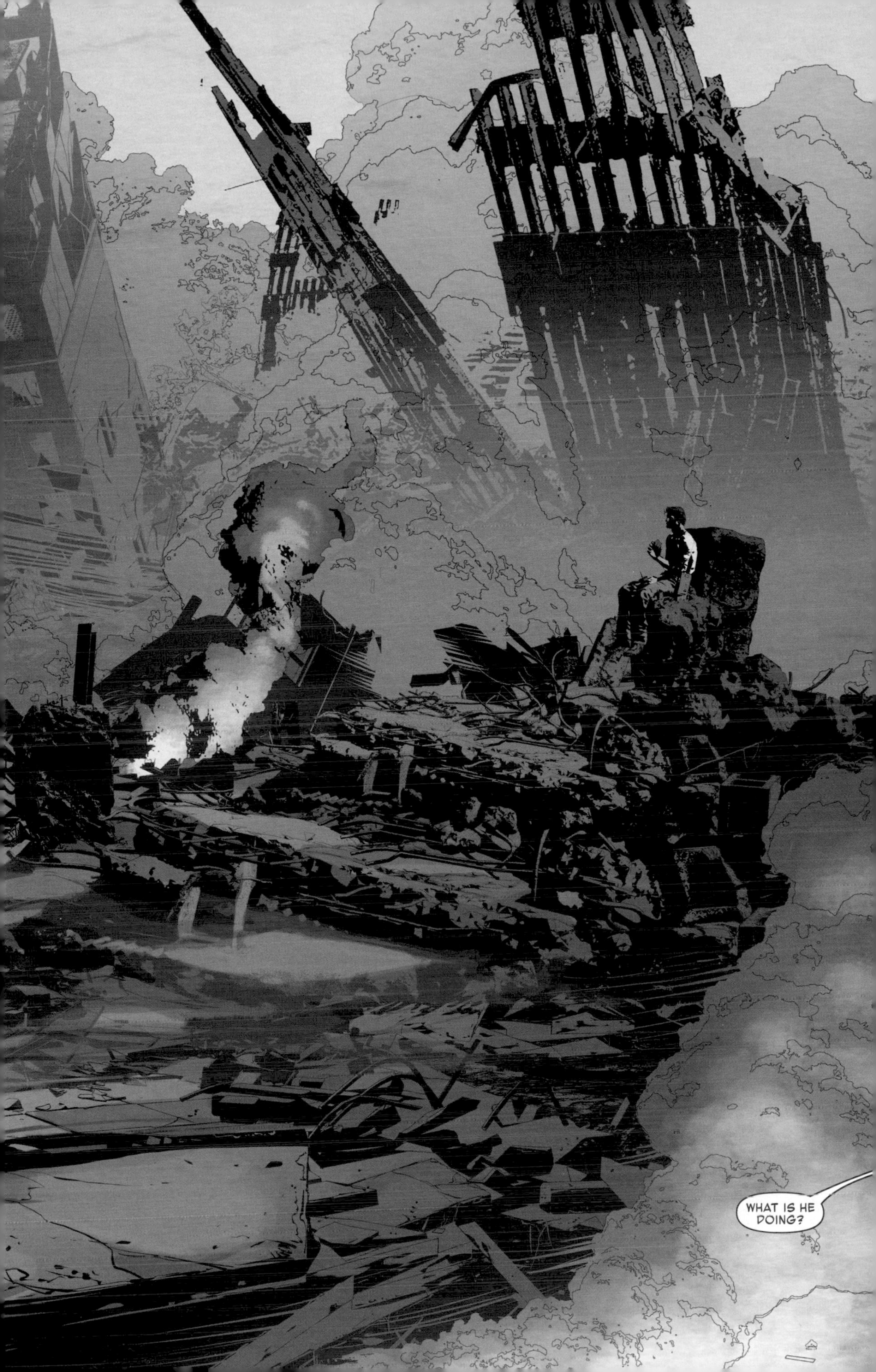
WHAT IS HE DOING?

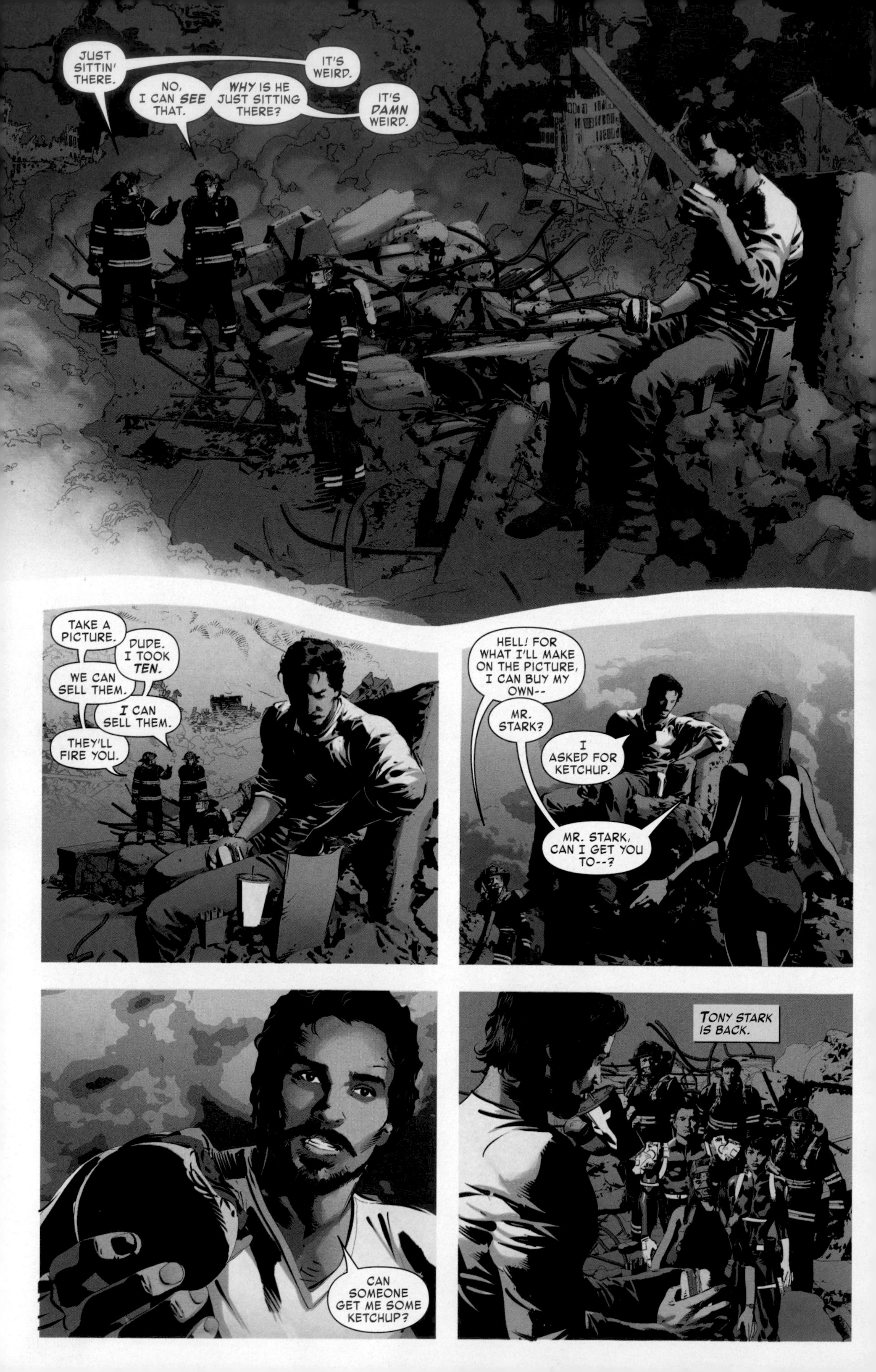

JUST SITTIN' THERE.
IT'S WEIRD.
NO, I CAN SEE THAT.
WHY IS HE JUST SITTING THERE?
IT'S DAMN WEIRD.
TAKE A PICTURE.
DUDE. I TOOK TEN.
WE CAN SELL THEM.
I CAN SELL THEM.
THEY'LL FIRE YOU.
HELL! FOR WHAT I'LL MAKE ON THE PICTURE, I CAN BUY MY OWN--
MR. STARK?
I ASKED FOR KETCHUP.
MR. STARK, CAN I GET YOU TO--?
CAN SOMEONE GET ME SOME KETCHUP?
TONY STARK IS BACK.

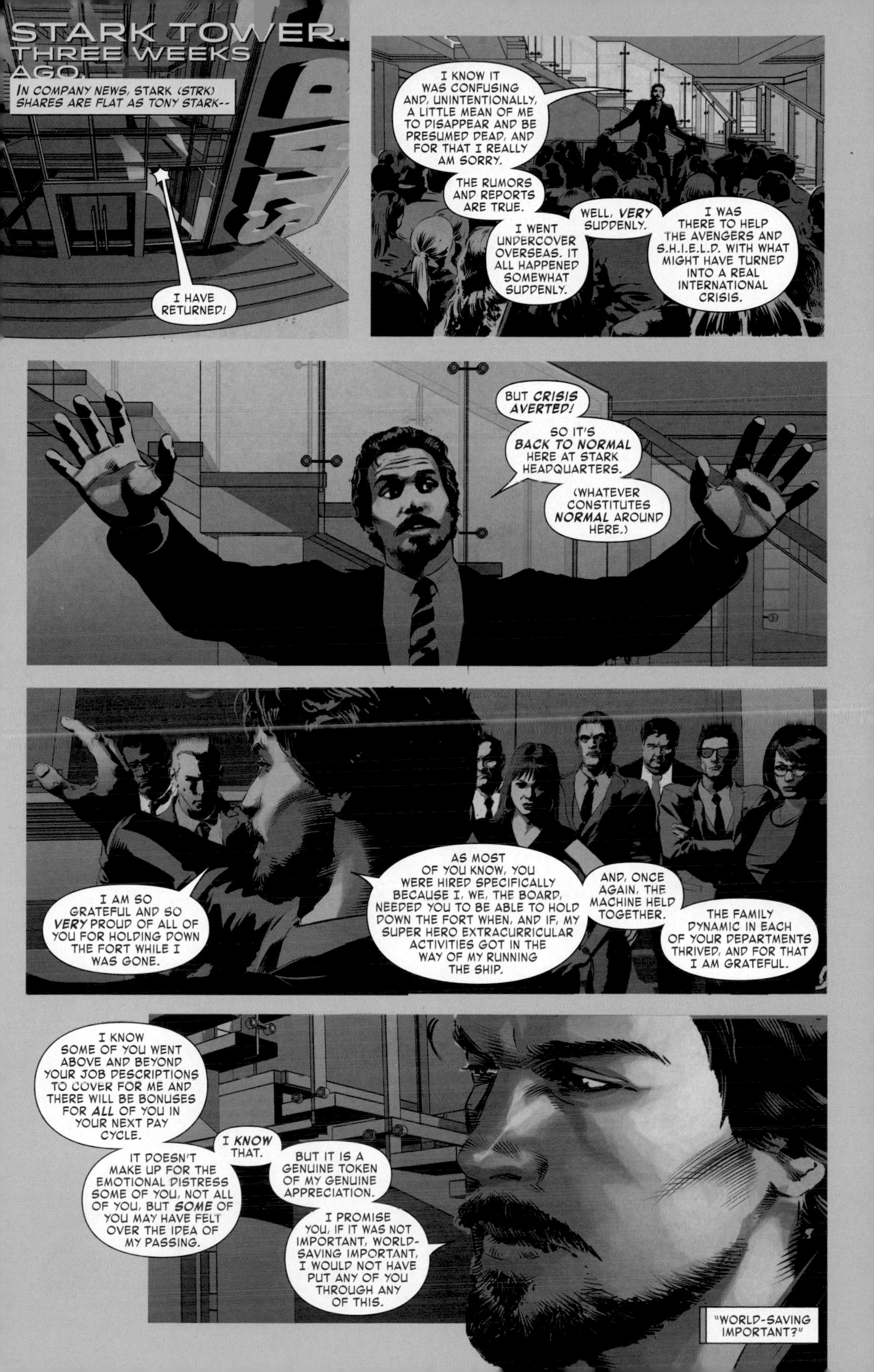
STARK TOWER. THREE WEEKS AGO.
IN COMPANY NEWS, STARK (STRK) SHARES ARE FLAT AS TONY STARK--
I HAVE RETURNED!
I KNOW IT WAS CONFUSING AND, UNINTENTIONALLY, A LITTLE MEAN OF ME TO DISAPPEAR AND BE PRESUMED DEAD, AND FOR THAT I REALLY AM SORRY.
THE RUMORS AND REPORTS ARE TRUE.
I WENT UNDERCOVER OVERSEAS. IT ALL HAPPENED SOMEWHAT SUDDENLY.
WELL, VERY SUDDENLY.
I WAS THERE TO HELP THE AVENGERS AND S.H.I.E.L.D. WITH WHAT MIGHT HAVE TURNED INTO A REAL INTERNATIONAL CRISIS.
BUT CRISIS AVERTED!
SO IT'S BACK TO NORMAL HERE AT STARK HEADQUARTERS.
(WHATEVER CONSTITUTES NORMAL AROUND HERE.)
I AM SO GRATEFUL AND SO VERY PROUD OF ALL OF YOU FOR HOLDING DOWN THE FORT WHILE I WAS GONE.
AS MOST OF YOU KNOW, YOU WERE HIRED SPECIFICALLY BECAUSE I, WE, THE BOARD, NEEDED YOU TO BE ABLE TO HOLD DOWN THE FORT WHEN, AND IF, MY SUPER HERO EXTRACURRICULAR ACTIVITIES GOT IN THE WAY OF MY RUNNING THE SHIP.
AND, ONCE AGAIN, THE MACHINE HELD TOGETHER.
THE FAMILY DYNAMIC IN EACH OF YOUR DEPARTMENTS THRIVED, AND FOR THAT I AM GRATEFUL.
I KNOW SOME OF YOU WENT ABOVE AND BEYOND YOUR JOB DESCRIPTIONS TO COVER FOR ME AND THERE WILL BE BONUSES FOR ALL OF YOU IN YOUR NEXT PAY CYCLE.
IT DOESN'T MAKE UP FOR THE EMOTIONAL DISTRESS SOME OF YOU, NOT ALL OF YOU, BUT SOME OF YOU MAY HAVE FELT OVER THE IDEA OF MY PASSING.
I KNOW THAT.
BUT IT IS A GENUINE TOKEN OF MY GENUINE APPRECIATION.
I PROMISE YOU, IF IT WAS NOT IMPORTANT, WORLD-SAVING IMPORTANT, I WOULD NOT HAVE PUT ANY OF YOU THROUGH ANY OF THIS.
"WORLD-SAVING IMPORTANT?"

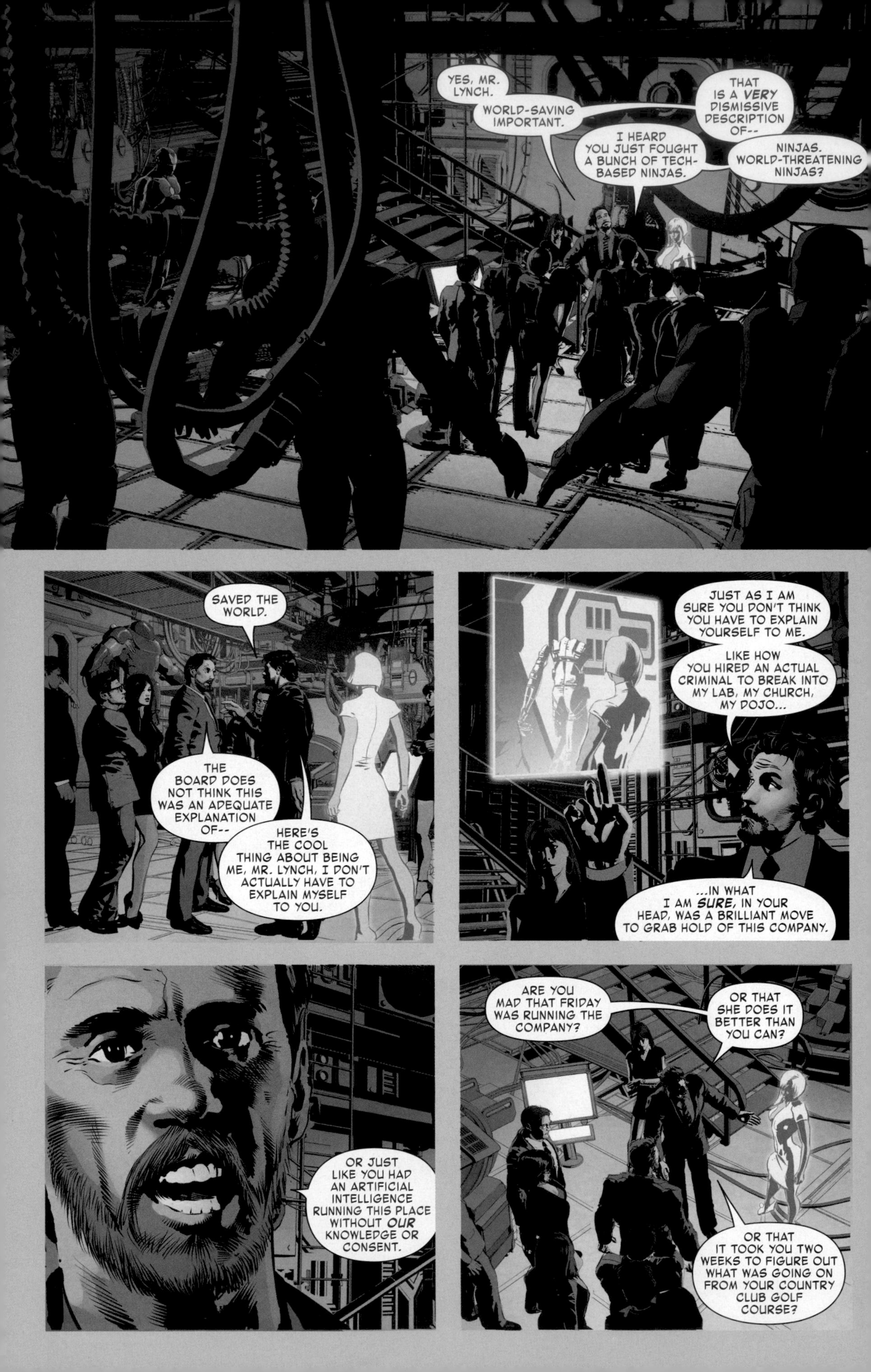
YES, MR. LYNCH.
WORLD-SAVING IMPORTANT.
THAT IS A VERY DISMISSIVE DESCRIPTION OF--
I HEARD YOU JUST FOUGHT A BUNCH OF TECH-BASED NINJAS.
NINJAS. WORLD-THREATENING NINJAS?
SAVED THE WORLD.
THE BOARD DOES NOT THINK THIS WAS AN ADEQUATE EXPLANATION OF--
HERE'S THE COOL THING ABOUT BEING ME, MR. LYNCH, I DON'T ACTUALLY HAVE TO EXPLAIN MYSELF TO YOU.
JUST AS I AM SURE YOU DON'T THINK YOU HAVE TO EXPLAIN YOURSELF TO ME.
LIKE HOW YOU HIRED AN ACTUAL CRIMINAL TO BREAK INTO MY LAB, MY CHURCH, MY DOJO...
...IN WHAT I AM SURE, IN YOUR HEAD, WAS A BRILLIANT MOVE TO GRAB HOLD OF THIS COMPANY.
OR JUST LIKE YOU HAD AN ARTIFICIAL INTELLIGENCE RUNNING THIS PLACE WITHOUT OUR KNOWLEDGE OR CONSENT.
ARE YOU MAD THAT FRIDAY WAS RUNNING THE COMPANY?
OR THAT SHE DOES IT BETTER THAN YOU CAN?
OR THAT IT TOOK YOU TWO WEEKS TO FIGURE OUT WHAT WAS GOING ON FROM YOUR COUNTRY CLUB GOLF COURSE?

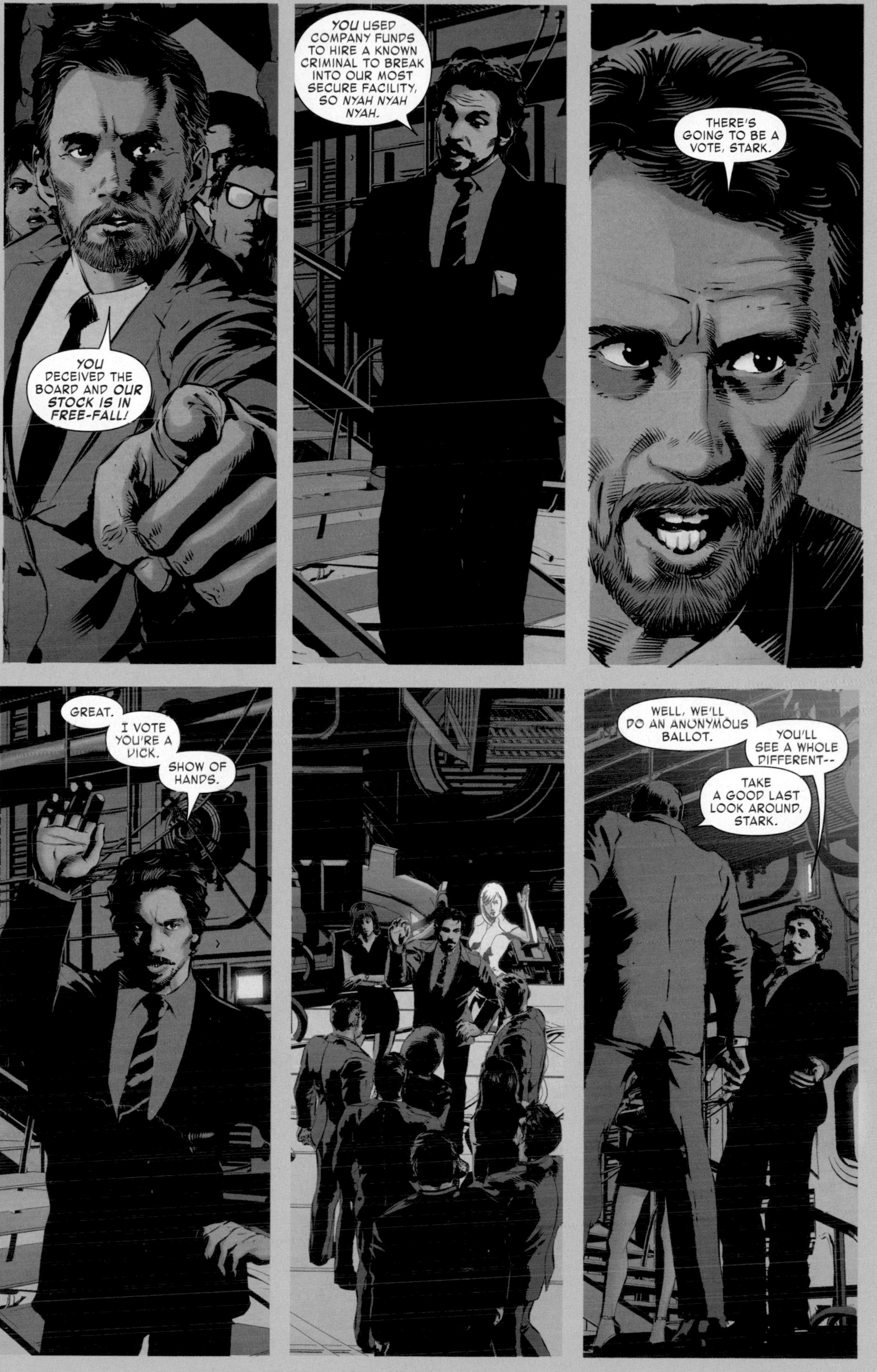
YOU DECEIVED THE BOARD AND OUR STOCK IS IN FREE-FALL!
YOU USED COMPANY FUNDS TO HIRE A KNOWN CRIMINAL TO BREAK INTO OUR MOST SECURE FACILITY, SO NYAH NYAH NYAH.
THERE'S GOING TO BE A VOTE, STARK.
GREAT.
I VOTE YOU'RE A DICK.
SHOW OF HANDS.
WELL, WE'LL DO AN ANONYMOUS BALLOT.
YOU'LL SEE A WHOLE DIFFERENT--
TAKE A GOOD LAST LOOK AROUND, STARK.

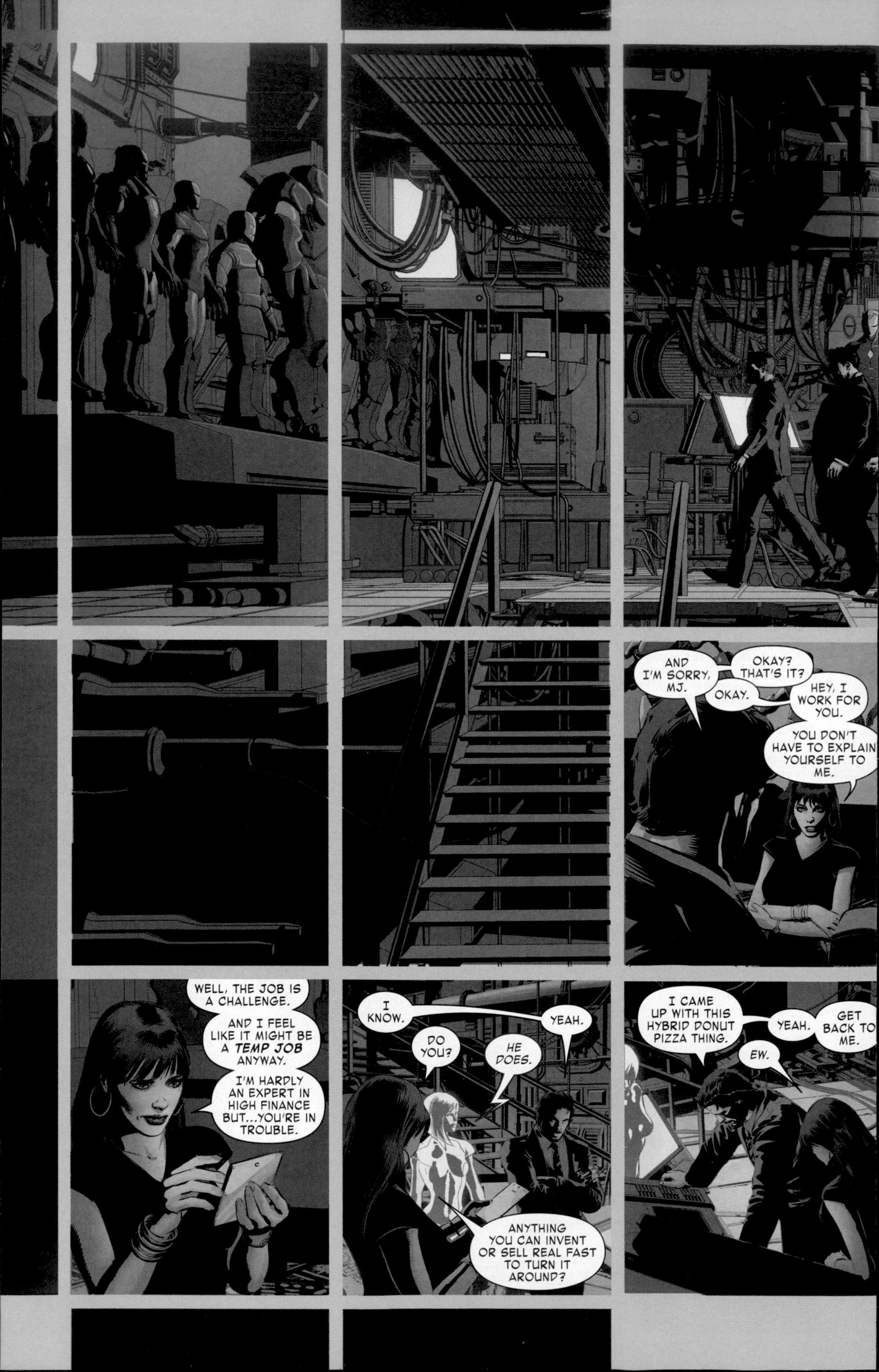
AND I'M SORRY, MJ.
OKAY? THAT'S IT?
OKAY.
HEY, I WORK FOR YOU.
YOU DON'T HAVE TO EXPLAIN YOURSELF TO ME.
WELL, THE JOB IS A CHALLENGE.
AND I FEEL LIKE IT MIGHT BE A TEMP JOB ANYWAY.
I'M HARDLY AN EXPERT IN HIGH FINANCE BUT...YOU'RE IN TROUBLE.
I KNOW.
YEAH.
DO YOU?
HE DOES.
ANYTHING YOU CAN INVENT OR SELL REAL FAST TO TURN IT AROUND?
I CAME UP WITH THIS HYBRID DONUT PIZZA THING.
YEAH.
GET BACK TO ME.
EW.

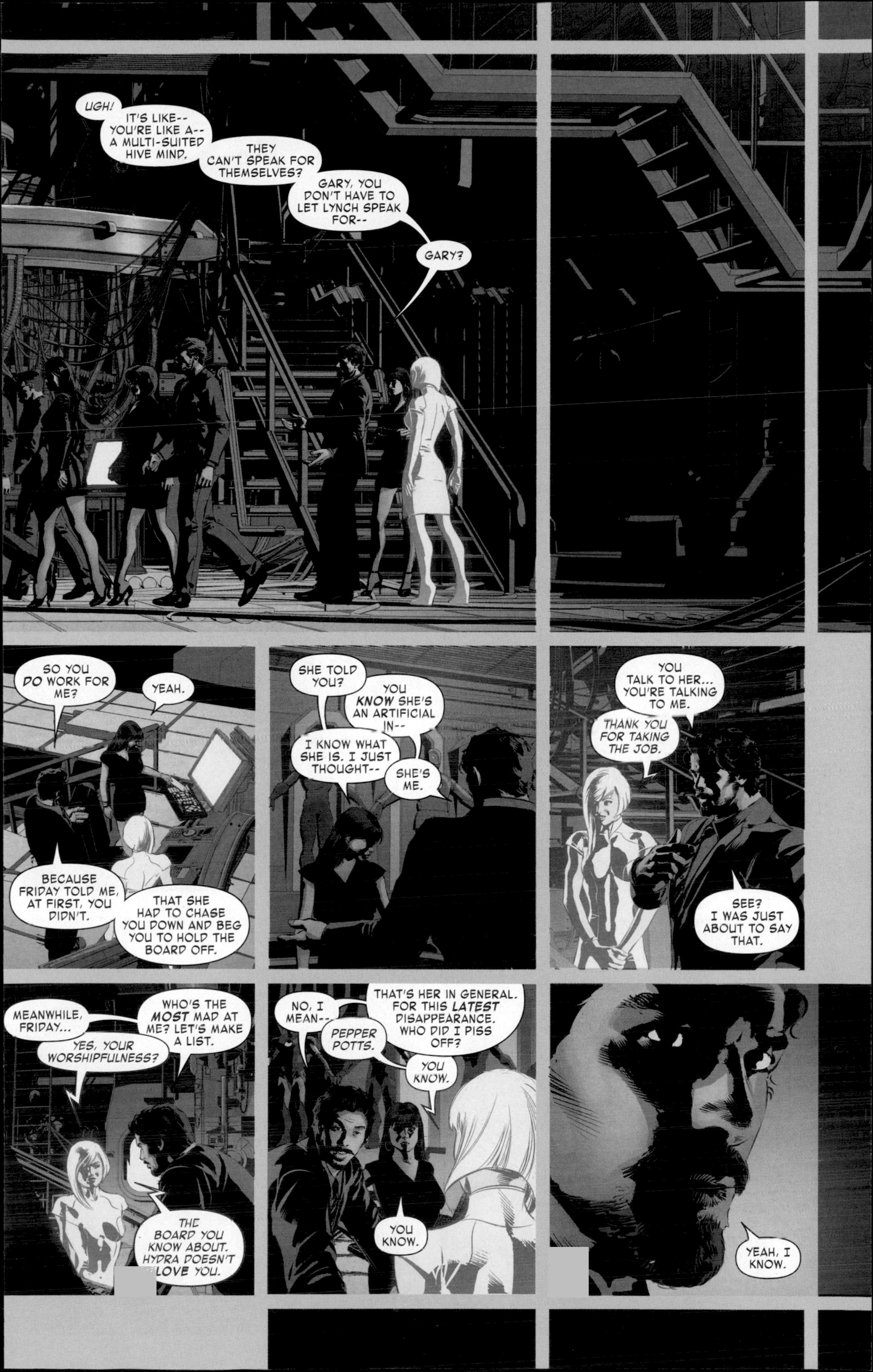
UGH!
IT'S LIKE-- YOU'RE LIKE A-- A MULTI-SUITED HIVE MIND.
THEY CAN'T SPEAK FOR THEMSELVES?
GARY, YOU DON'T HAVE TO LET LYNCH SPEAK FOR--
GARY?
SO YOU DO WORK FOR ME?
YEAH.
BECAUSE FRIDAY TOLD ME, AT FIRST, YOU DIDN'T.
THAT SHE HAD TO CHASE YOU DOWN AND BEG YOU TO HOLD THE BOARD OFF.
SHE TOLD YOU?
YOU KNOW SHE'S AN ARTIFICIAL IN--
I KNOW WHAT SHE IS. I JUST THOUGHT--
SHE'S ME.
YOU TALK TO HER... YOU'RE TALKING TO ME.
THANK YOU FOR TAKING THE JOB.
SEE? I WAS JUST ABOUT TO SAY THAT.
MEANWHILE, FRIDAY...
YES, YOUR WORSHIPFULNESS?
WHO'S THE MOST MAD AT ME? LET'S MAKE A LIST.
THE BOARD YOU KNOW ABOUT. HYDRA DOESN'T LOVE YOU.
NO, I MEAN--
PEPPER POTTS.
THAT'S HER IN GENERAL. FOR THIS LATEST DISAPPEARANCE. WHO DID I PISS OFF?
YOU KNOW.
YOU KNOW.
YEAH, I KNOW.

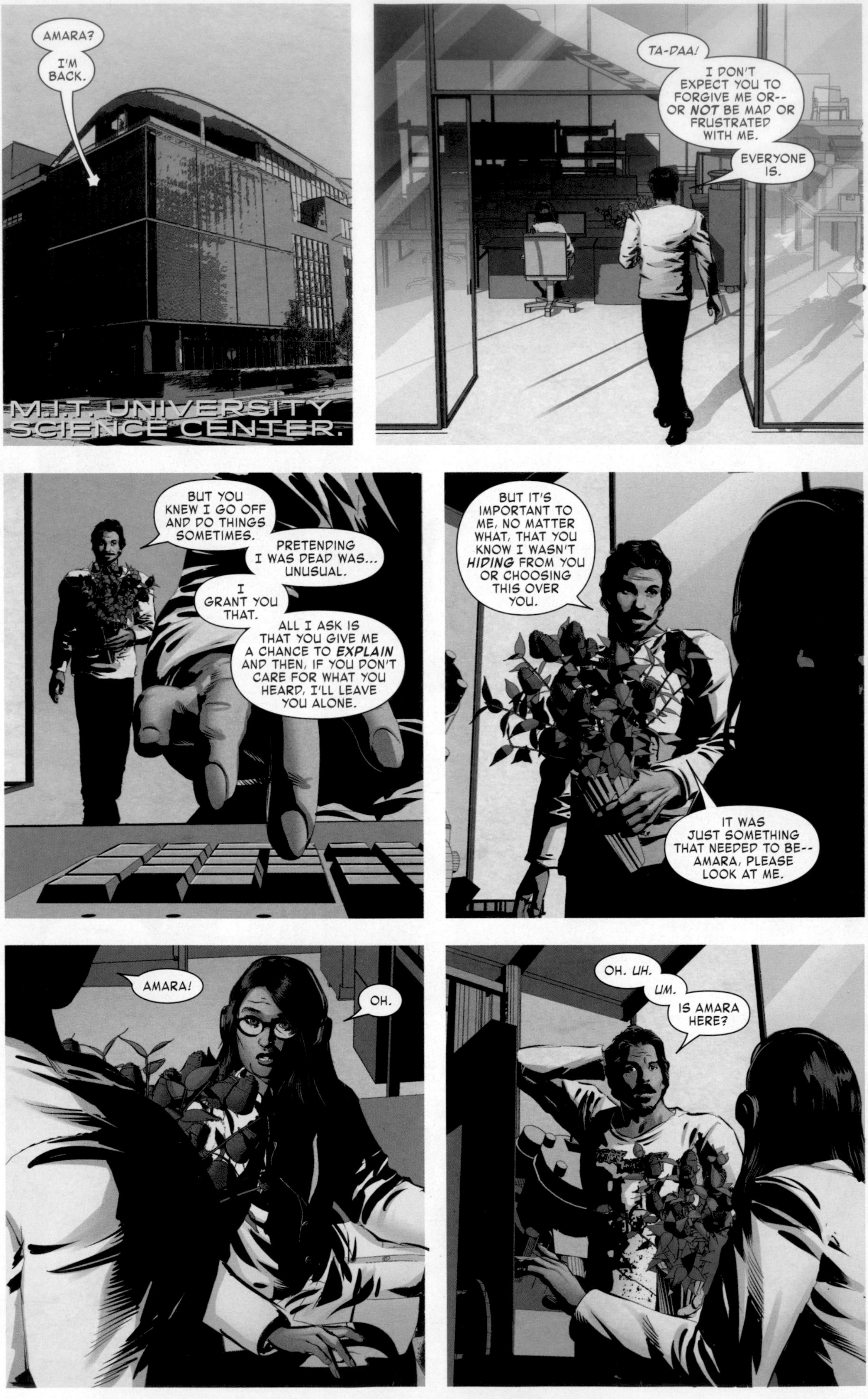
AMARA?
I'M BACK.
M.I.T. UNIVERSITY SCIENCE CENTER.
TA-DAA!
I DON'T EXPECT YOU TO FORGIVE ME OR-- OR NOT BE MAD OR FRUSTRATED WITH ME.
EVERYONE IS.
BUT YOU KNEW I GO OFF AND DO THINGS SOMETIMES.
PRETENDING I WAS DEAD WAS... UNUSUAL.
I GRANT YOU THAT.
ALL I ASK IS THAT YOU GIVE ME A CHANCE TO EXPLAIN AND THEN, IF YOU DON'T CARE FOR WHAT YOU HEARD, I'LL LEAVE YOU ALONE.
BUT IT'S IMPORTANT TO ME, NO MATTER WHAT, THAT YOU KNOW I WASN'T HIDING FROM YOU OR CHOOSING THIS OVER YOU.
IT WAS JUST SOMETHING THAT NEEDED TO BE-- AMARA, PLEASE LOOK AT ME.
AMARA!
OH.
OH. UH.
UM.
IS AMARA HERE?

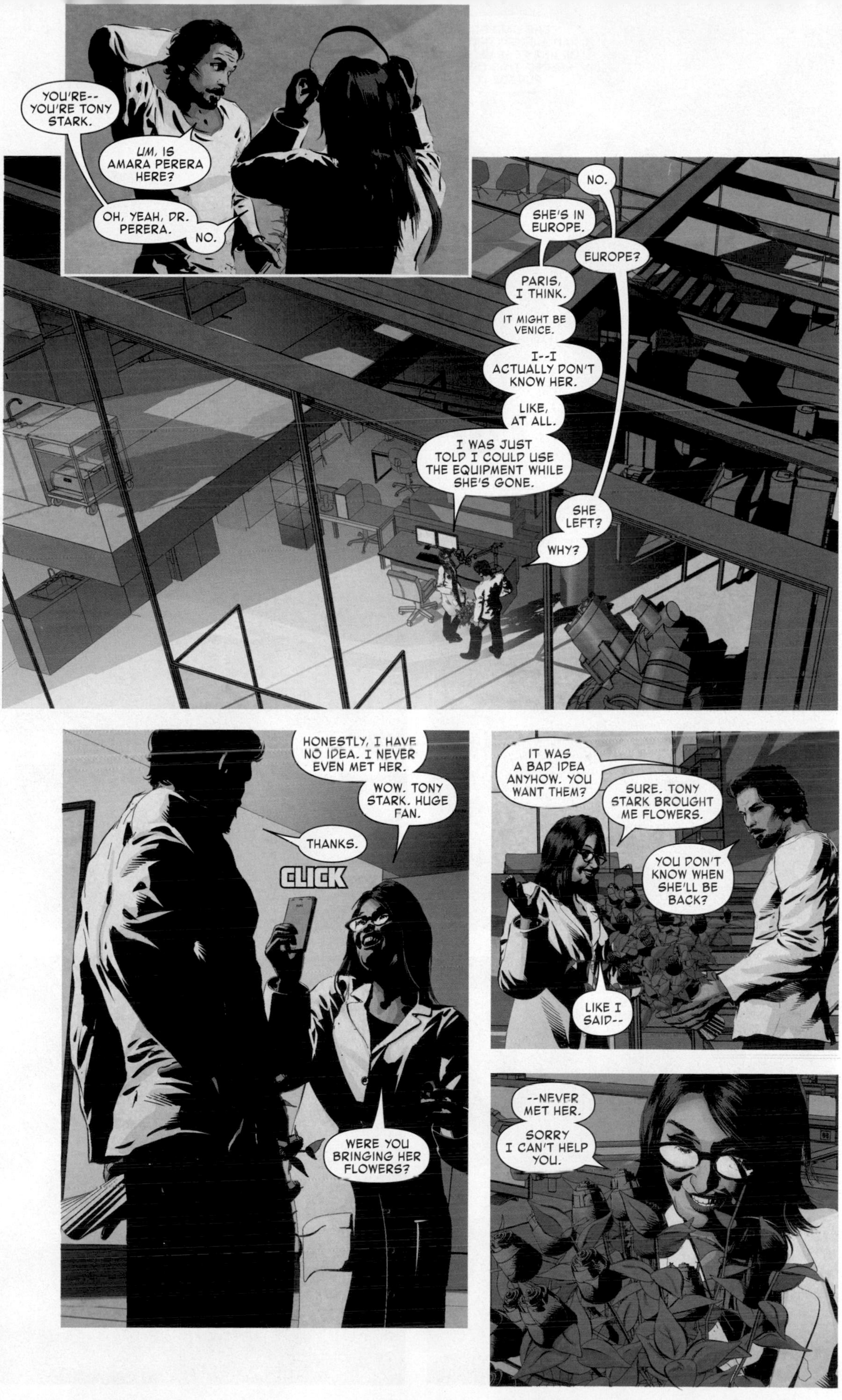
YOU'RE-- YOU'RE TONY STARK.
UM, IS AMARA PERERA HERE?
OH, YEAH, DR. PERERA.
NO.
NO.
SHE'S IN EUROPE.
EUROPE?
PARIS, I THINK.
IT MIGHT BE VENICE.
I--I ACTUALLY DON'T KNOW HER.
LIKE, AT ALL.
I WAS JUST TOLD I COULD USE THE EQUIPMENT WHILE SHE'S GONE.
SHE LEFT?
WHY?
HONESTLY, I HAVE NO IDEA. I NEVER EVEN MET HER.
WOW. TONY STARK. HUGE FAN.
THANKS.
CLICK
WERE YOU BRINGING HER FLOWERS?
IT WAS A BAD IDEA ANYHOW. YOU WANT THEM?
SURE. TONY STARK BROUGHT ME FLOWERS.
YOU DON'T KNOW WHEN SHE'LL BE BACK?
LIKE I SAID--
--NEVER MET HER.
SORRY I CAN'T HELP YOU.

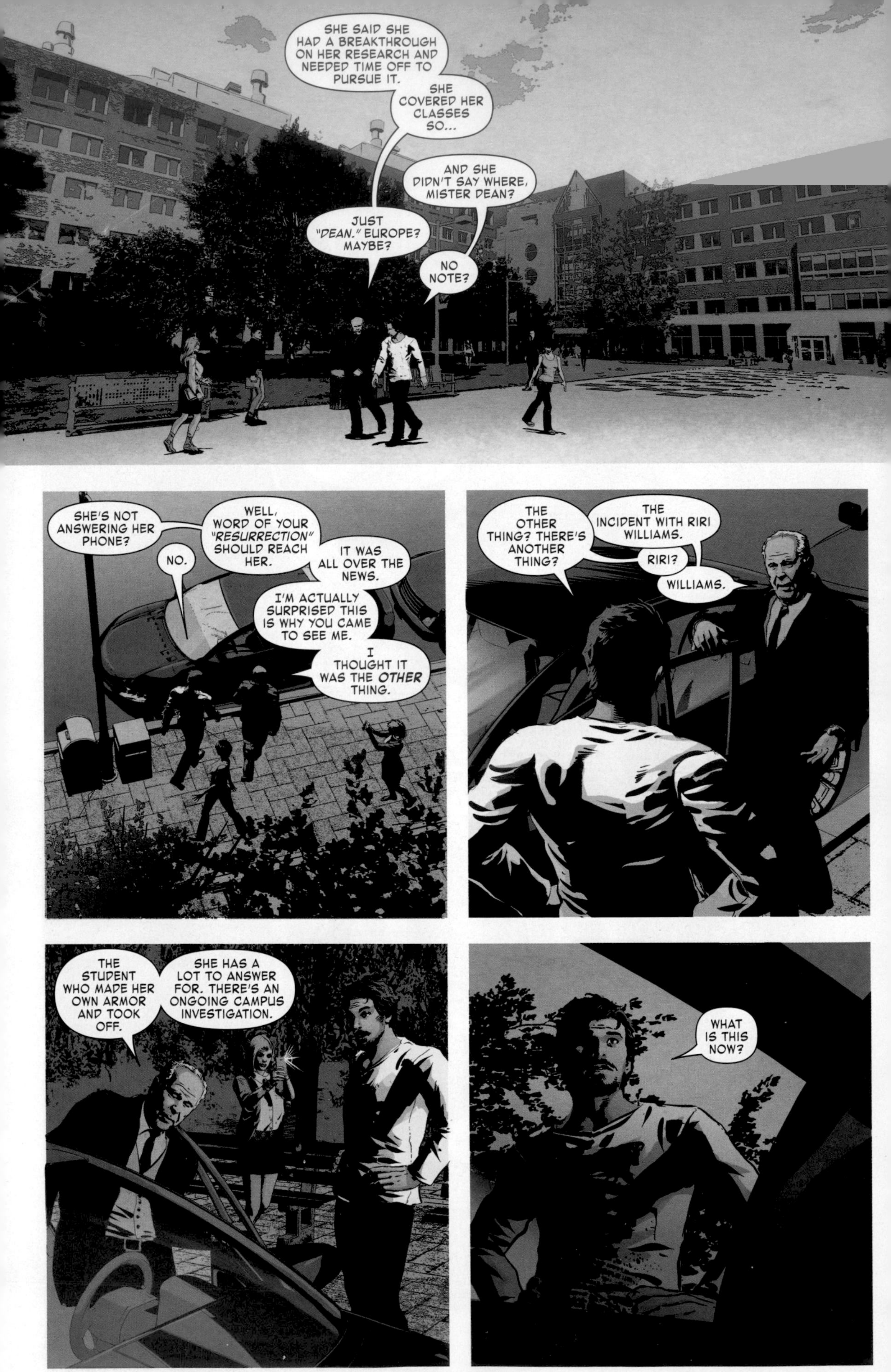
SHE SAID SHE HAD A BREAKTHROUGH ON HER RESEARCH AND NEEDED TIME OFF TO PURSUE IT.
SHE COVERED HER CLASSES SO...
AND SHE DIDN'T SAY WHERE, MISTER DEAN?
JUST "DEAN." EUROPE? MAYBE?
NO NOTE?
SHE'S NOT ANSWERING HER PHONE?
NO.
WELL, WORD OF YOUR "RESURRECTION" SHOULD REACH HER.
IT WAS ALL OVER THE NEWS.
I'M ACTUALLY SURPRISED THIS IS WHY YOU CAME TO SEE ME.
I THOUGHT IT WAS THE OTHER THING.
THE OTHER THING? THERE'S ANOTHER THING?
THE INCIDENT WITH RIRI WILLIAMS.
RIRI?
WILLIAMS.
THE STUDENT WHO MADE HER OWN ARMOR AND TOOK OFF.
SHE HAS A LOT TO ANSWER FOR. THERE'S AN ONGOING CAMPUS INVESTIGATION.
WHAT IS THIS NOW?

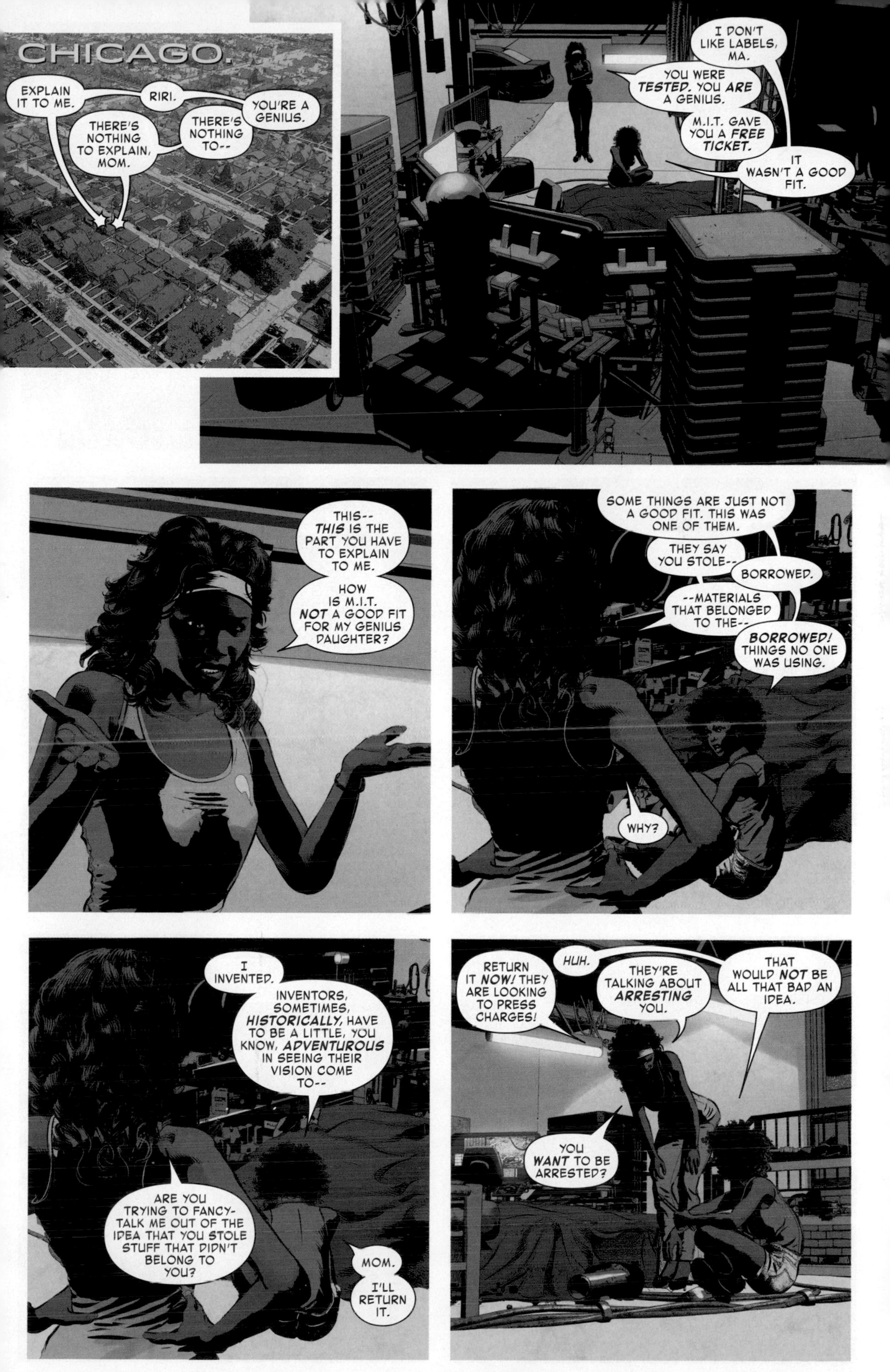
CHICAGO.
EXPLAIN IT TO ME.
RIRI.
YOU'RE A GENIUS.
THERE'S NOTHING TO EXPLAIN, MOM.
THERE'S NOTHING TO--
I DON'T LIKE LABELS, MA.
YOU WERE TESTED. YOU ARE A GENIUS.
M.I.T. GAVE YOU A FREE TICKET.
IT WASN'T A GOOD FIT.
THIS-- THIS IS THE PART YOU HAVE TO EXPLAIN TO ME.
HOW IS M.I.T. NOT A GOOD FIT FOR MY GENIUS DAUGHTER?
SOME THINGS ARE JUST NOT A GOOD FIT. THIS WAS ONE OF THEM.
THEY SAY YOU STOLE--
BORROWED.
--MATERIALS THAT BELONGED TO THE--
BORROWED! THINGS NO ONE WAS USING.
WHY?
I INVENTED.
INVENTORS, SOMETIMES, HISTORICALLY, HAVE TO BE A LITTLE, YOU KNOW, ADVENTUROUS IN SEEING THEIR VISION COME TO--
ARE YOU TRYING TO FANCY-TALK ME OUT OF THE IDEA THAT YOU STOLE STUFF THAT DIDN'T BELONG TO YOU?
MOM.
I'LL RETURN IT.
RETURN IT NOW! THEY ARE LOOKING TO PRESS CHARGES!
HUH.
THEY'RE TALKING ABOUT ARRESTING YOU.
THAT WOULD NOT BE ALL THAT BAD AN IDEA.
YOU WANT TO BE ARRESTED?

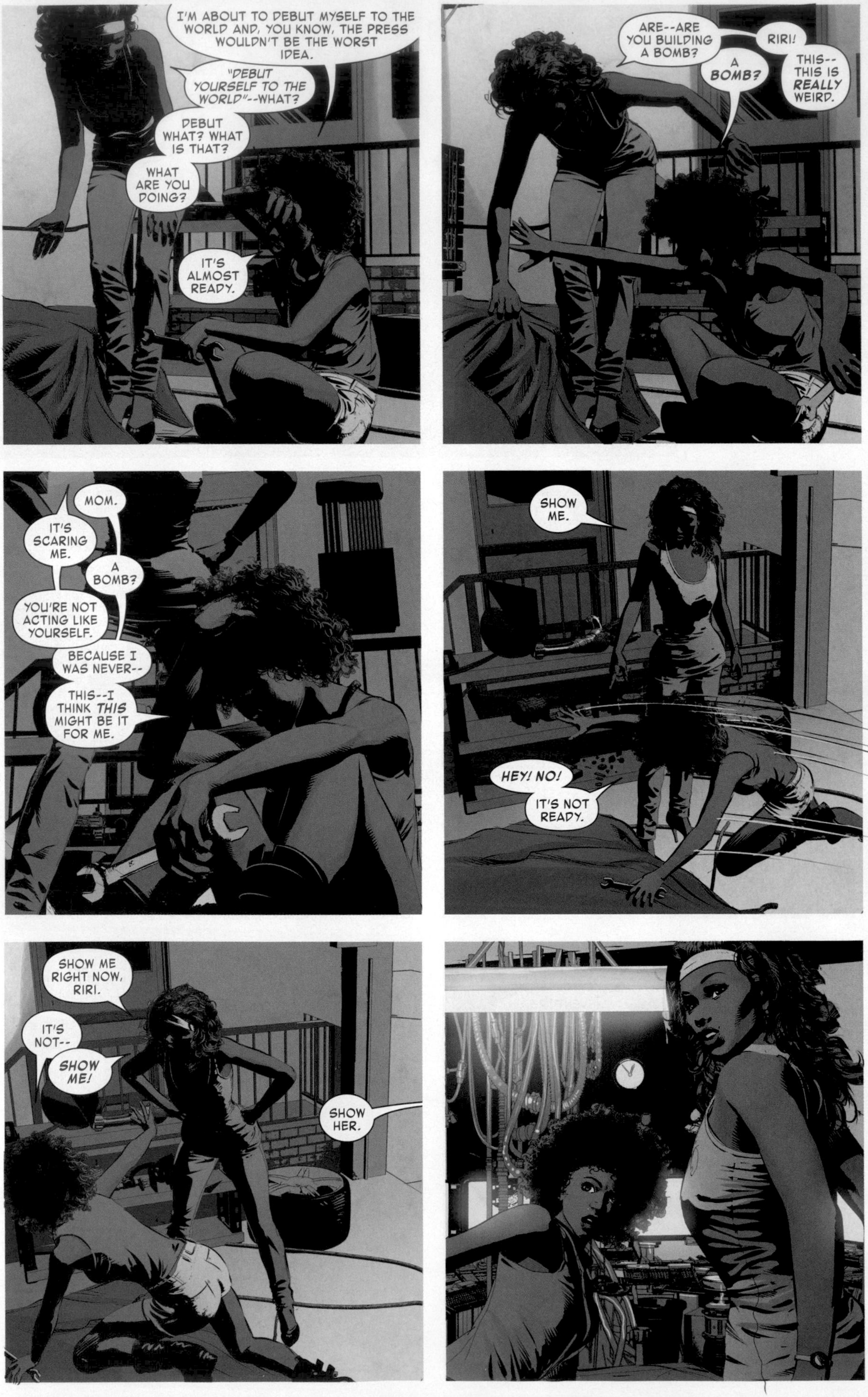

I'M ABOUT TO DEBUT MYSELF TO THE WORLD AND, YOU KNOW, THE PRESS WOULDN'T BE THE WORST IDEA.
"DEBUT YOURSELF TO THE WORLD"--WHAT?
DEBUT WHAT? WHAT IS THAT?
WHAT ARE YOU DOING?
IT'S ALMOST READY.
ARE--ARE YOU BUILDING A BOMB?
A BOMB?
RIRI!
THIS--THIS IS REALLY WEIRD.
MOM.
IT'S SCARING ME.
A BOMB?
YOU'RE NOT ACTING LIKE YOURSELF.
BECAUSE I WAS NEVER--
THIS--I THINK THIS MIGHT BE IT FOR ME.
SHOW ME.
HEY! NO!
IT'S NOT READY.
SHOW ME RIGHT NOW, RIRI.
IT'S NOT--
SHOW ME!
SHOW HER.

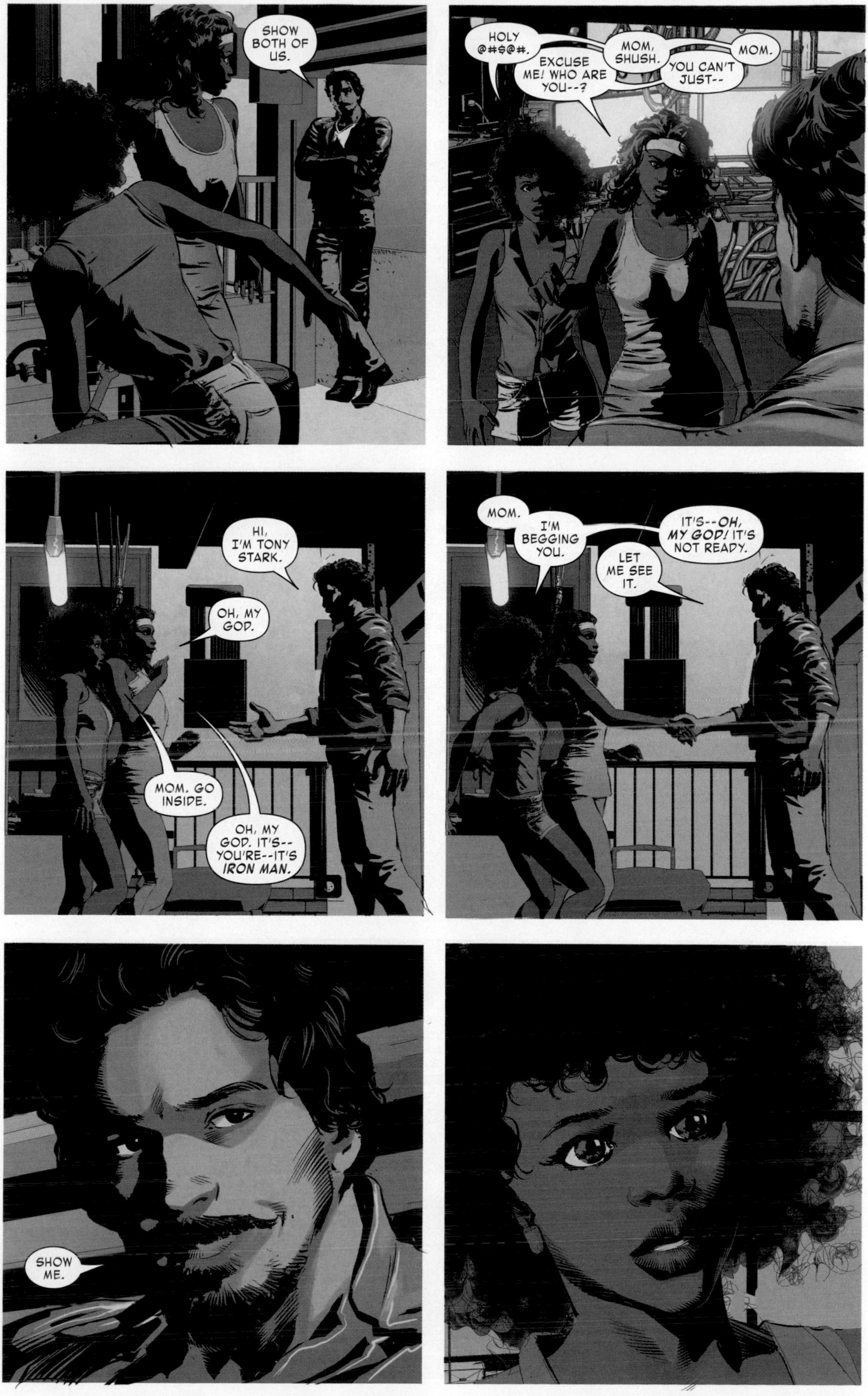
SHOW BOTH OF US.
HOLY @#$@#.
EXCUSE ME! WHO ARE YOU--?
MOM, SHUSH.
MOM.
YOU CAN'T JUST--
HI, I'M TONY STARK.
OH, MY GOD.
MOM. GO INSIDE.
OH, MY GOD. IT'S-- YOU'RE--IT'S *IRON MAN.*
MOM.
I'M BEGGING YOU.
IT'S--*OH, MY GOD!* IT'S NOT READY.
LET ME SEE IT.
SHOW ME.

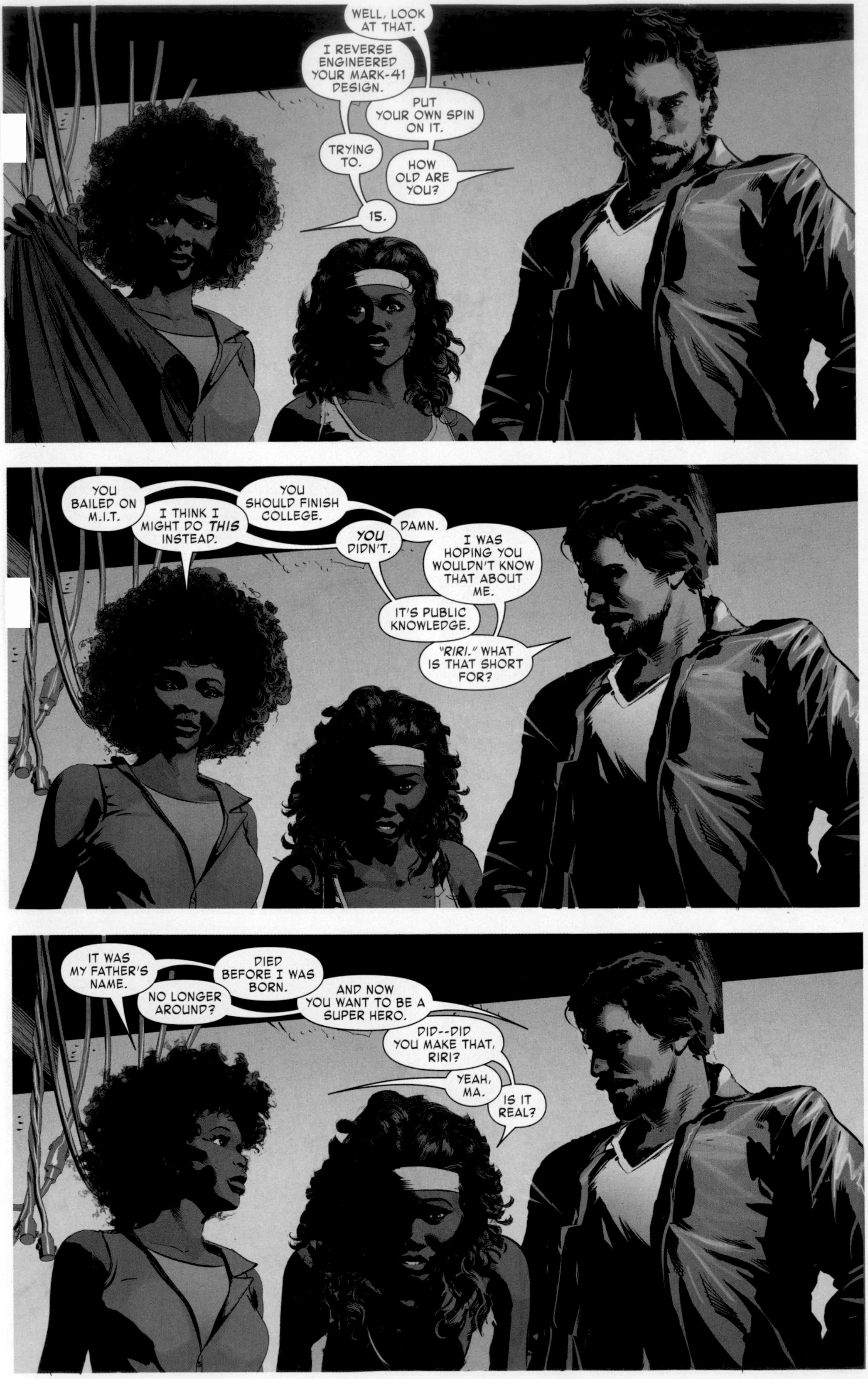
WELL, LOOK AT THAT.
I REVERSE ENGINEERED YOUR MARK-41 DESIGN.
PUT YOUR OWN SPIN ON IT.
TRYING TO.
HOW OLD ARE YOU?
15.
YOU BAILED ON M.I.T.
YOU SHOULD FINISH COLLEGE.
I THINK I MIGHT DO *THIS* INSTEAD.
YOU DIDN'T.
DAMN.
I WAS HOPING YOU WOULDN'T KNOW THAT ABOUT ME.
IT'S PUBLIC KNOWLEDGE.
"*RIRI*." WHAT IS THAT SHORT FOR?
IT WAS MY FATHER'S NAME.
NO LONGER AROUND?
DIED BEFORE I WAS BORN.
AND NOW YOU WANT TO BE A SUPER HERO.
DID--DID YOU MAKE THAT, RIRI?
YEAH, MA.
IS IT REAL?

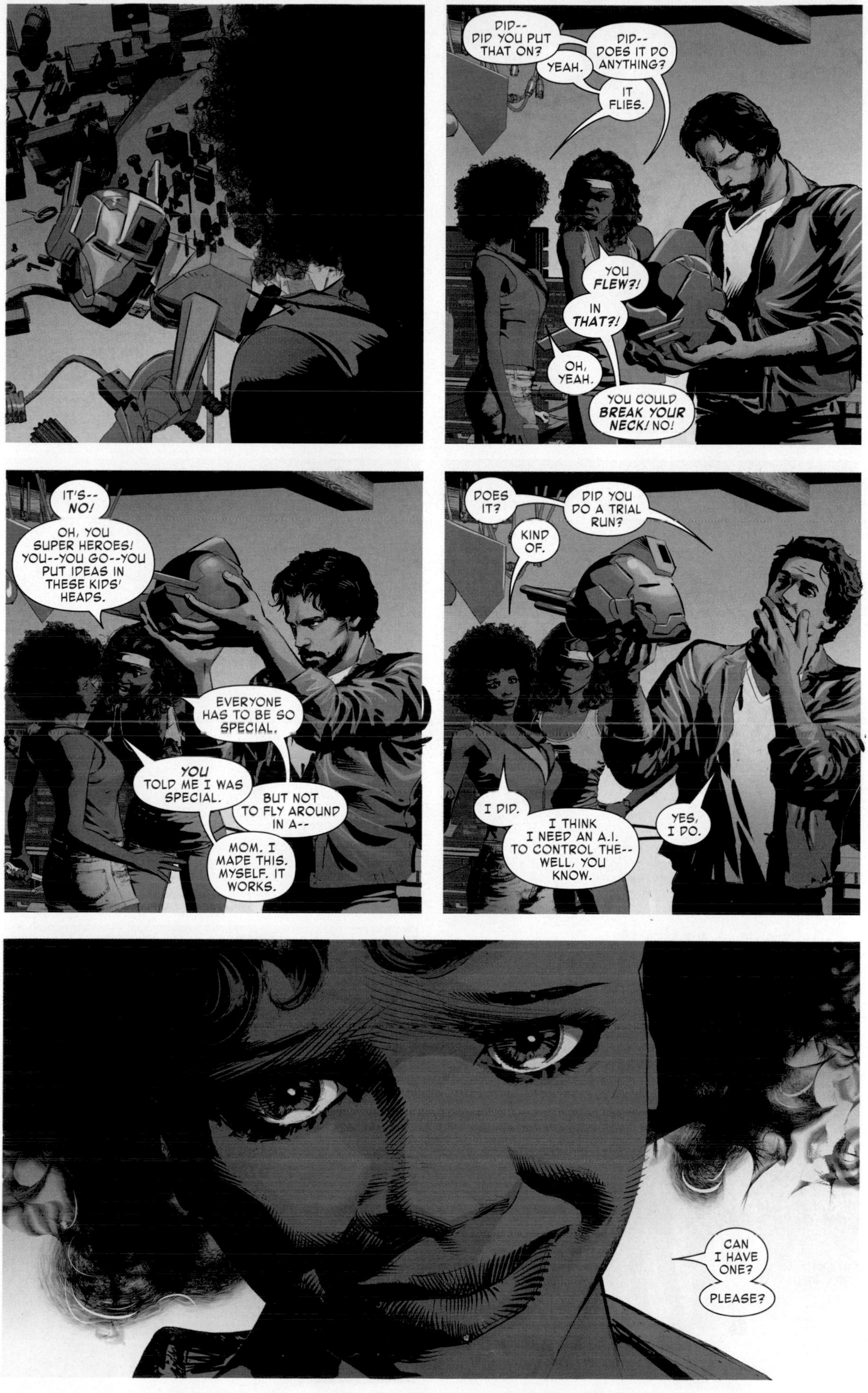
DID--
DID YOU PUT THAT ON?
YEAH.
DID--
DOES IT DO ANYTHING?
IT FLIES.
YOU FLEW?!
IN THAT?!
OH, YEAH.
YOU COULD BREAK YOUR NECK! NO!
IT'S-- NO!
OH, YOU SUPER HEROES! YOU--YOU GO--YOU PUT IDEAS IN THESE KIDS' HEADS.
EVERYONE HAS TO BE SO SPECIAL.
YOU TOLD ME I WAS SPECIAL.
BUT NOT TO FLY AROUND IN A--
MOM. I MADE THIS. MYSELF. IT WORKS.
DOES IT?
DID YOU DO A TRIAL RUN?
KIND OF.
I DID.
I THINK I NEED AN A.I. TO CONTROL THE-- WELL, YOU KNOW.
YES, I DO.
CAN I HAVE ONE?
PLEASE?

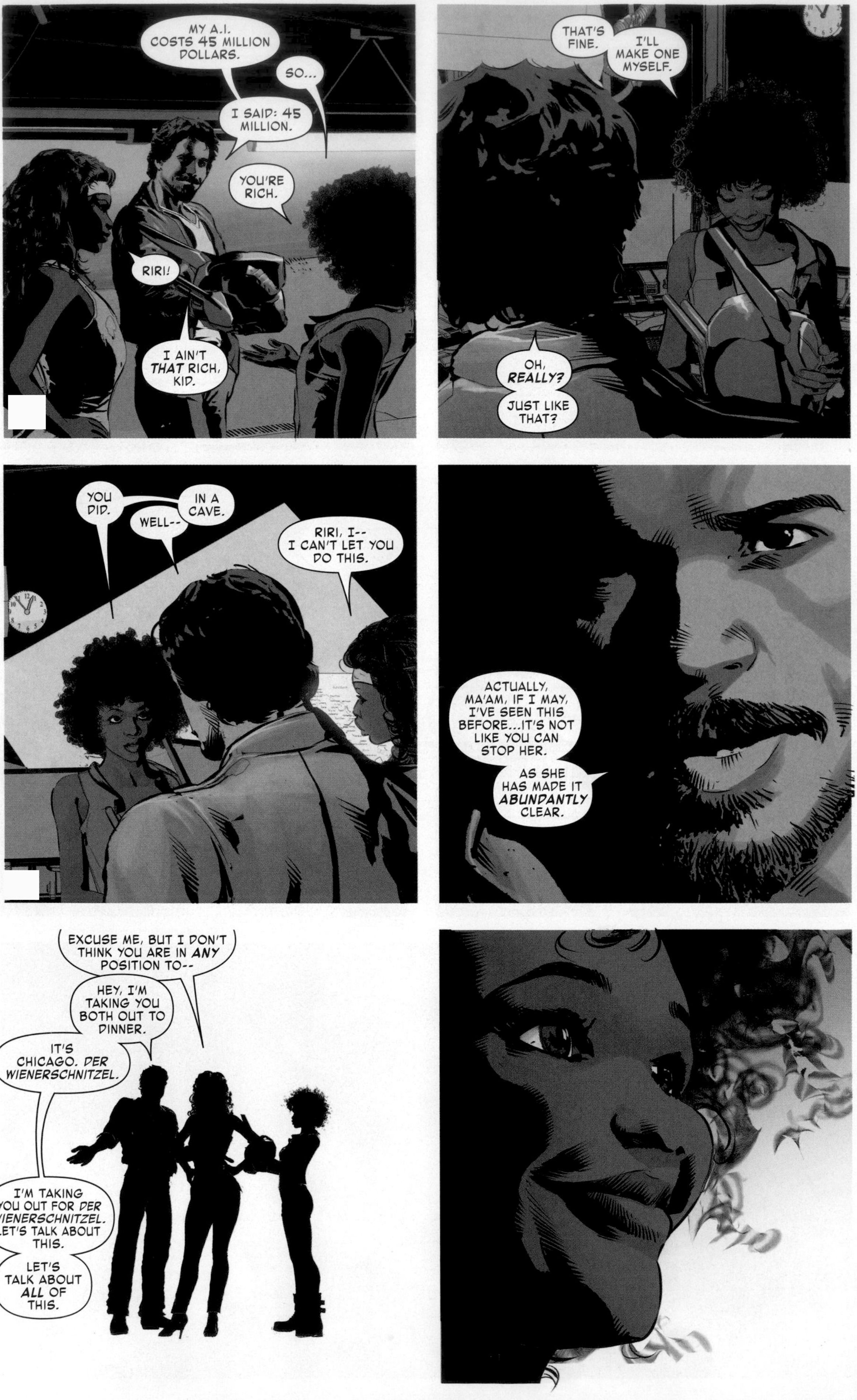
MY A.I. COSTS 45 MILLION DOLLARS.
SO...
I SAID: 45 MILLION.
YOU'RE RICH.
RIRI!
I AIN'T *THAT* RICH, KID.
THAT'S FINE.
I'LL MAKE ONE MYSELF.
OH, *REALLY?*
JUST LIKE THAT?
YOU DID.
IN A CAVE.
WELL--
RIRI, I-- I CAN'T LET YOU DO THIS.
ACTUALLY, MA'AM, IF I MAY, I'VE SEEN THIS BEFORE...IT'S NOT LIKE YOU CAN STOP HER.
AS SHE HAS MADE IT *ABUNDANTLY* CLEAR.
EXCUSE ME, BUT I DON'T THINK YOU ARE IN *ANY* POSITION TO--
HEY, I'M TAKING YOU BOTH OUT TO DINNER.
IT'S CHICAGO. *DER WIENERSCHNITZEL.*
I'M TAKING YOU OUT FOR *DER WIENERSCHNITZEL.* LET'S TALK ABOUT THIS.
LET'S TALK ABOUT *ALL* OF THIS.

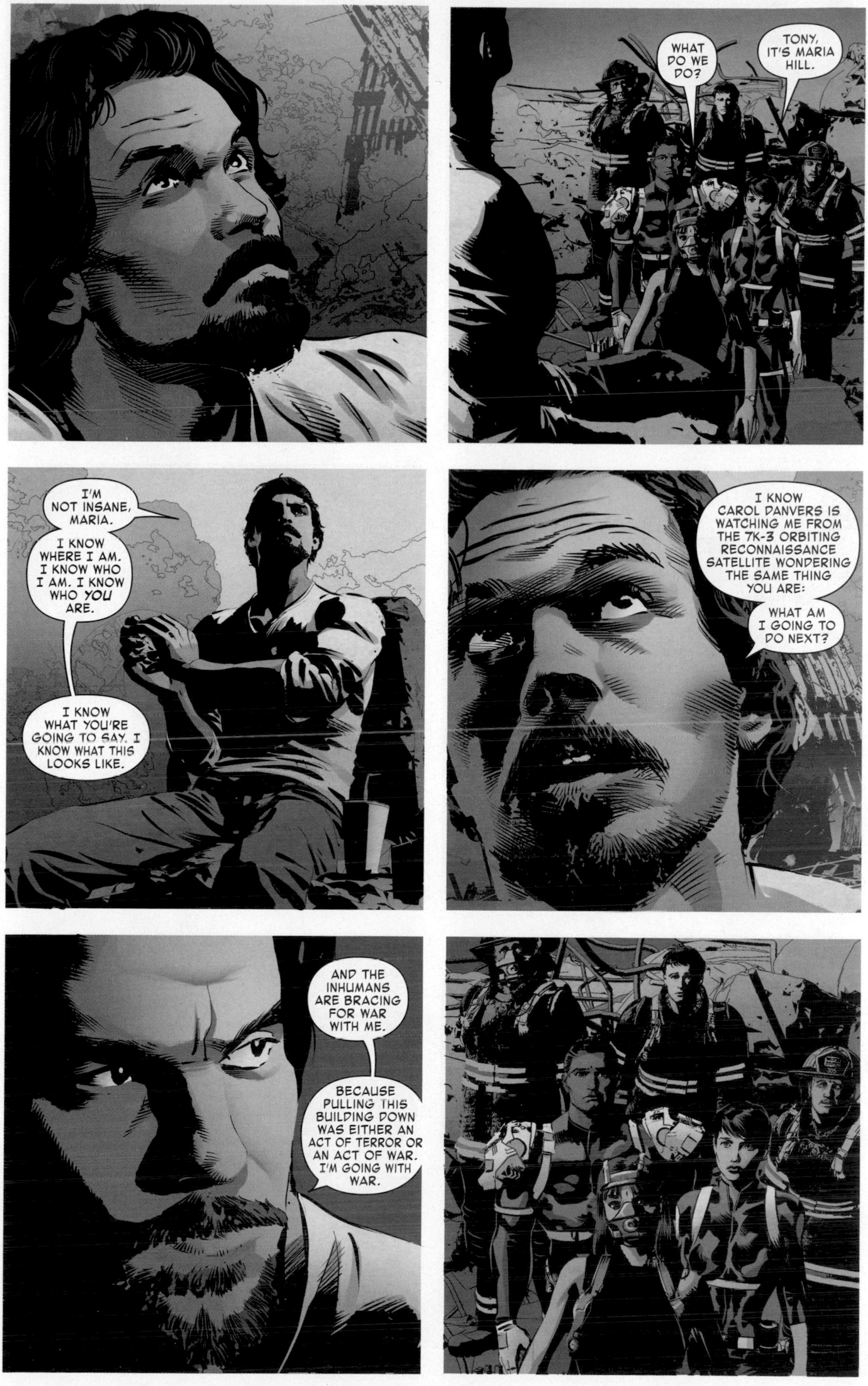
WHAT DO WE DO?
TONY, IT'S MARIA HILL.
I'M NOT INSANE, MARIA.
I KNOW WHERE I AM. I KNOW WHO I AM. I KNOW WHO YOU ARE.
I KNOW WHAT YOU'RE GOING TO SAY. I KNOW WHAT THIS LOOKS LIKE.
I KNOW CAROL DANVERS IS WATCHING ME FROM THE 7K-3 ORBITING RECONNAISSANCE SATELLITE WONDERING THE SAME THING YOU ARE:
WHAT AM I GOING TO DO NEXT?
AND THE INHUMANS ARE BRACING FOR WAR WITH ME.
BECAUSE PULLING THIS BUILDING DOWN WAS EITHER AN ACT OF TERROR OR AN ACT OF WAR. I'M GOING WITH WAR.

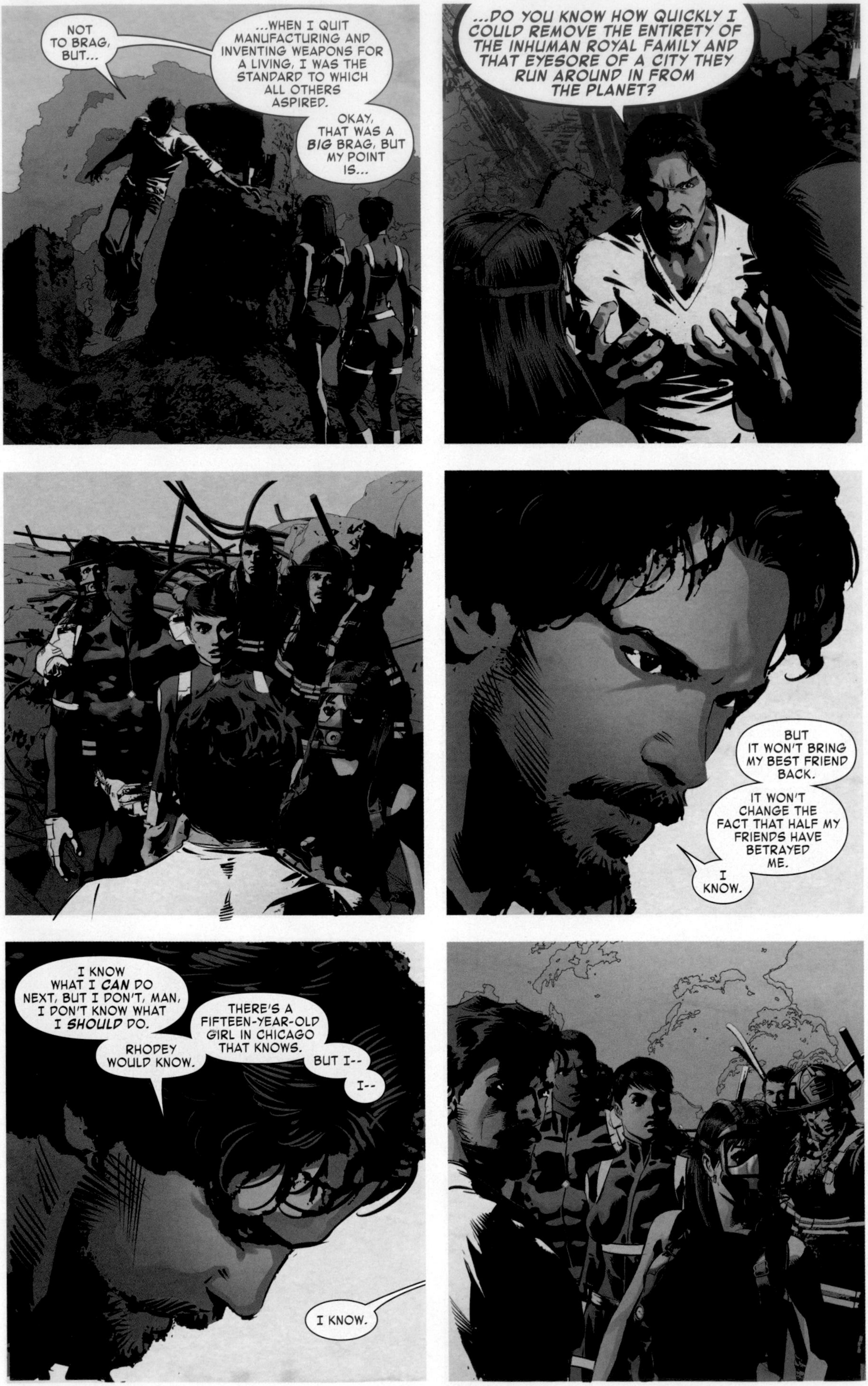
NOT TO BRAG, BUT...
...WHEN I QUIT MANUFACTURING AND INVENTING WEAPONS FOR A LIVING, I WAS THE STANDARD TO WHICH ALL OTHERS ASPIRED.
OKAY, THAT WAS A BIG BRAG, BUT MY POINT IS...
...DO YOU KNOW HOW QUICKLY I COULD REMOVE THE ENTIRETY OF THE INHUMAN ROYAL FAMILY AND THAT EYESORE OF A CITY THEY RUN AROUND IN FROM THE PLANET?
BUT IT WON'T BRING MY BEST FRIEND BACK.
IT WON'T CHANGE THE FACT THAT HALF MY FRIENDS HAVE BETRAYED ME.
I KNOW.
I KNOW WHAT I CAN DO NEXT, BUT I DON'T, MAN, I DON'T KNOW WHAT I SHOULD DO.
RHODEY WOULD KNOW.
THERE'S A FIFTEEN-YEAR-OLD GIRL IN CHICAGO THAT KNOWS.
BUT I--
I--
I KNOW.

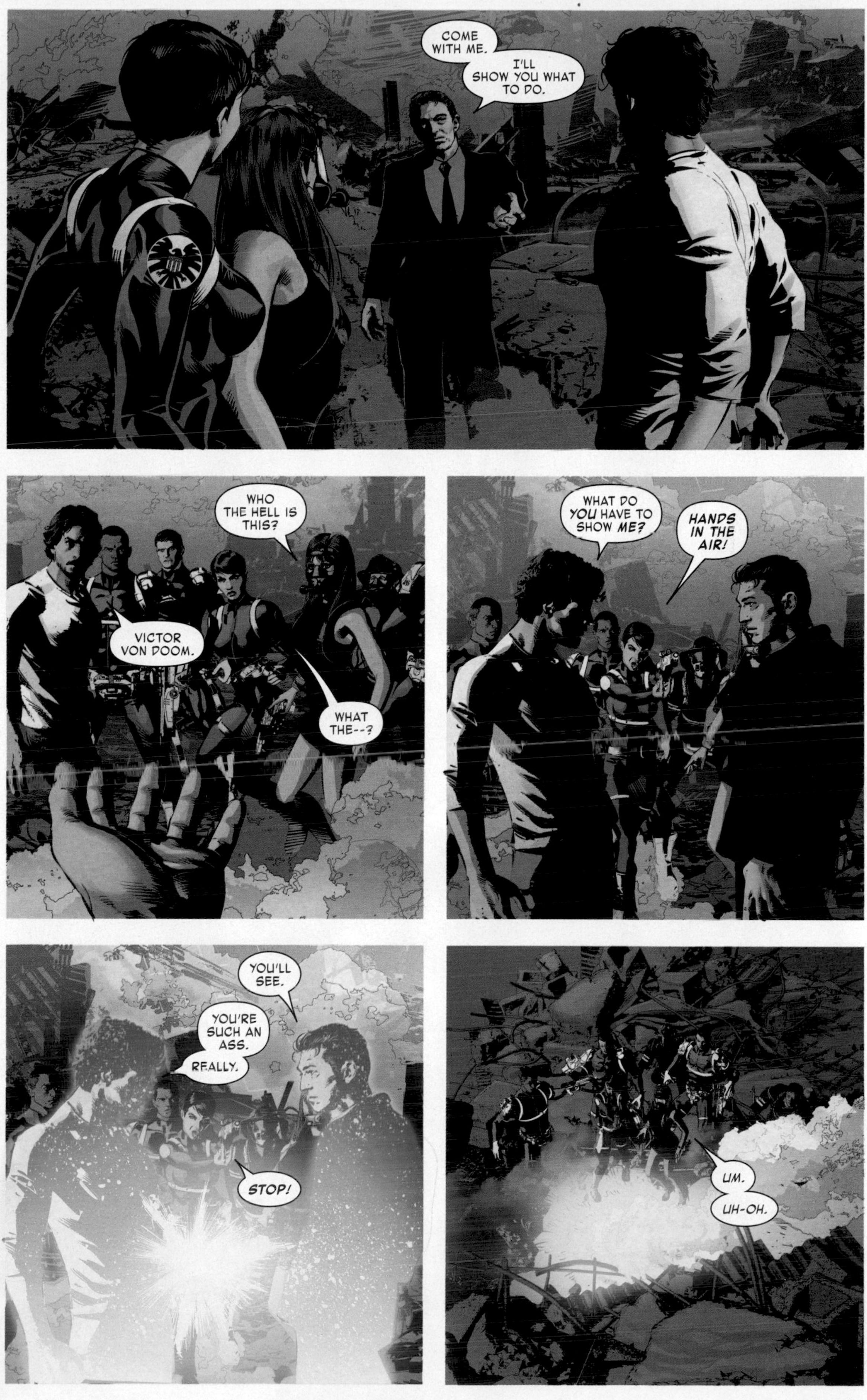
COME WITH ME.
I'LL SHOW YOU WHAT TO DO.
WHO THE HELL IS THIS?
VICTOR VON DOOM.
WHAT THE--?
WHAT DO YOU HAVE TO SHOW ME?
HANDS IN THE AIR!
YOU'LL SEE.
YOU'RE SUCH AN ASS.
REALLY.
STOP!
UM.
UH-OH.

#13

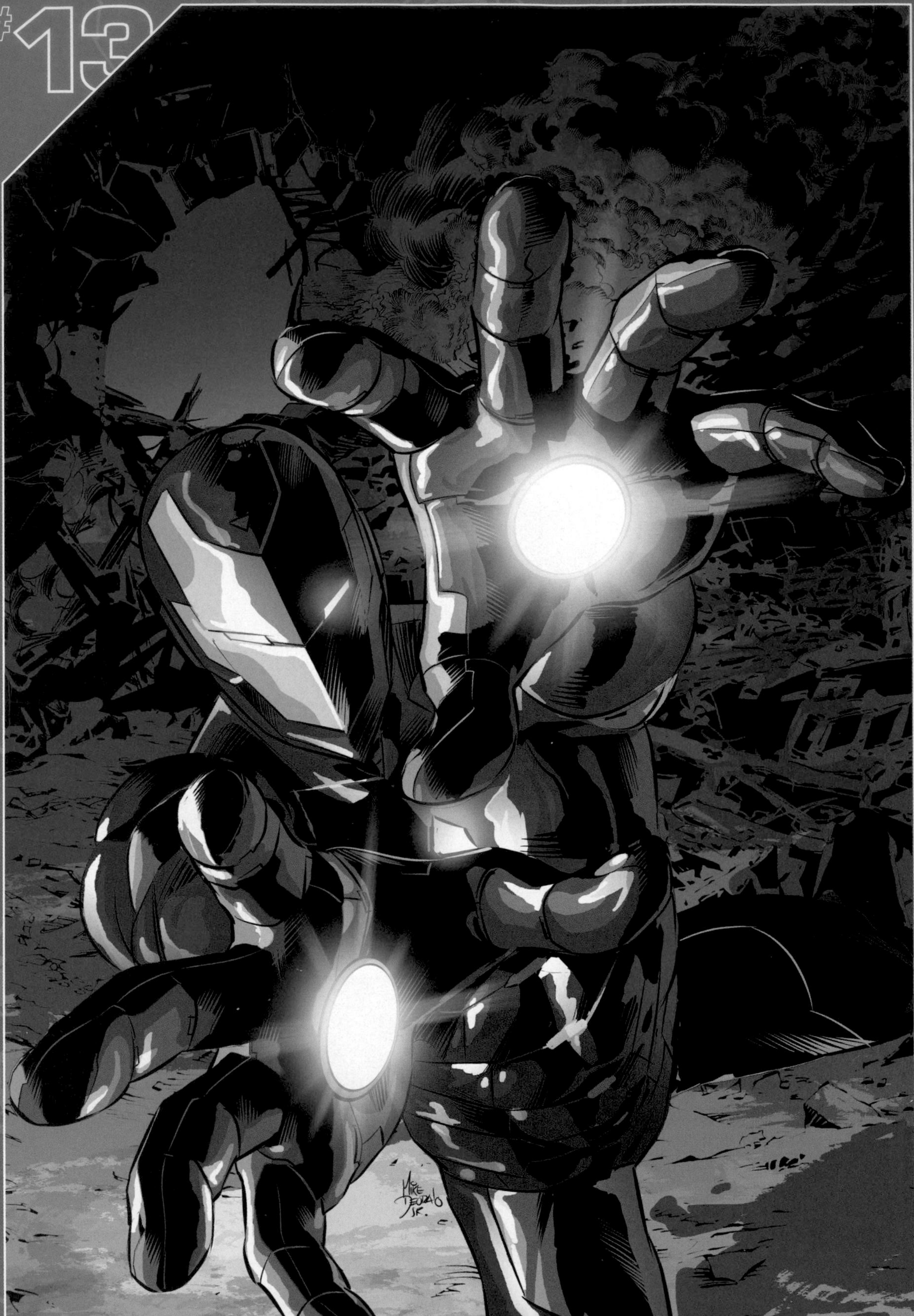

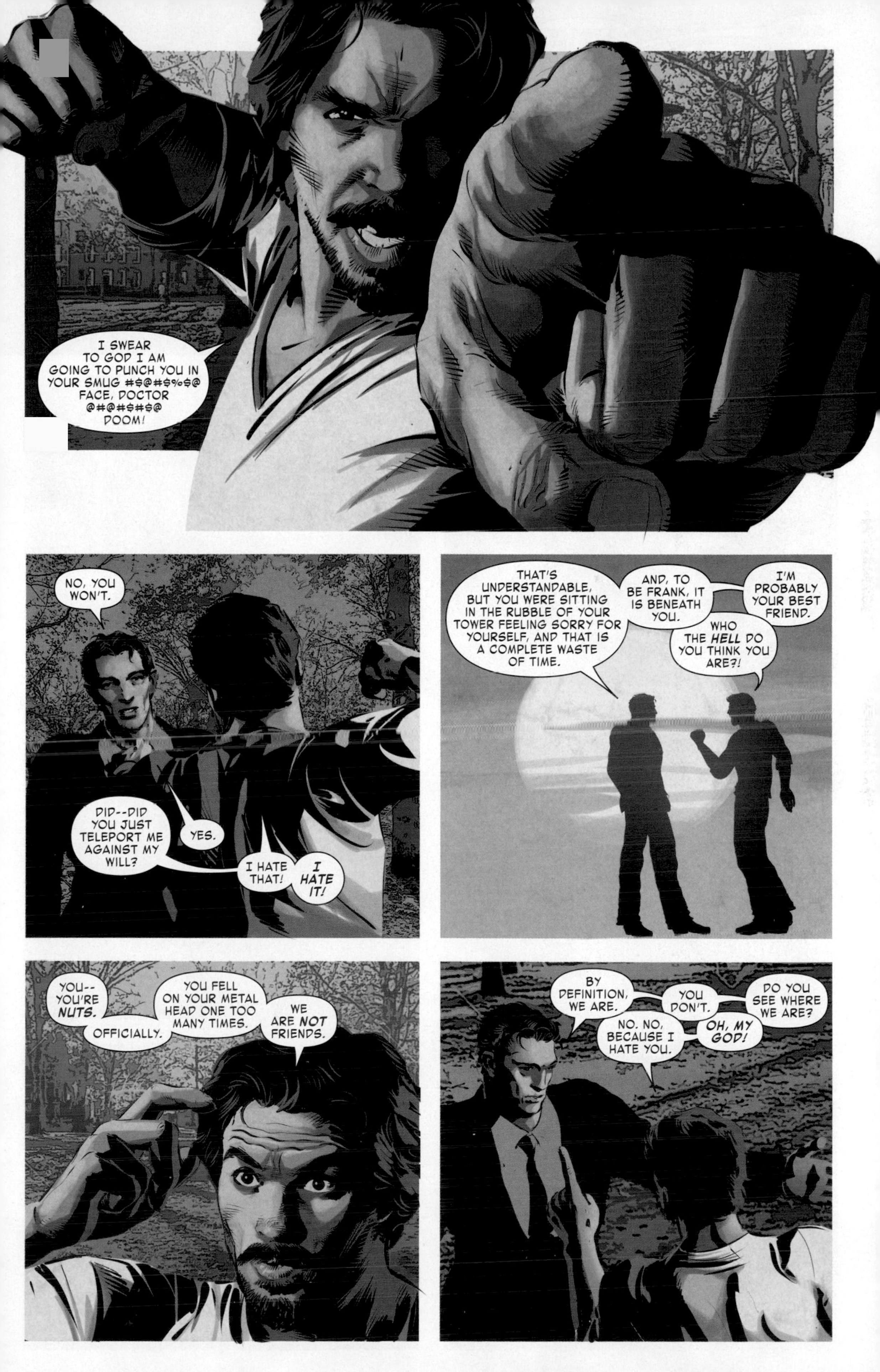
I SWEAR TO GOD I AM GOING TO PUNCH YOU IN YOUR SMUG #$@#$%$@ FACE, DOCTOR @#@#$#$@ DOOM!
NO, YOU WON'T.
DID--DID YOU JUST TELEPORT ME AGAINST MY WILL?
YES.
I HATE THAT!
I HATE IT!
THAT'S UNDERSTANDABLE, BUT YOU WERE SITTING IN THE RUBBLE OF YOUR TOWER FEELING SORRY FOR YOURSELF, AND THAT IS A COMPLETE WASTE OF TIME.
AND, TO BE FRANK, IT IS BENEATH YOU.
I'M PROBABLY YOUR BEST FRIEND.
WHO THE HELL DO YOU THINK YOU ARE?!
YOU-- YOU'RE NUTS.
OFFICIALLY.
YOU FELL ON YOUR METAL HEAD ONE TOO MANY TIMES.
WE ARE NOT FRIENDS.
BY DEFINITION, WE ARE.
YOU DON'T.
DO YOU SEE WHERE WE ARE?
NO. NO, BECAUSE I HATE YOU.
OH, MY GOD!

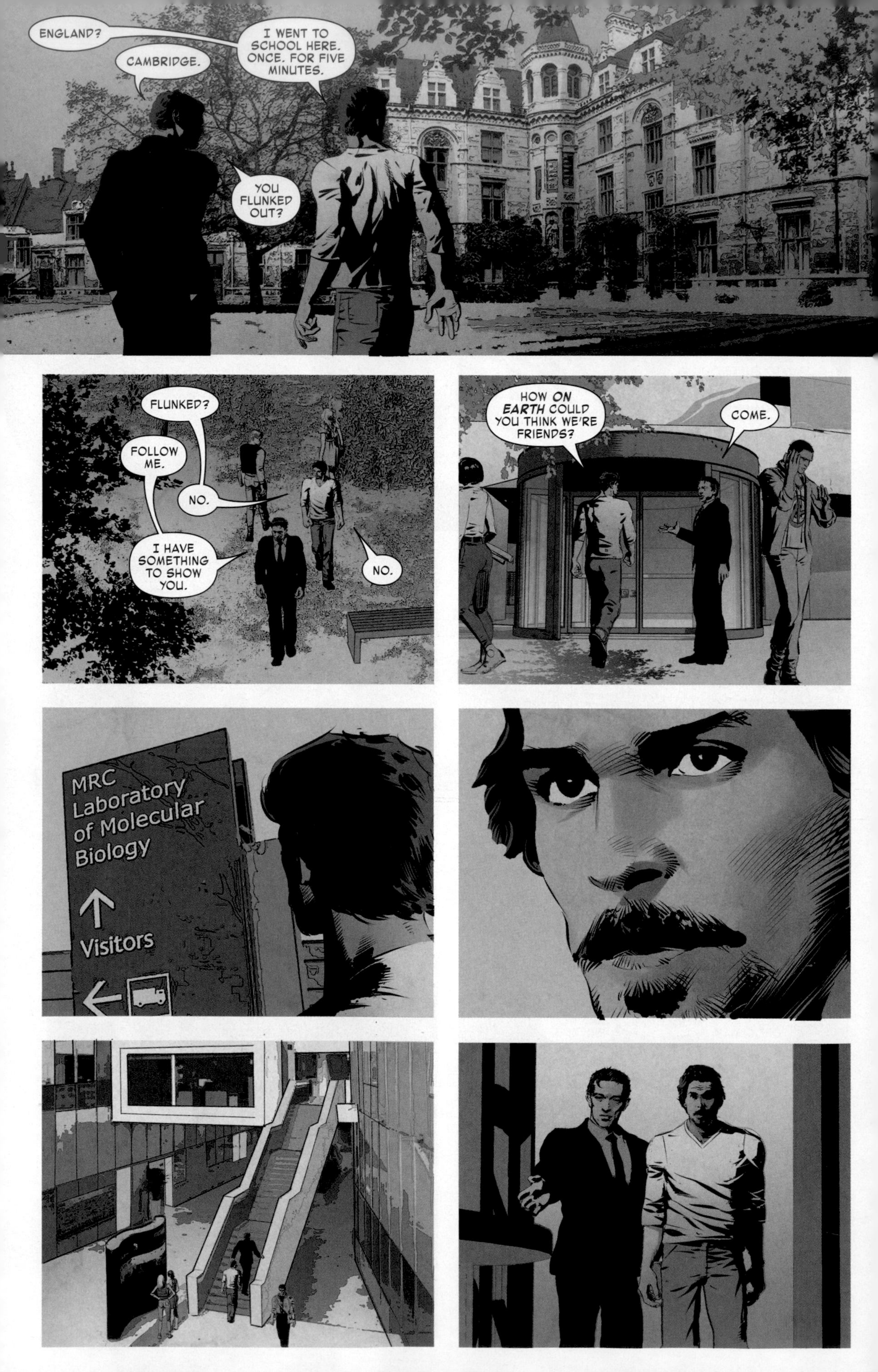
ENGLAND?
CAMBRIDGE.
I WENT TO SCHOOL HERE. ONCE. FOR FIVE MINUTES.
YOU FLUNKED OUT?
FLUNKED?
FOLLOW ME.
NO.
I HAVE SOMETHING TO SHOW YOU.
NO.
HOW ON EARTH COULD YOU THINK WE'RE FRIENDS?
COME.
MRC Laboratory of Molecular Biology
Visitors

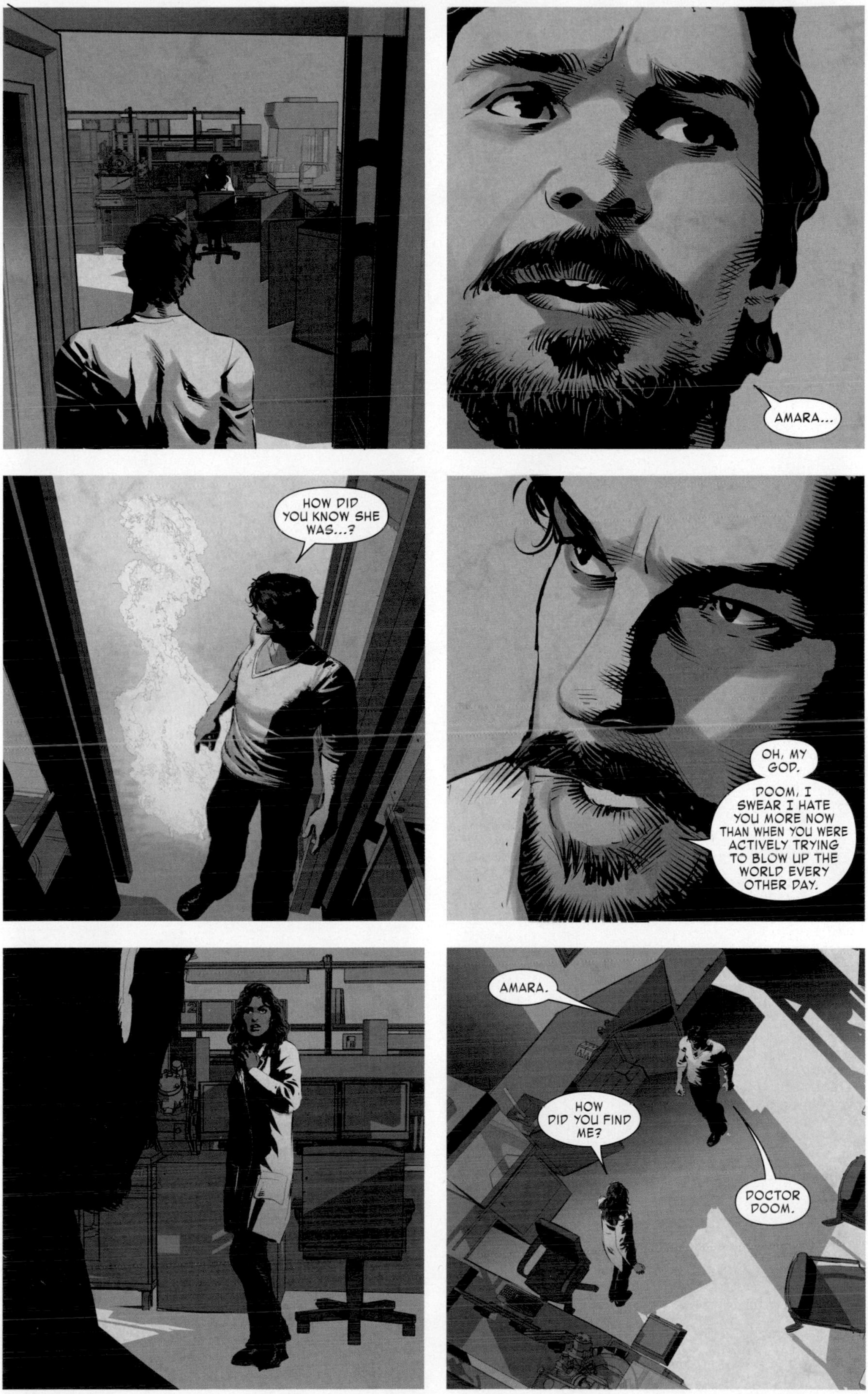
AMARA...
HOW DID YOU KNOW SHE WAS...?
OH, MY GOD.
DOOM, I SWEAR I HATE YOU MORE NOW THAN WHEN YOU WERE ACTIVELY TRYING TO BLOW UP THE WORLD EVERY OTHER DAY.
AMARA.
HOW DID YOU FIND ME?
DOCTOR DOOM.

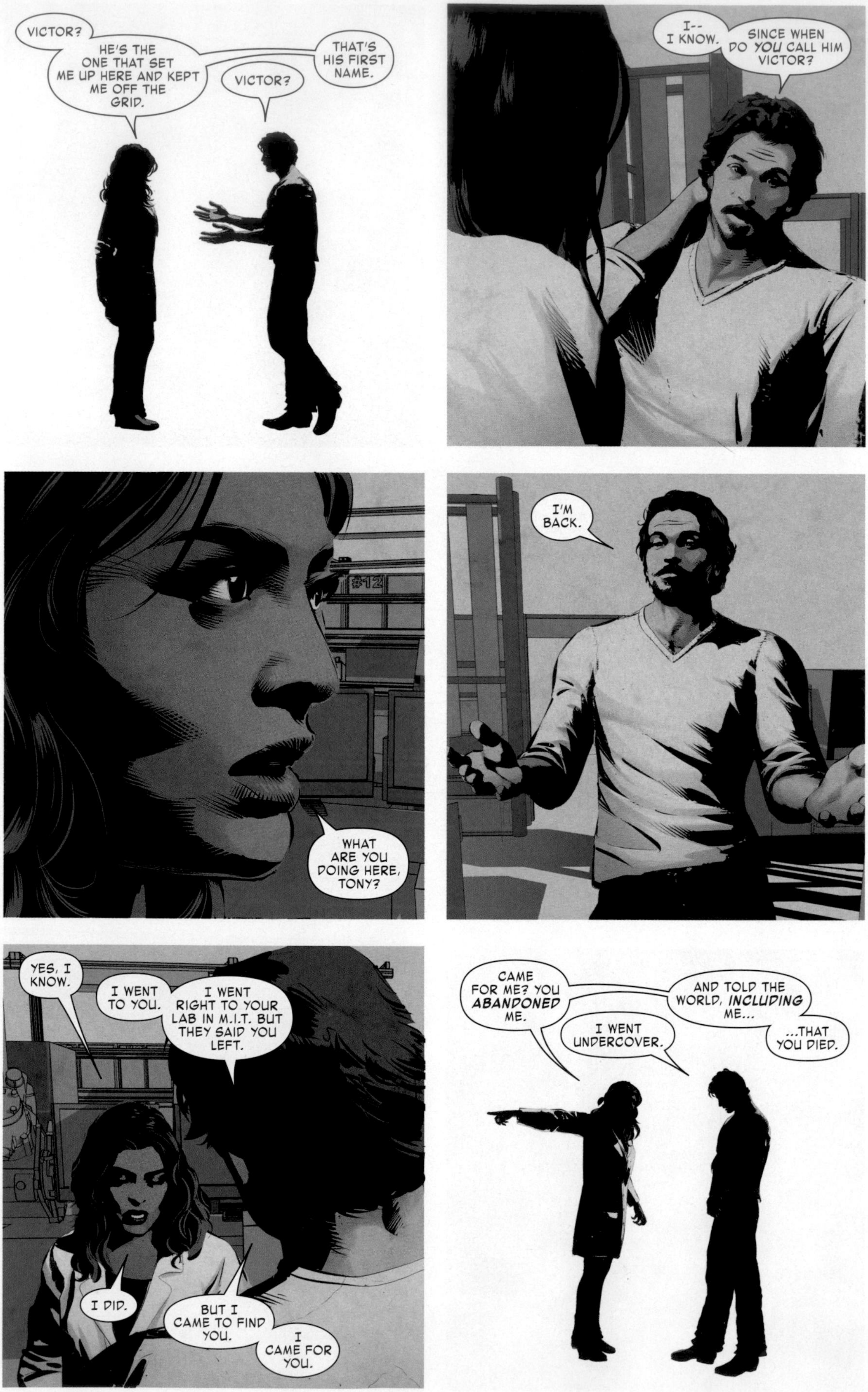

VICTOR?
HE'S THE ONE THAT SET ME UP HERE AND KEPT ME OFF THE GRID.
VICTOR?
THAT'S HIS FIRST NAME.
I-- I KNOW.
SINCE WHEN DO *YOU* CALL HIM VICTOR?
#12
WHAT ARE YOU DOING HERE, TONY?
I'M BACK.
YES, I KNOW.
I WENT TO YOU.
I WENT RIGHT TO YOUR LAB IN M.I.T. BUT THEY SAID YOU LEFT.
I DID.
BUT I CAME TO FIND YOU.
I CAME FOR YOU.
CAME FOR ME? YOU ***ABANDONED*** ME.
AND TOLD THE WORLD, ***INCLUDING*** ME...
I WENT UNDERCOVER.
...THAT YOU DIED.

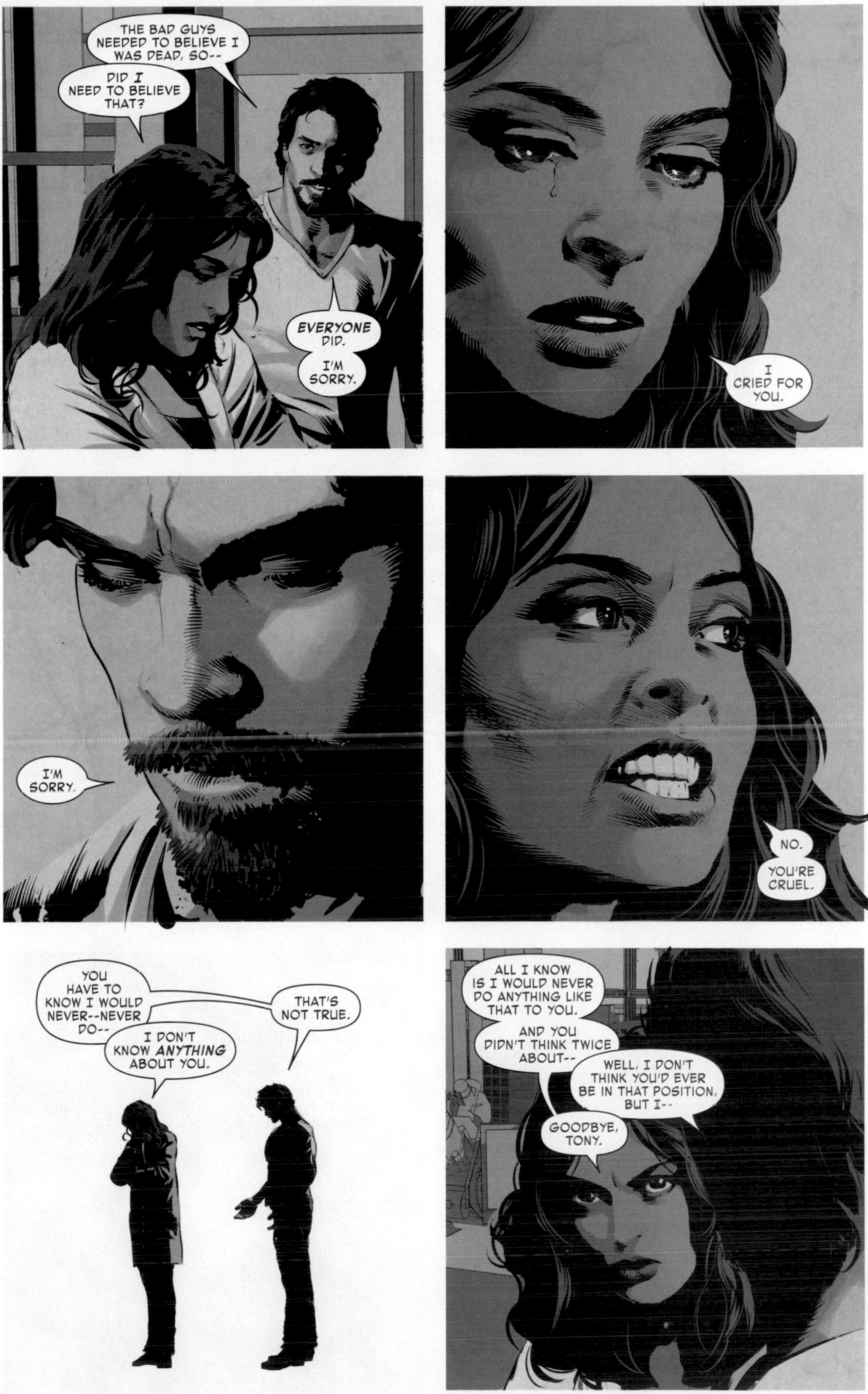
THE BAD GUYS NEEDED TO BELIEVE I WAS DEAD, SO--
DID I NEED TO BELIEVE THAT?
EVERYONE DID.
I'M SORRY.
I CRIED FOR YOU.
I'M SORRY.
NO.
YOU'RE CRUEL.
YOU HAVE TO KNOW I WOULD NEVER--NEVER DO--
THAT'S NOT TRUE.
I DON'T KNOW ANYTHING ABOUT YOU.
ALL I KNOW IS I WOULD NEVER DO ANYTHING LIKE THAT TO YOU.
AND YOU DIDN'T THINK TWICE ABOUT--
WELL, I DON'T THINK YOU'D EVER BE IN THAT POSITION, BUT I--
GOODBYE, TONY.

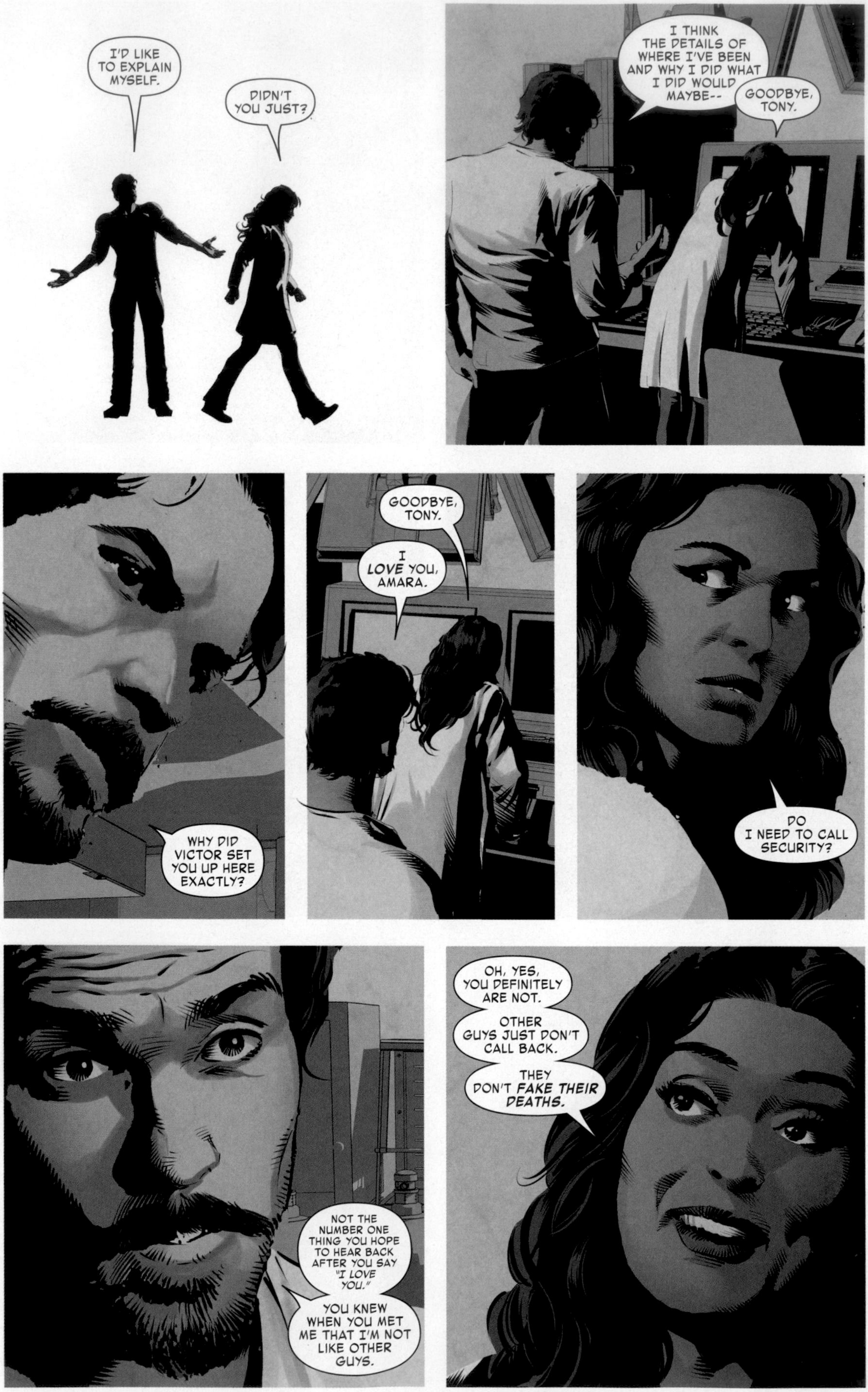
I'D LIKE TO EXPLAIN MYSELF.
DIDN'T YOU JUST?
I THINK THE DETAILS OF WHERE I'VE BEEN AND WHY I DID WHAT I DID WOULD MAYBE--
GOODBYE, TONY.
WHY DID VICTOR SET YOU UP HERE EXACTLY?
GOODBYE, TONY.
I *LOVE* YOU, AMARA.
DO I NEED TO CALL SECURITY?
NOT THE NUMBER ONE THING YOU HOPE TO HEAR BACK AFTER YOU SAY *"I LOVE YOU."*
YOU KNEW WHEN YOU MET ME THAT I'M NOT LIKE OTHER GUYS.
OH, YES, YOU DEFINITELY ARE NOT.
OTHER GUYS JUST DON'T CALL BACK.
THEY DON'T *FAKE THEIR DEATHS.*

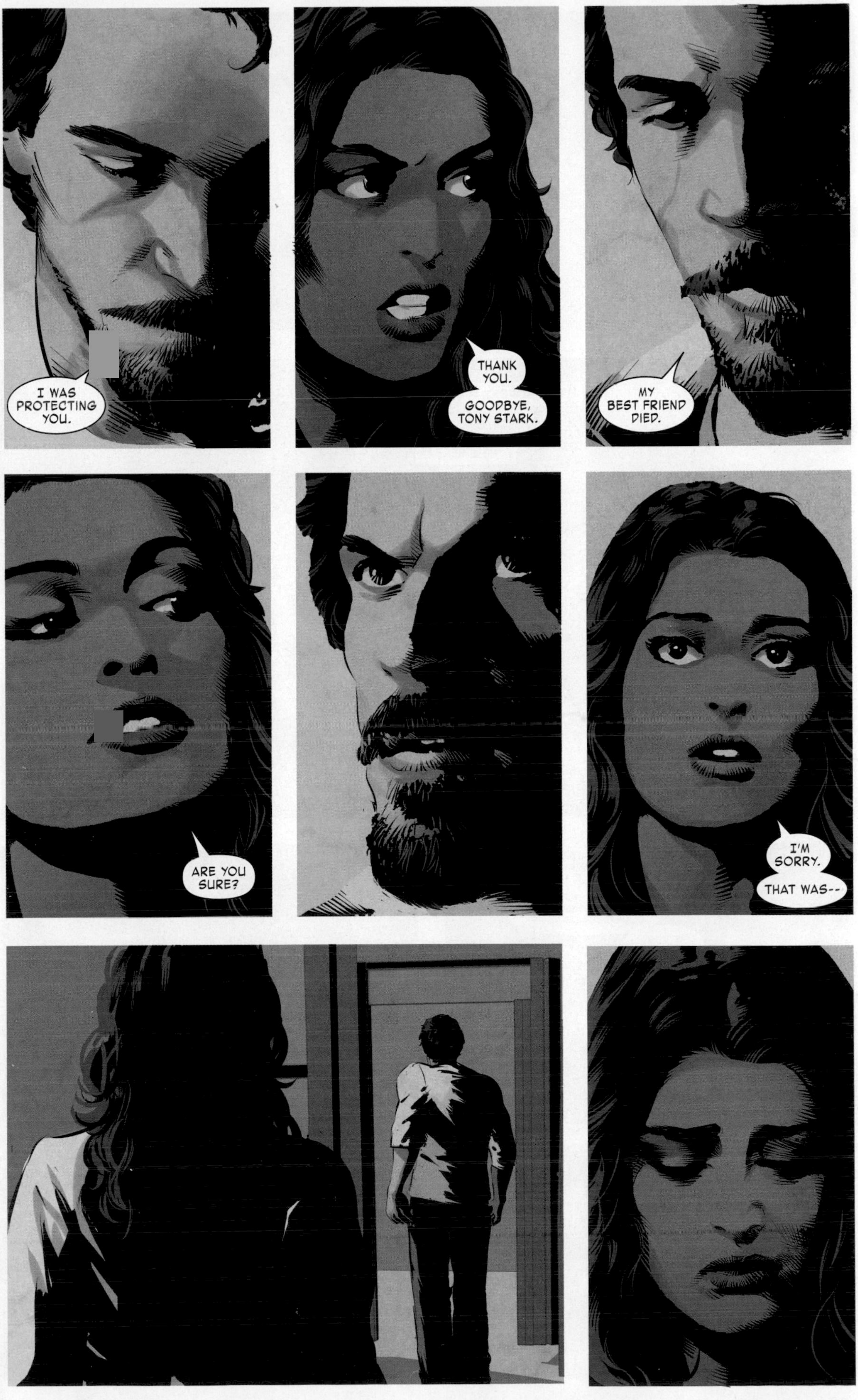
I WAS PROTECTING YOU.
THANK YOU.
GOODBYE, TONY STARK.
MY BEST FRIEND DIED.
ARE YOU SURE?
I'M SORRY.
THAT WAS--

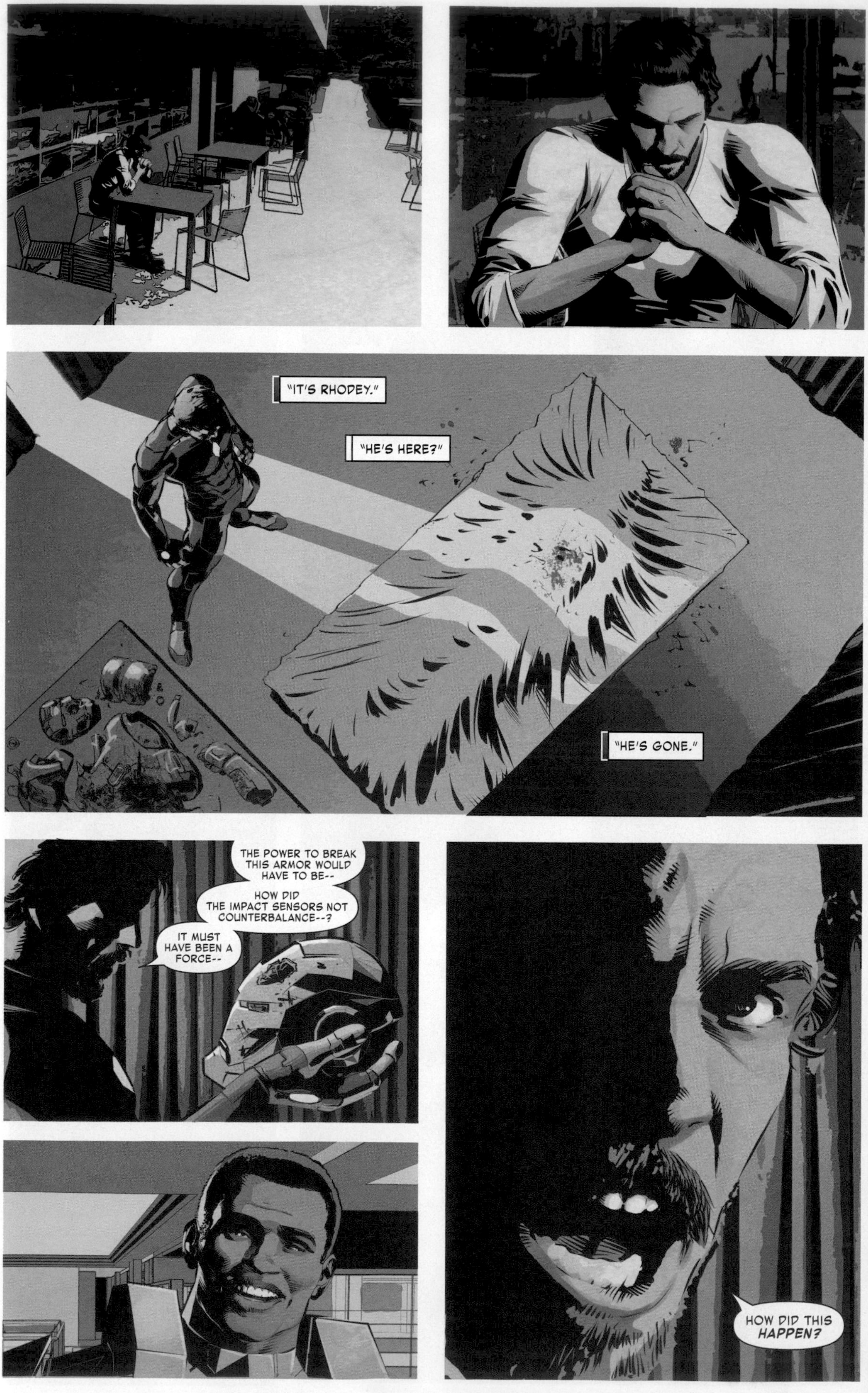

"IT'S RHODEY."
"HE'S HERE?"
"HE'S GONE."
THE POWER TO BREAK THIS ARMOR WOULD HAVE TO BE--
HOW DID THE IMPACT SENSORS NOT COUNTERBALANCE--?
IT MUST HAVE BEEN A FORCE--
HOW DID THIS *HAPPEN?*

James "Rhodey" Rhodes,
A.K.A. War Machine, is Dead
Stark Stock in Free Fall
War Machine Memorial
Open to the Public
...s Desperate
...erstood
...Wanted for
... by Defense Council
...rvel
...e World

...to the Public
Inhumans Desperate
to be Understood

Tony Stark Wanted for
Questioning by Defense Coun...

Captain Marvel
Updates the World

THIS IS COLONEL CAROL DANVERS SPEAKING FOR THE ULTIMATES.

IN THE INTEREST OF FULL DISCLOSURE, THIS MESSAGE IS BEING BEAMED WORLDWIDE.

I HAVE JUST RETURNED FROM A DIPLOMATIC MEETING WITH A LONGTIME ALLY AND BENEFCATOR TO THE ENTIRE PLANET...

SOMEONE I AM SO PROUD TO CALL FRIEND...

KING T'CHALLA, THE BLACK PANTHER.

ONE OF THE GREAT JOYS OF MY LIFE IS THAT I GET TO SPEND REAL TIME WITH THESE GREAT HEROES OF SUCH SHEER STRENGTH AND COMPASSION.

T'CHALLA IS, BY ANY DEFINITION, THE REAL DEAL. SO SMART. SUCH A PRESENCE. SUCH A GREAT LEADER TO HIS PEOPLE.

AND HE AND I, WELL, WE TALKED ABOUT THE FUTURE.

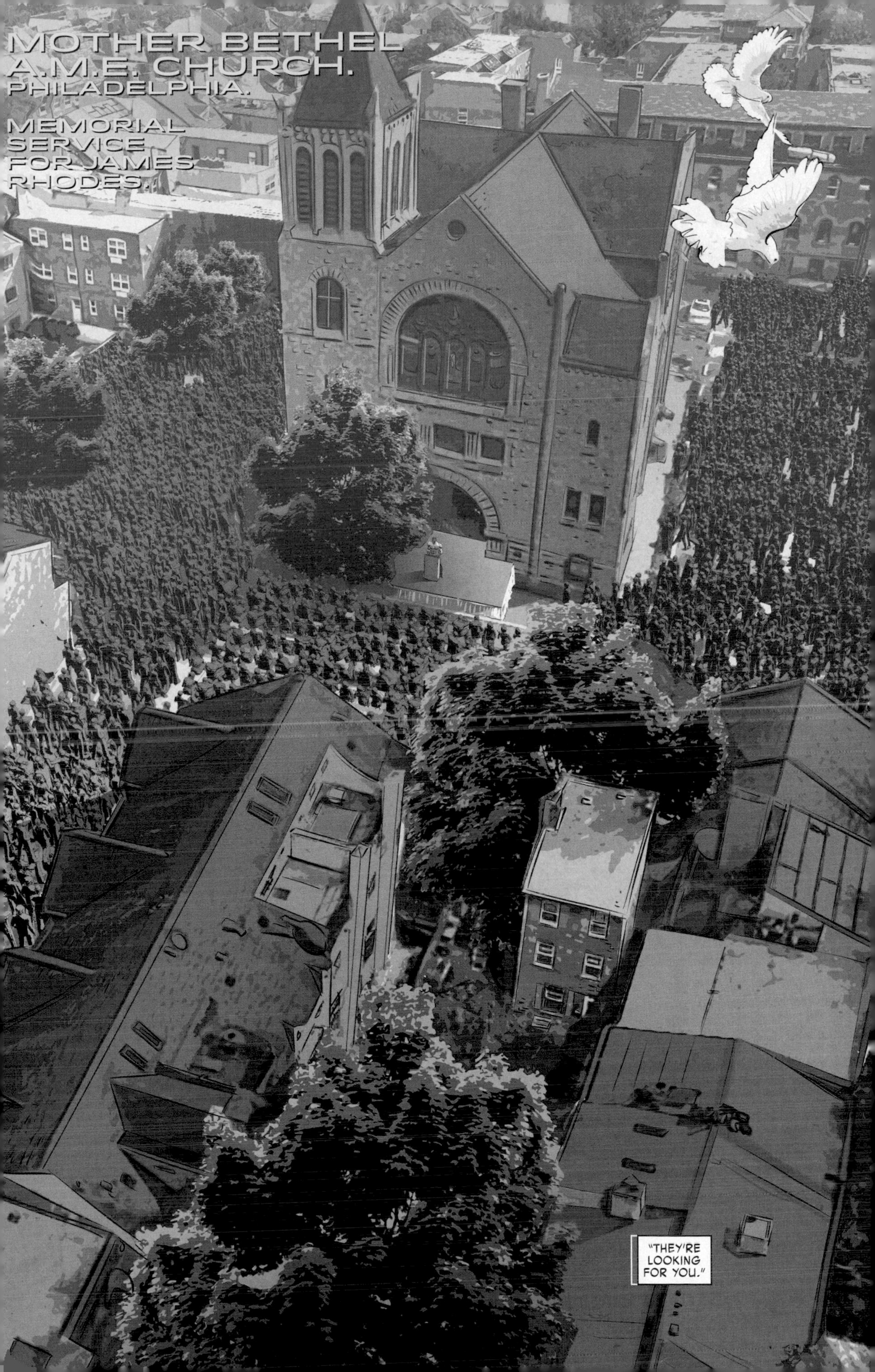
MOTHER BETHEL A.M.E. CHURCH.
PHILADELPHIA.
MEMORIAL SERVICE FOR JAMES RHODES.
"THEY'RE LOOKING FOR YOU."

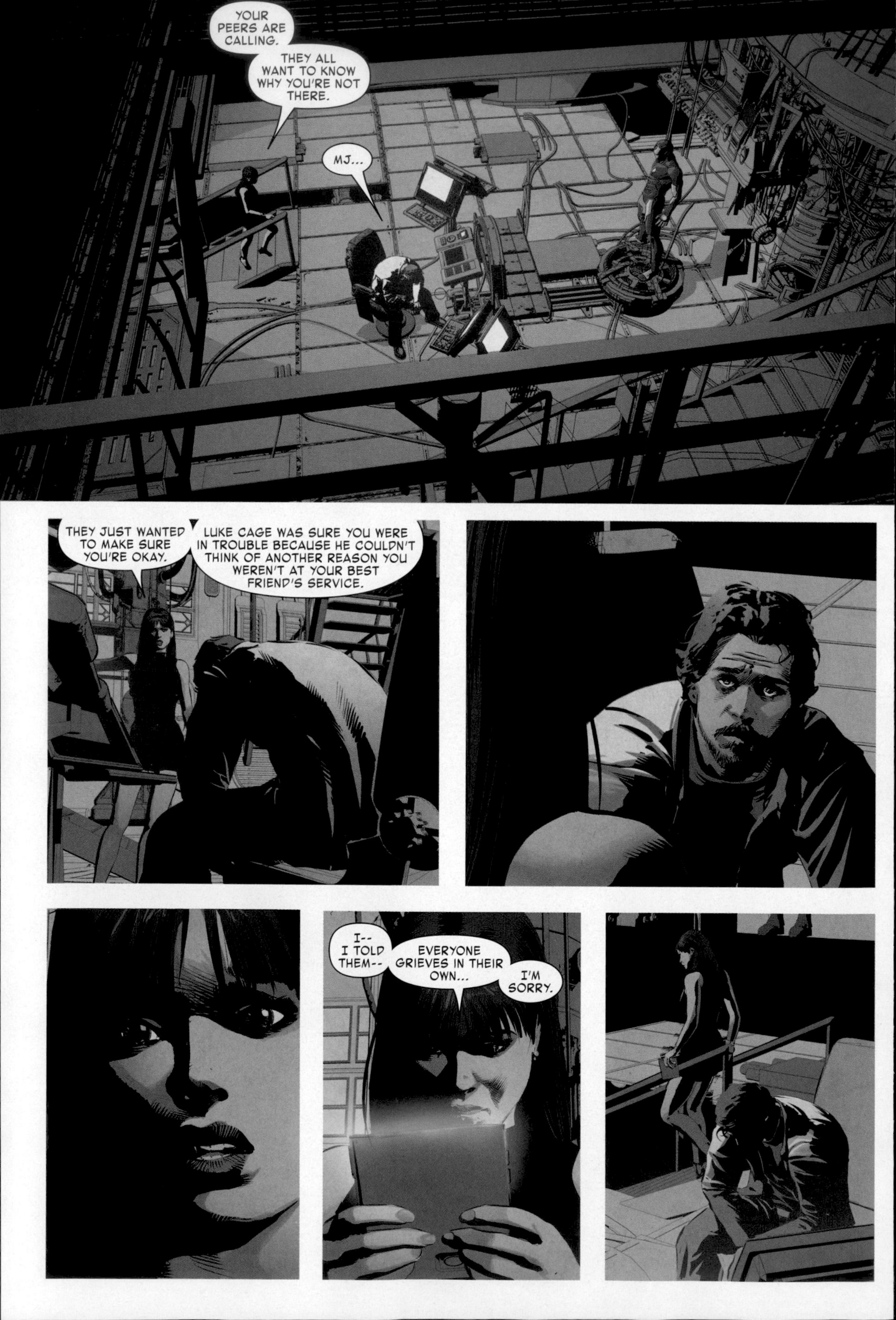
YOUR PEERS ARE CALLING.
THEY ALL WANT TO KNOW WHY YOU'RE NOT THERE.
MJ...
THEY JUST WANTED TO MAKE SURE YOU'RE OKAY.
LUKE CAGE WAS SURE YOU WERE IN TROUBLE BECAUSE HE COULDN'T THINK OF ANOTHER REASON YOU WEREN'T AT YOUR BEST FRIEND'S SERVICE.
I-- I TOLD THEM--
EVERYONE GRIEVES IN THEIR OWN...
I'M SORRY.

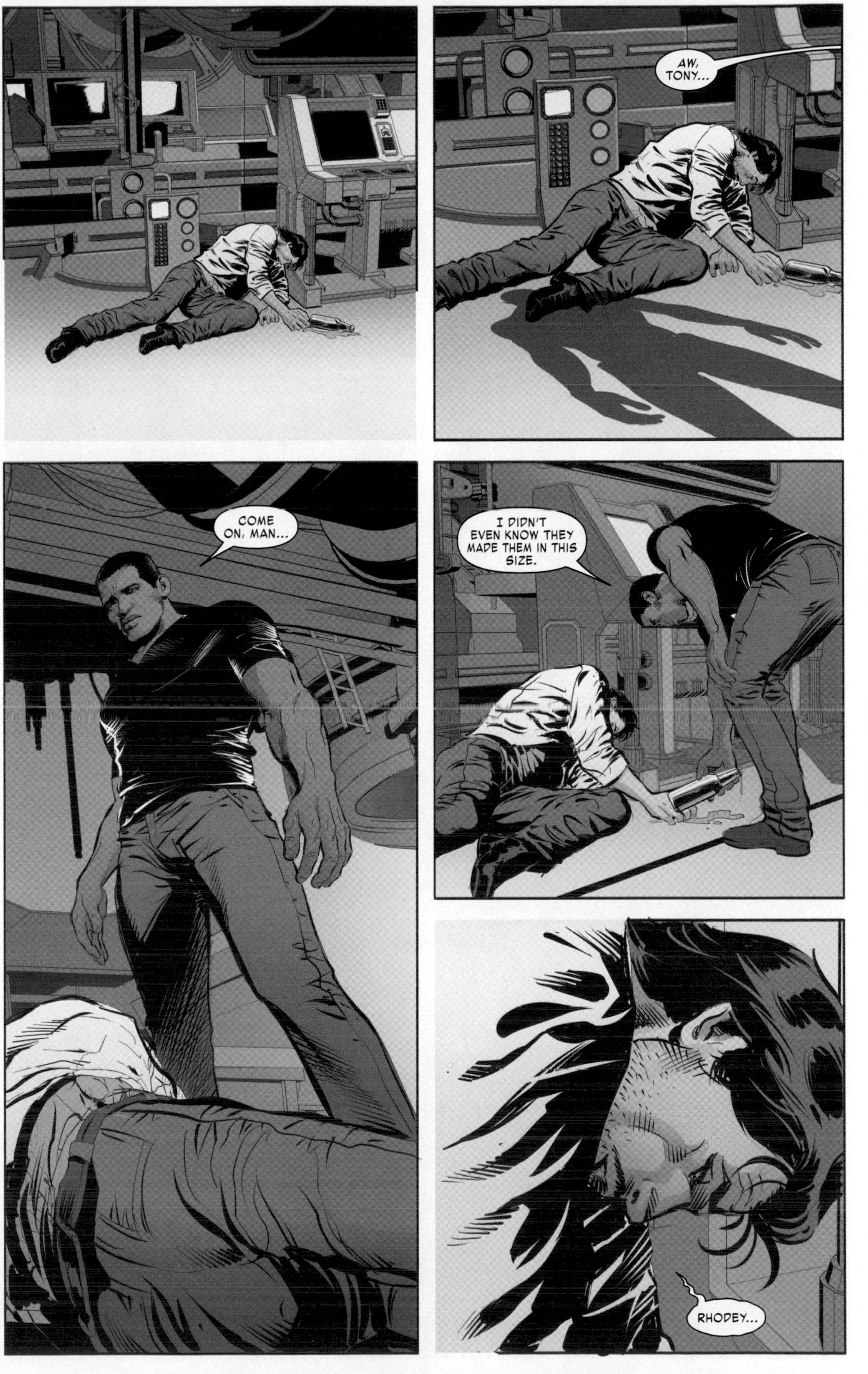
AW, TONY...
COME ON, MAN...
I DIDN'T EVEN KNOW THEY MADE THEM IN THIS SIZE.
RHODEY...

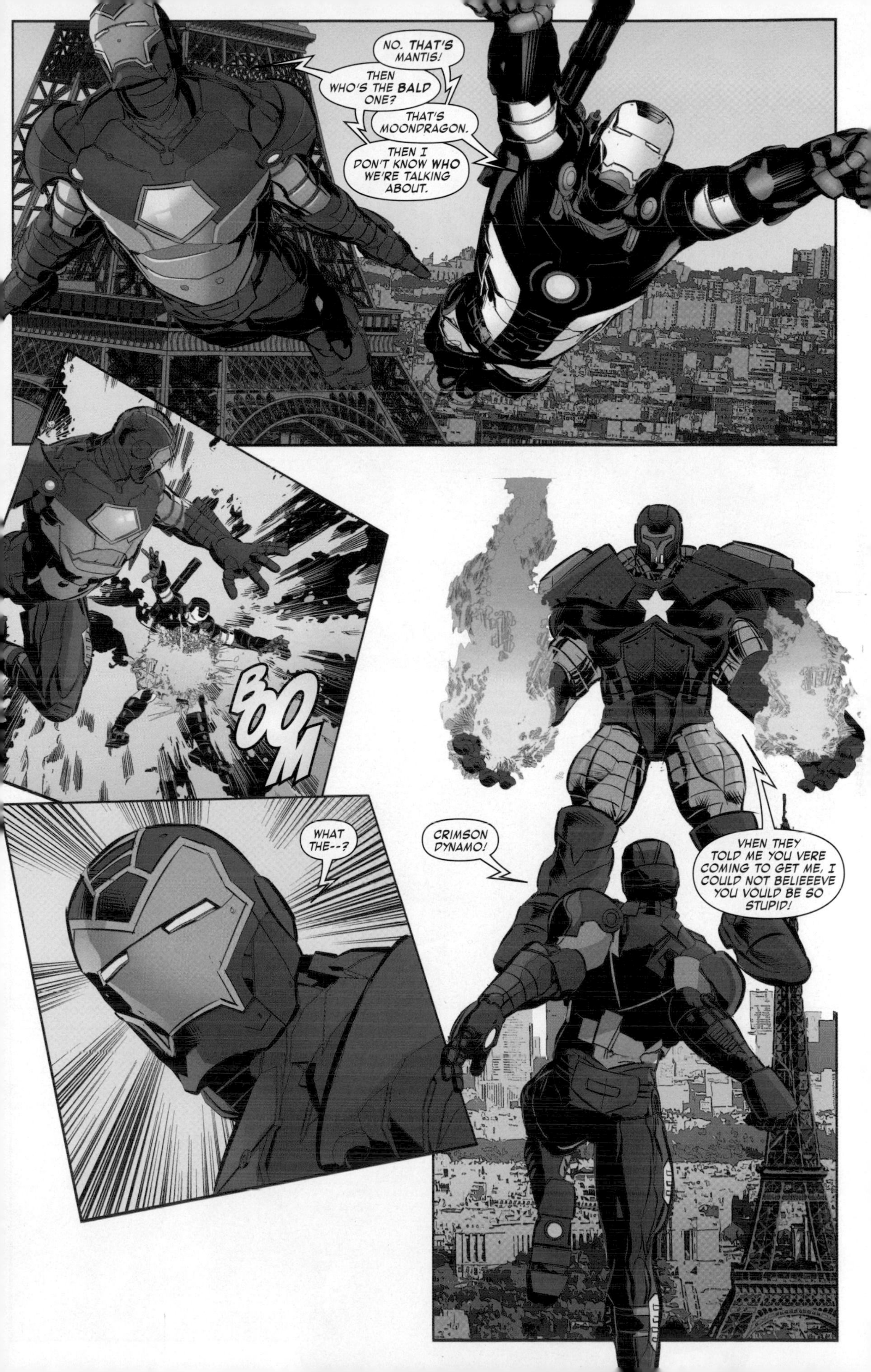
NO. THAT'S MANTIS!
THEN WHO'S THE BALD ONE?
THAT'S MOONDRAGON.
THEN I DON'T KNOW WHO WE'RE TALKING ABOUT.
BOOM
WHAT THE--?
CRIMSON DYNAMO!
VHEN THEY TOLD ME YOU VERE COMING TO GET ME, I COULD NOT BELIEEEVE YOU VOULD BE SO STUPID!

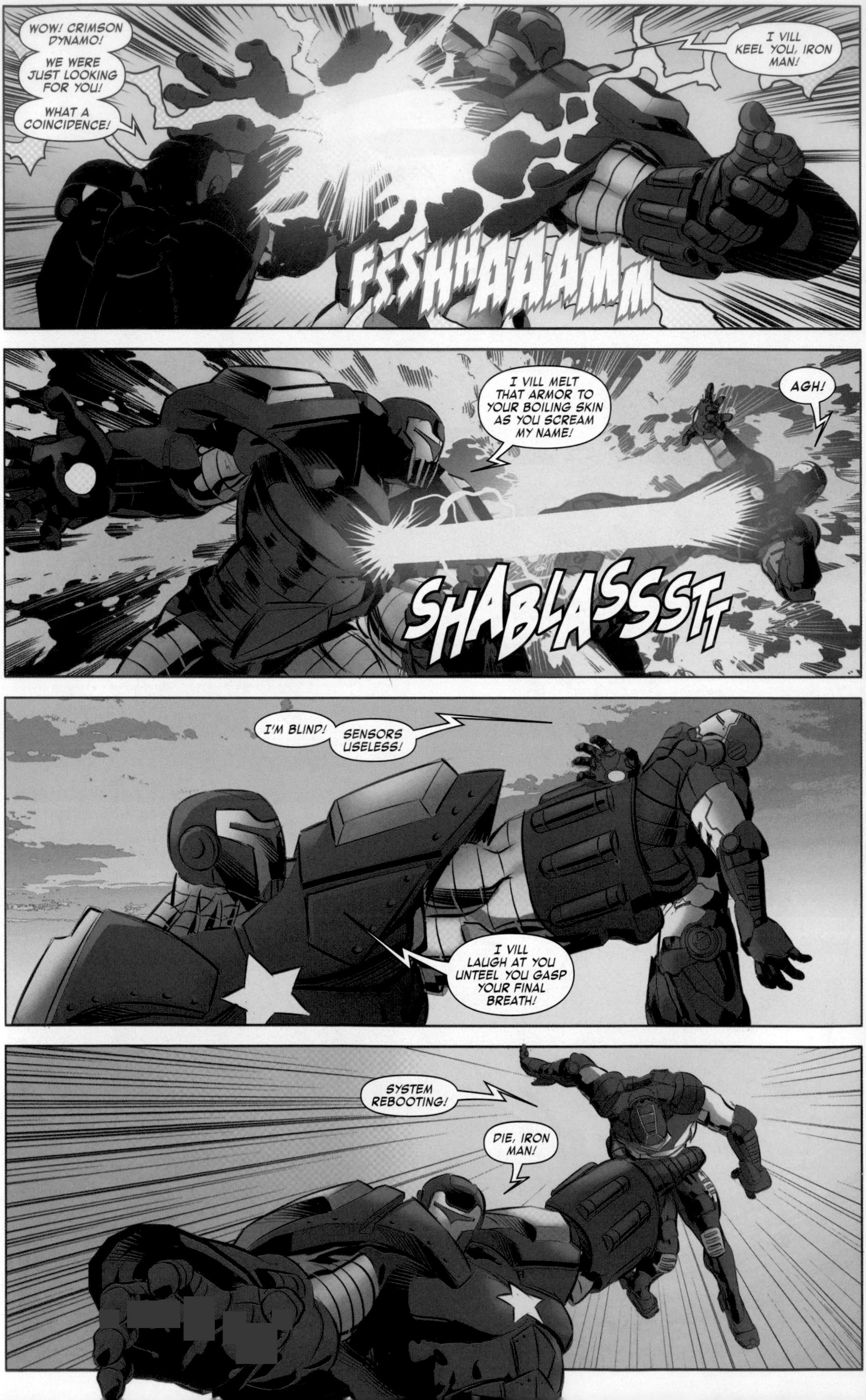
WOW! CRIMSON DYNAMO!
WE WERE JUST LOOKING FOR YOU!
WHAT A COINCIDENCE!
I VILL KEEL YOU, IRON MAN!
FSSHHAAAAMM
I VILL MELT THAT ARMOR TO YOUR BOILING SKIN AS YOU SCREAM MY NAME!
AGH!
SHABLASSSSTT
I'M BLIND!
SENSORS USELESS!
I VILL LAUGH AT YOU UNTEEL YOU GASP YOUR FINAL BREATH!
SYSTEM REBOOTING!
DIE, IRON MAN!

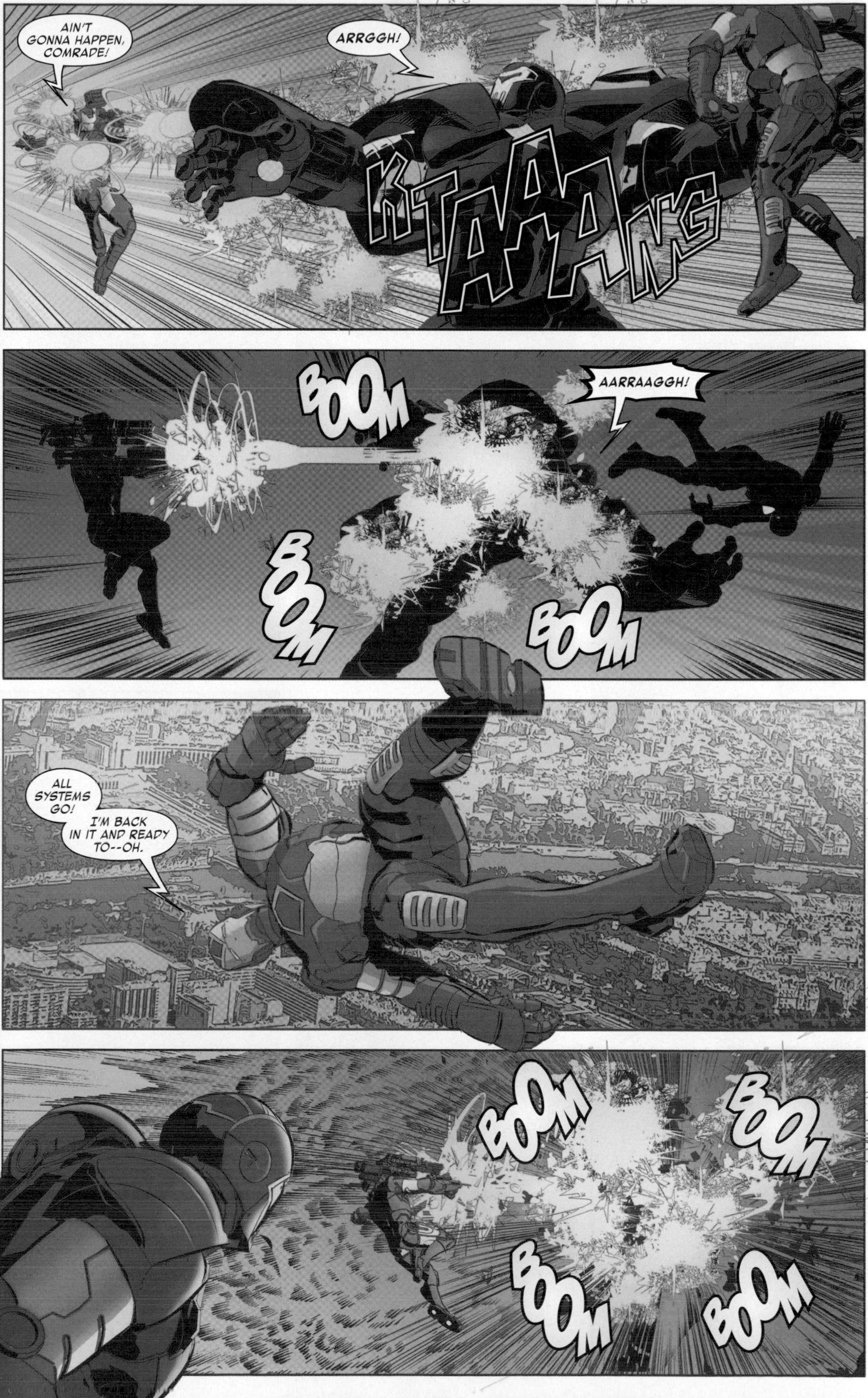
AIN'T GONNA HAPPEN, COMRADE!
ARRGGH!
KTAAAANG
BOOM
AARRAAGGH!
BOOM
BOOM
ALL SYSTEMS GO!
I'M BACK IN IT AND READY TO--OH.
BOOM
BOOM
BOOM
BOOM

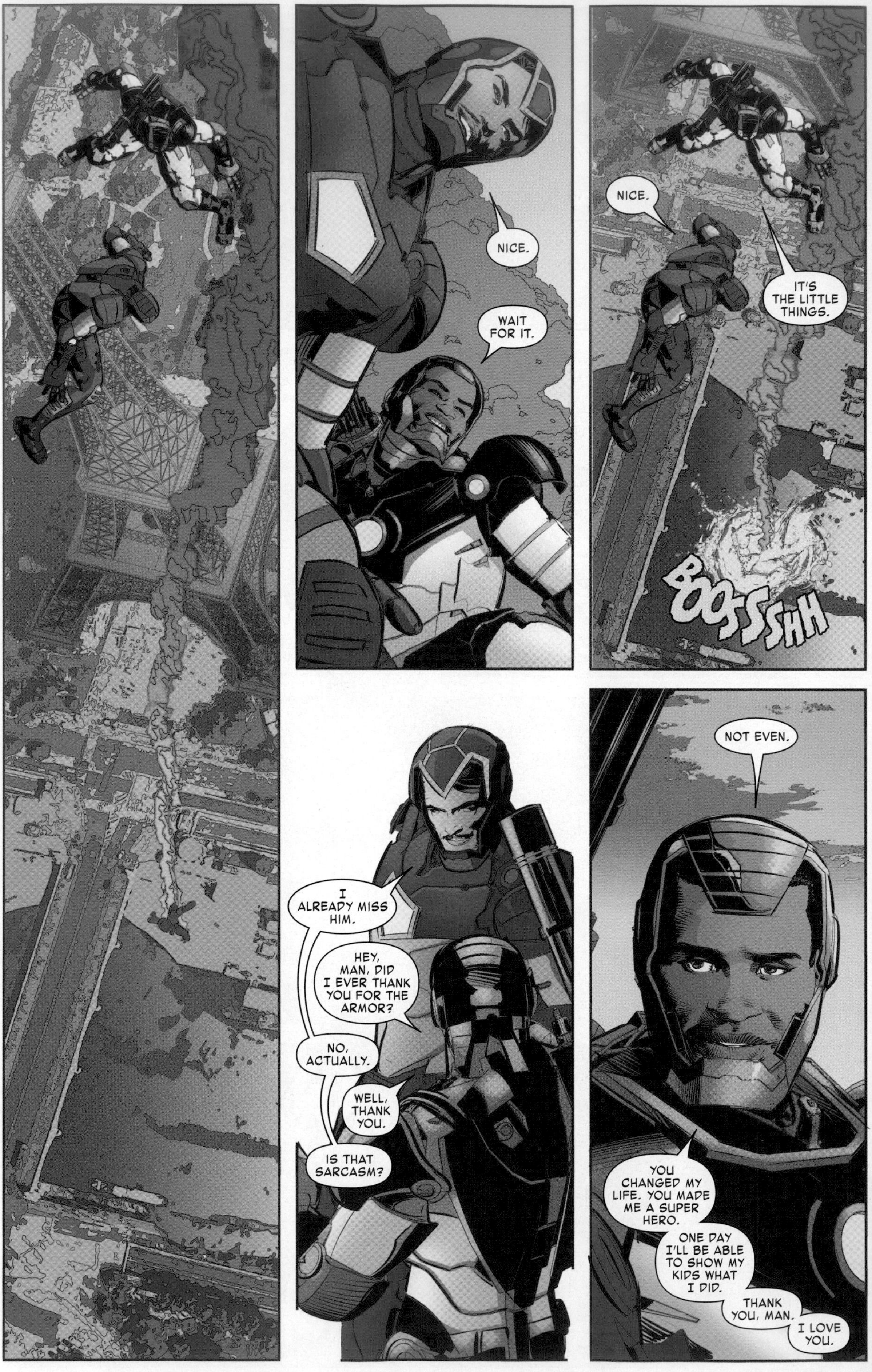
NICE.
WAIT FOR IT.
NICE.
IT'S THE LITTLE THINGS.
BOOSSHH
I ALREADY MISS HIM.
HEY, MAN, DID I EVER THANK YOU FOR THE ARMOR?
NO, ACTUALLY.
WELL, THANK YOU.
IS THAT SARCASM?
NOT EVEN.
YOU CHANGED MY LIFE. YOU MADE ME A SUPER HERO.
ONE DAY I'LL BE ABLE TO SHOW MY KIDS WHAT I DID.
THANK YOU, MAN.
I LOVE YOU.

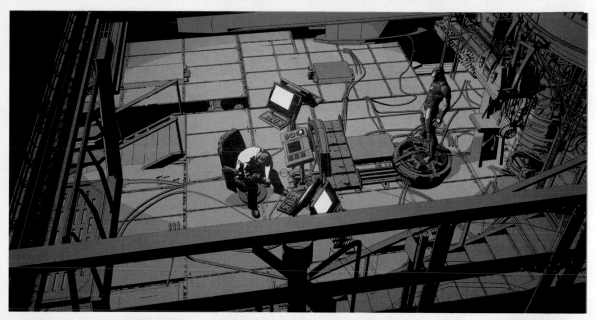

THINK MAYBE I NEED A MEETING.

NO. YOU DON'T.

YOU NEED TO REFOCUS.

GET YOUR COMPANY AFLOAT.

FIND YOUR FOOTING AGAIN AND STOP WALLOWING.

DOOM.

YOU KEEP DISTRACTING YOURSELF.

NOW YOU HAVE *THIS* TO DISTRACT YOURSELF WITH.

DOOM.

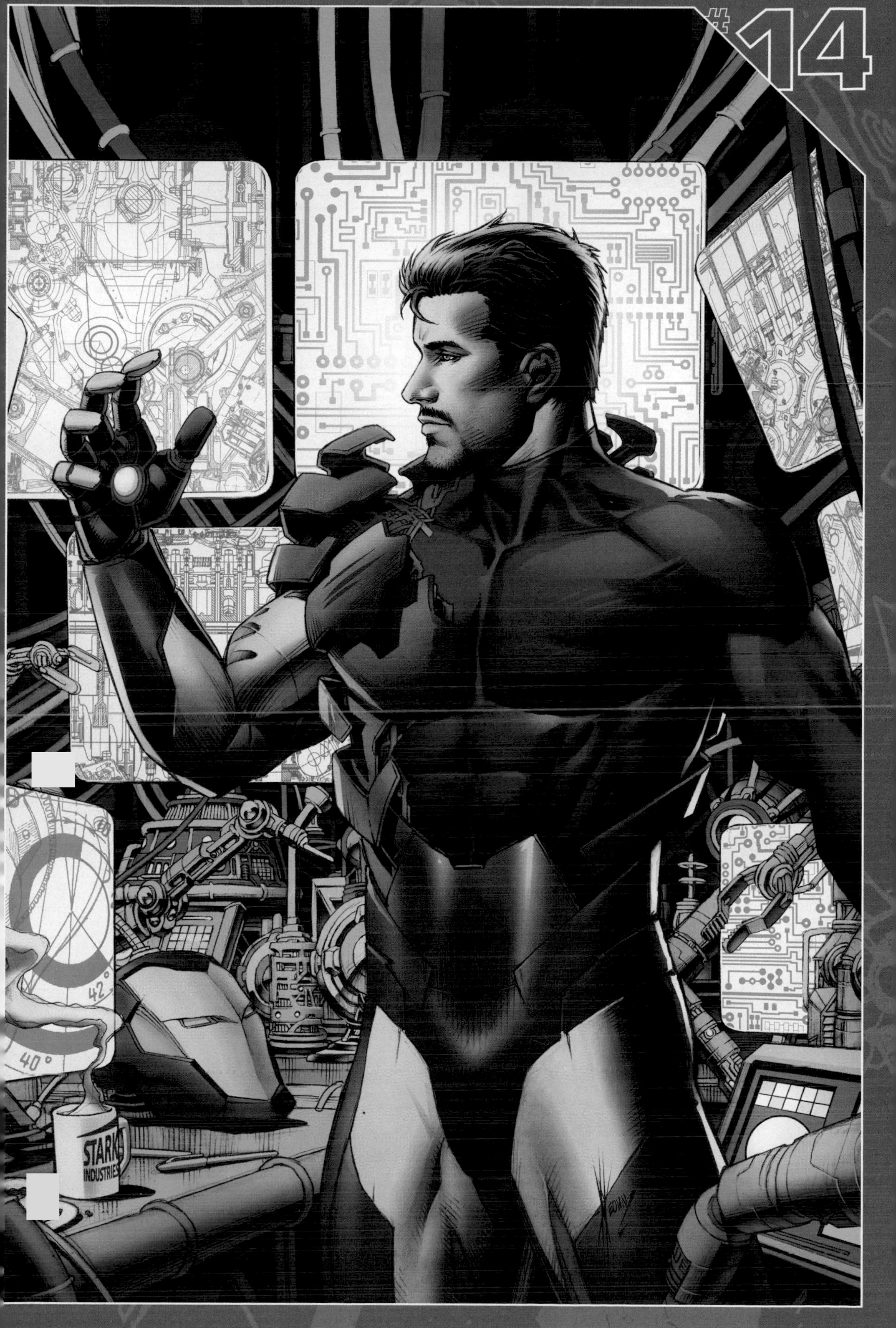
#14
42°
40°
STARK INDUSTRIES

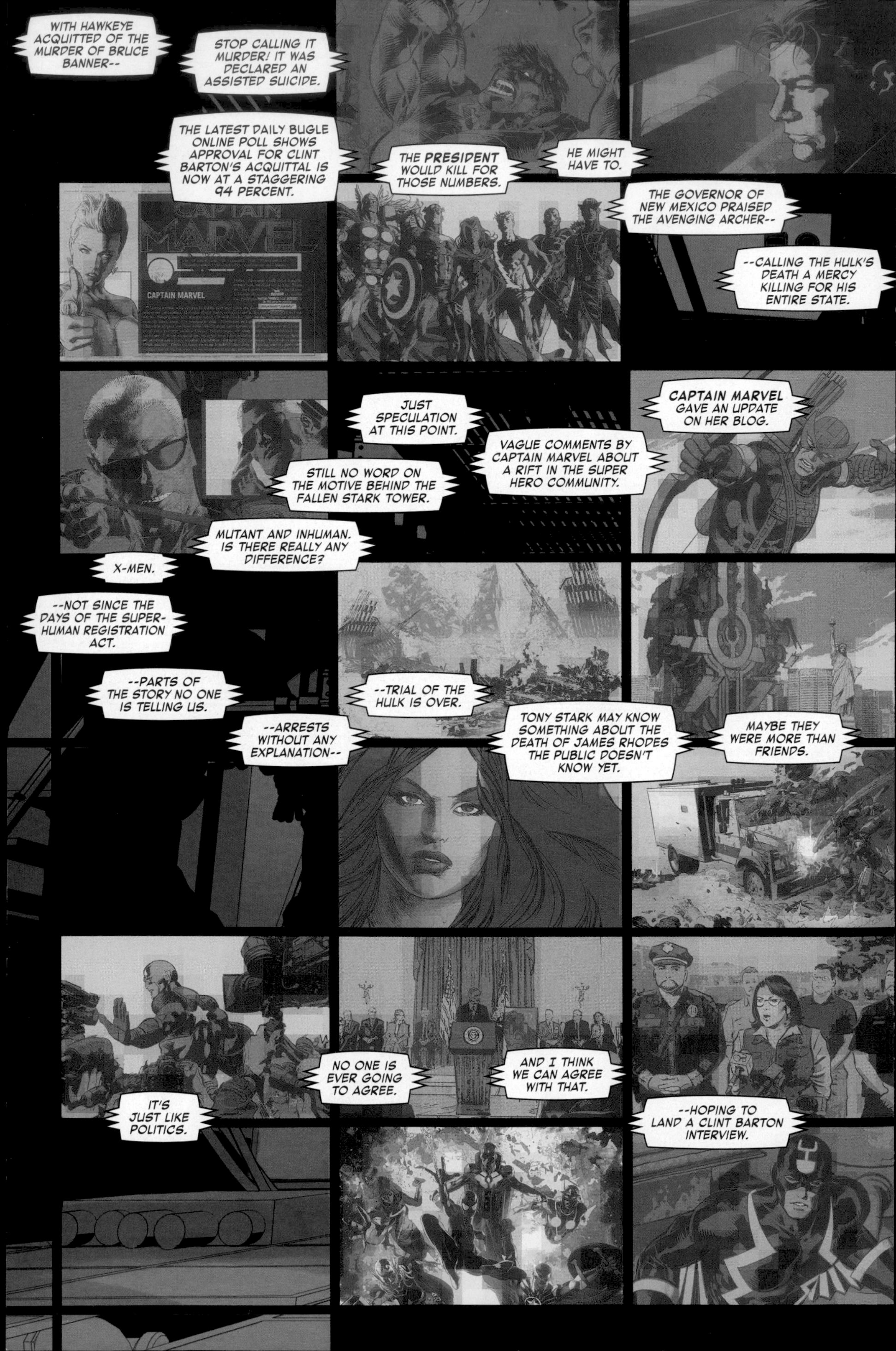

WITH HAWKEYE ACQUITTED OF THE MURDER OF BRUCE BANNER--
STOP CALLING IT MURDER! IT WAS DECLARED AN ASSISTED SUICIDE.
THE LATEST DAILY BUGLE ONLINE POLL SHOWS APPROVAL FOR CLINT BARTON'S ACQUITTAL IS NOW AT A STAGGERING 94 PERCENT.
THE PRESIDENT WOULD KILL FOR THOSE NUMBERS.
HE MIGHT HAVE TO.
CAPTAIN MARVEL
CAPTAIN MARVEL
THE GOVERNOR OF NEW MEXICO PRAISED THE AVENGING ARCHER--
--CALLING THE HULK'S DEATH A MERCY KILLING FOR HIS ENTIRE STATE.
JUST SPECULATION AT THIS POINT.
CAPTAIN MARVEL GAVE AN UPDATE ON HER BLOG.
VAGUE COMMENTS BY CAPTAIN MARVEL ABOUT A RIFT IN THE SUPER HERO COMMUNITY.
STILL NO WORD ON THE MOTIVE BEHIND THE FALLEN STARK TOWER.
MUTANT AND INHUMAN. IS THERE REALLY ANY DIFFERENCE?
X-MEN.
--NOT SINCE THE DAYS OF THE SUPER-HUMAN REGISTRATION ACT.
--PARTS OF THE STORY NO ONE IS TELLING US.
--TRIAL OF THE HULK IS OVER.
--ARRESTS WITHOUT ANY EXPLANATION--
TONY STARK MAY KNOW SOMETHING ABOUT THE DEATH OF JAMES RHODES THE PUBLIC DOESN'T KNOW YET.
MAYBE THEY WERE MORE THAN FRIENDS.
NO ONE IS EVER GOING TO AGREE.
AND I THINK WE CAN AGREE WITH THAT.
IT'S JUST LIKE POLITICS.
--HOPING TO LAND A CLINT BARTON INTERVIEW.

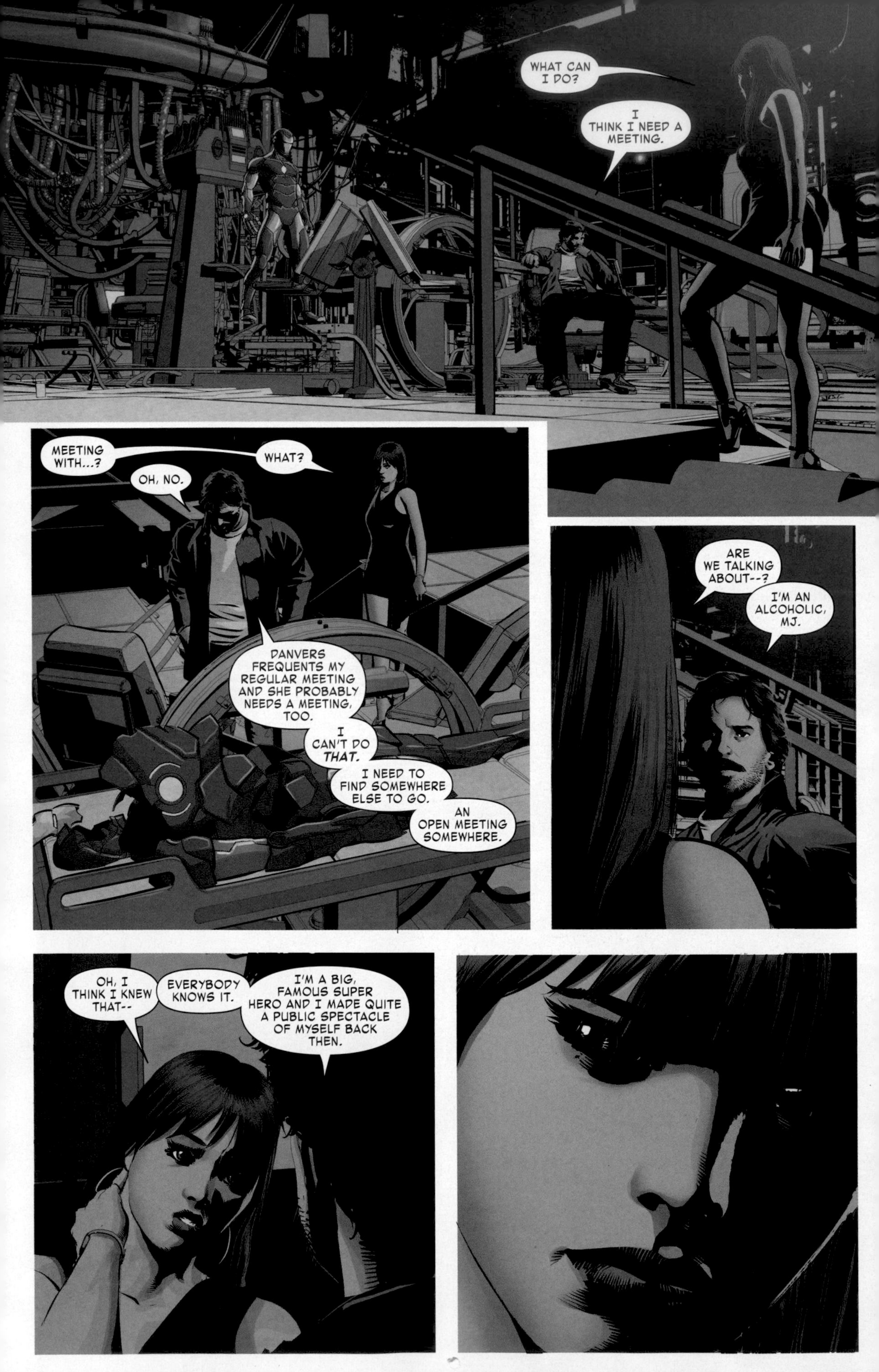
WHAT CAN I DO?
I THINK I NEED A MEETING.
MEETING WITH...?
WHAT?
OH, NO.
DANVERS FREQUENTS MY REGULAR MEETING AND SHE PROBABLY NEEDS A MEETING, TOO.
I CAN'T DO *THAT.*
I NEED TO FIND SOMEWHERE ELSE TO GO.
AN OPEN MEETING SOMEWHERE.
ARE WE TALKING ABOUT--?
I'M AN ALCOHOLIC, MJ.
OH, I THINK I KNEW THAT--
EVERYBODY KNOWS IT.
I'M A BIG, FAMOUS SUPER HERO AND I MADE QUITE A PUBLIC SPECTACLE OF MYSELF BACK THEN.

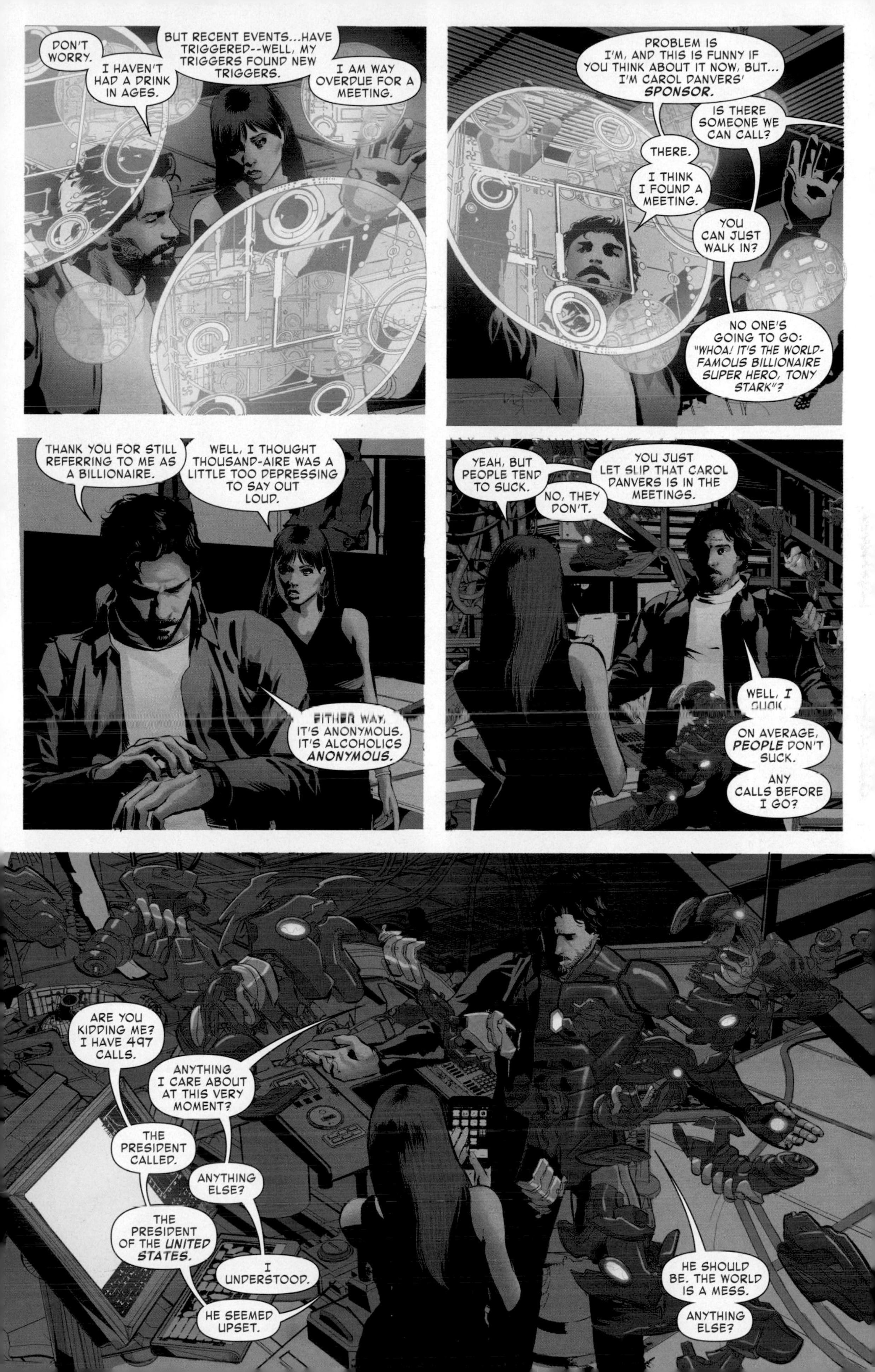
DON'T WORRY.
I HAVEN'T HAD A DRINK IN AGES.
BUT RECENT EVENTS...HAVE TRIGGERED--WELL, MY TRIGGERS FOUND NEW TRIGGERS.
I AM WAY OVERDUE FOR A MEETING.
PROBLEM IS I'M, AND THIS IS FUNNY IF YOU THINK ABOUT IT NOW, BUT... I'M CAROL DANVERS' SPONSOR.
IS THERE SOMEONE WE CAN CALL?
THERE.
I THINK I FOUND A MEETING.
YOU CAN JUST WALK IN?
NO ONE'S GOING TO GO: "WHOA! IT'S THE WORLD-FAMOUS BILLIONAIRE SUPER HERO, TONY STARK"?
THANK YOU FOR STILL REFERRING TO ME AS A BILLIONAIRE.
WELL, I THOUGHT THOUSAND-AIRE WAS A LITTLE TOO DEPRESSING TO SAY OUT LOUD.
EITHER WAY, IT'S ANONYMOUS. IT'S ALCOHOLICS ANONYMOUS.
YEAH, BUT PEOPLE TEND TO SUCK.
YOU JUST LET SLIP THAT CAROL DANVERS IS IN THE MEETINGS.
NO, THEY DON'T.
WELL, I SUCK.
ON AVERAGE, PEOPLE DON'T SUCK.
ANY CALLS BEFORE I GO?
ARE YOU KIDDING ME? I HAVE 497 CALLS.
ANYTHING I CARE ABOUT AT THIS VERY MOMENT?
THE PRESIDENT CALLED.
ANYTHING ELSE?
THE PRESIDENT OF THE UNITED STATES.
I UNDERSTOOD.
HE SEEMED UPSET.
HE SHOULD BE. THE WORLD IS A MESS.
ANYTHING ELSE?

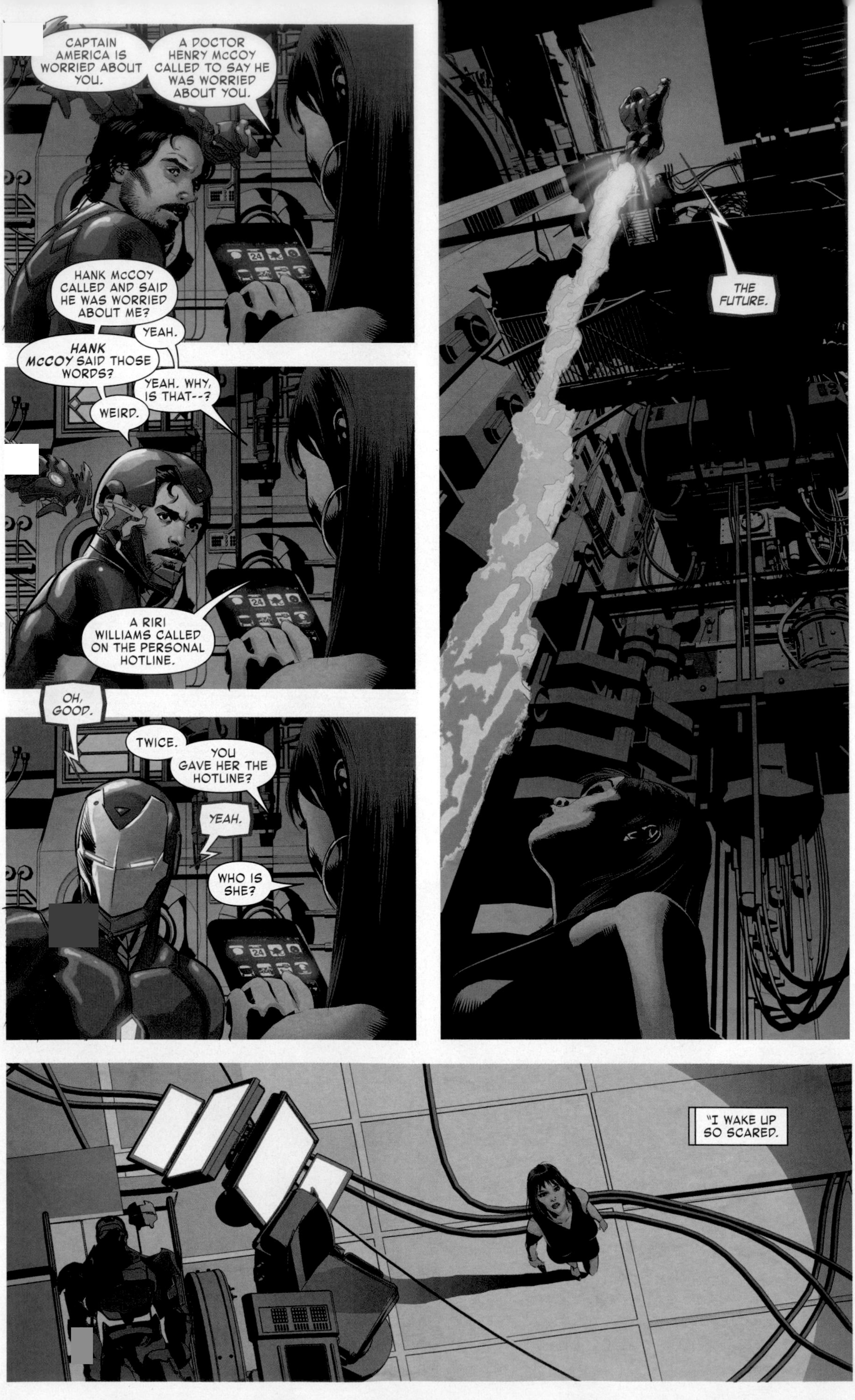
CAPTAIN AMERICA IS WORRIED ABOUT YOU.
A DOCTOR HENRY McCOY CALLED TO SAY HE WAS WORRIED ABOUT YOU.
HANK McCOY CALLED AND SAID HE WAS WORRIED ABOUT ME?
YEAH.
HANK McCOY SAID THOSE WORDS?
YEAH. WHY, IS THAT--?
WEIRD.
A RIRI WILLIAMS CALLED ON THE PERSONAL HOTLINE.
OH, GOOD.
TWICE.
YOU GAVE HER THE HOTLINE?
YEAH.
WHO IS SHE?
THE FUTURE.
"I WAKE UP SO SCARED.

IT'S INTERESTING, WHAT HE JUST SAID.

I'M ACTUALLY IN LAW ENFORCEMENT AND I DO THE SAME THING.

YES, BECAUSE OF THE JOB, I TEND TO SEE THINGS AT THEIR WORST...

I SEE PEOPLE AT THEIR WORST, AT THEIR MOST DIRE.

I UNDERSTAND THAT MY PERSPECTIVE CAN BE WARPED.

BUT I WAKE UP--THIS IS MY ROUTINE--I WAKE UP, I GRAB MY TABLET, WHICH I HAVE TAKEN TO SLEEPING WITH, I OPEN IT...

...AND THE FIRST THING I DO AFTER MY GLORIOUS FIVE HOURS OF SLEEP...

...IS LOOK TO SEE IF THE WORLD IS STILL TURNING.

TO MAKE SURE WE'RE NOT BEING DESTROYED.

TO MAKE SURE WE'RE NOT AT WAR.

THIS IS THE FIRST THING I DO.

I WAKE UP AND MAKE SURE THE WORLD IS STILL TURNING.

EVERY DAY.

AND IT HIT ME, THAT IS INSANE.

IT'S INSANE THAT THE WORLD--THAT THE WORLD IS SO OUT OF CONTROL THAT LITERALLY ANY DAY COULD BE THE LAST...

...OR THE BEGINNING OF A WHOLE NEW HORROR THAT WOULD--

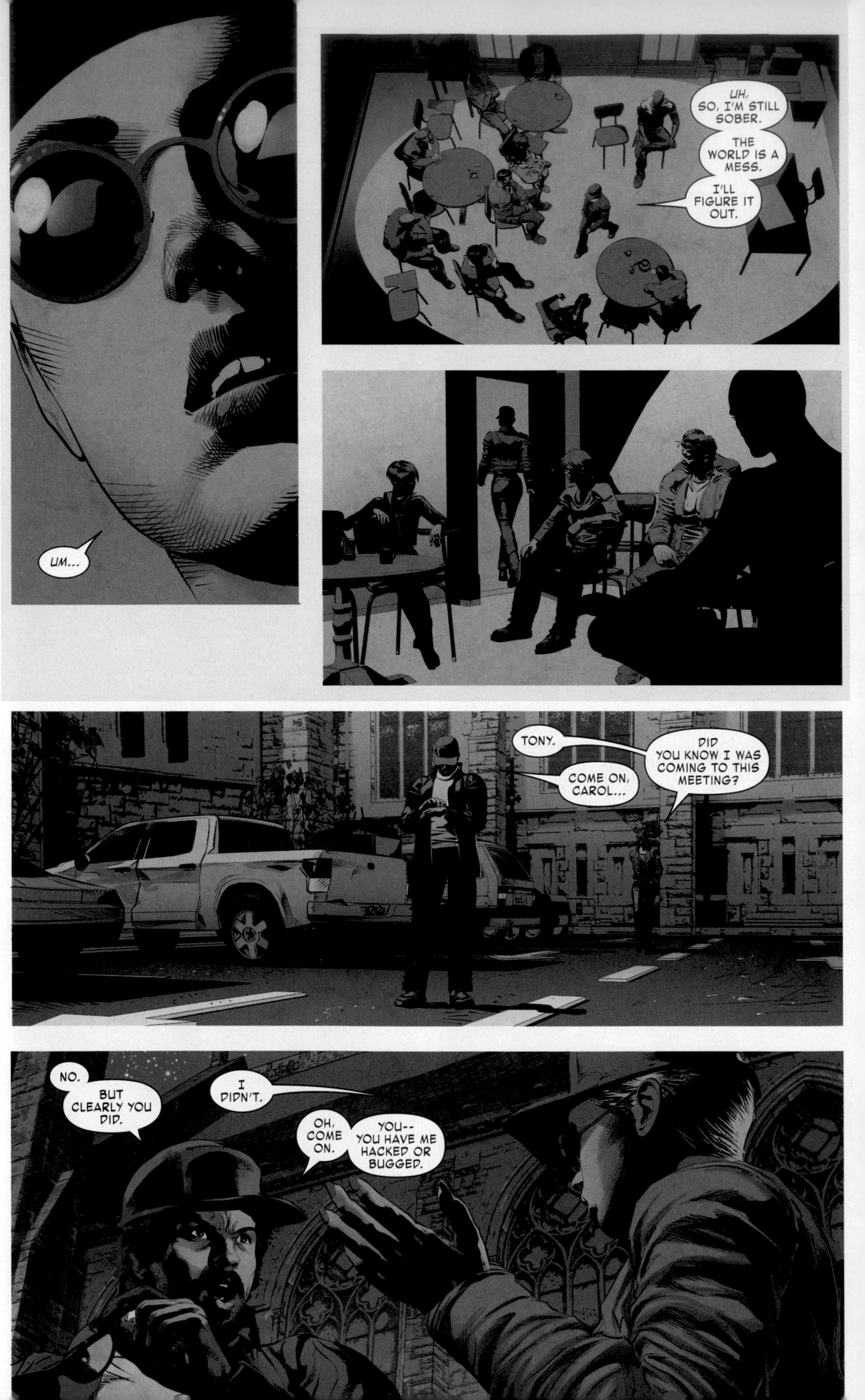
UM...
UH, SO, I'M STILL SOBER.
THE WORLD IS A MESS.
I'LL FIGURE IT OUT.
TONY.
COME ON, CAROL...
DID YOU KNOW I WAS COMING TO THIS MEETING?
NO.
BUT CLEARLY YOU DID.
I DIDN'T.
OH, COME ON.
YOU-- YOU HAVE ME HACKED OR BUGGED.

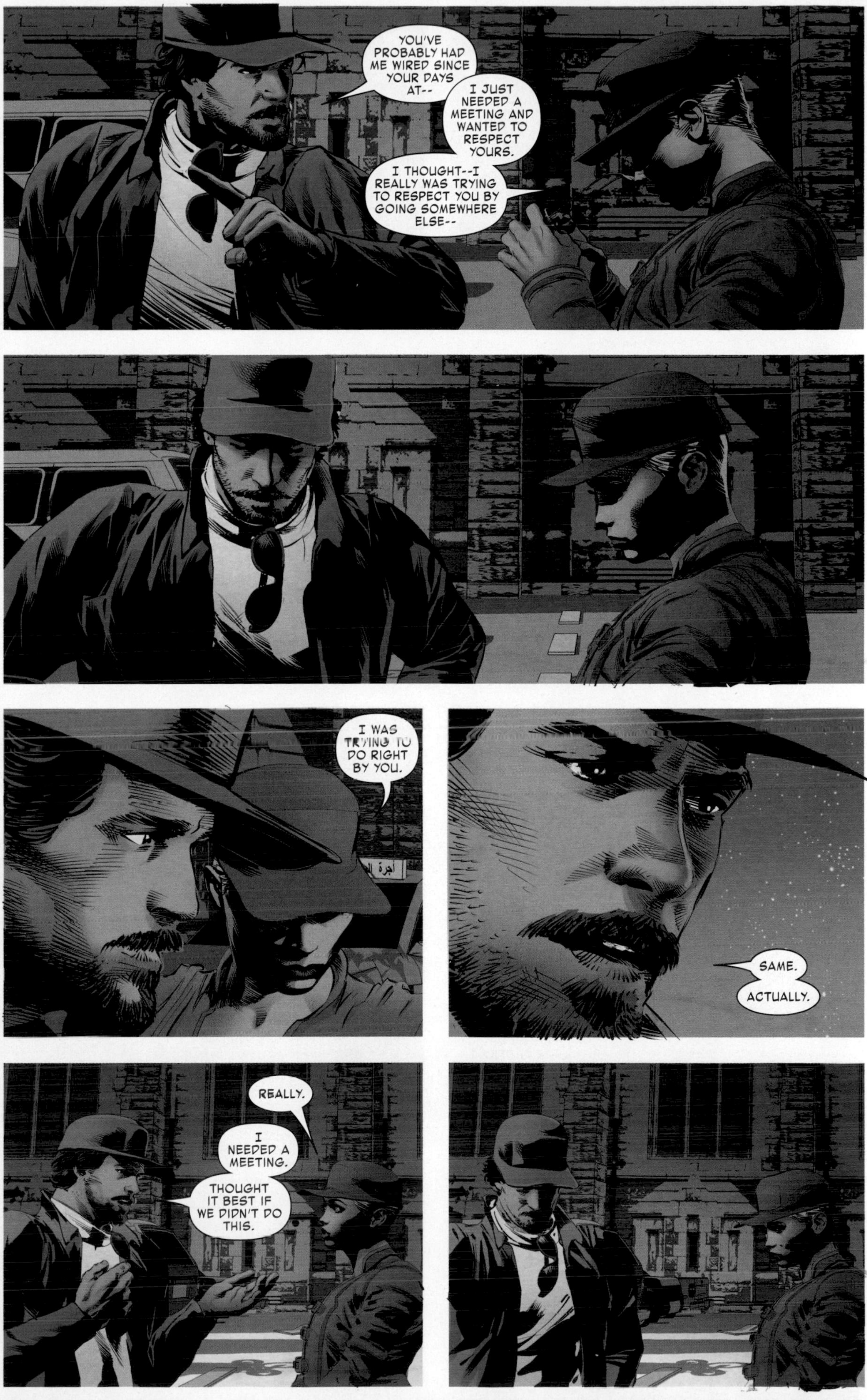
YOU'VE PROBABLY HAD ME WIRED SINCE YOUR DAYS AT--
I JUST NEEDED A MEETING AND WANTED TO RESPECT YOURS.
I THOUGHT--I REALLY WAS TRYING TO RESPECT YOU BY GOING SOMEWHERE ELSE--
I WAS TRYING TO DO RIGHT BY YOU.
SAME.
ACTUALLY.
REALLY.
I NEEDED A MEETING.
THOUGHT IT BEST IF WE DIDN'T DO THIS.

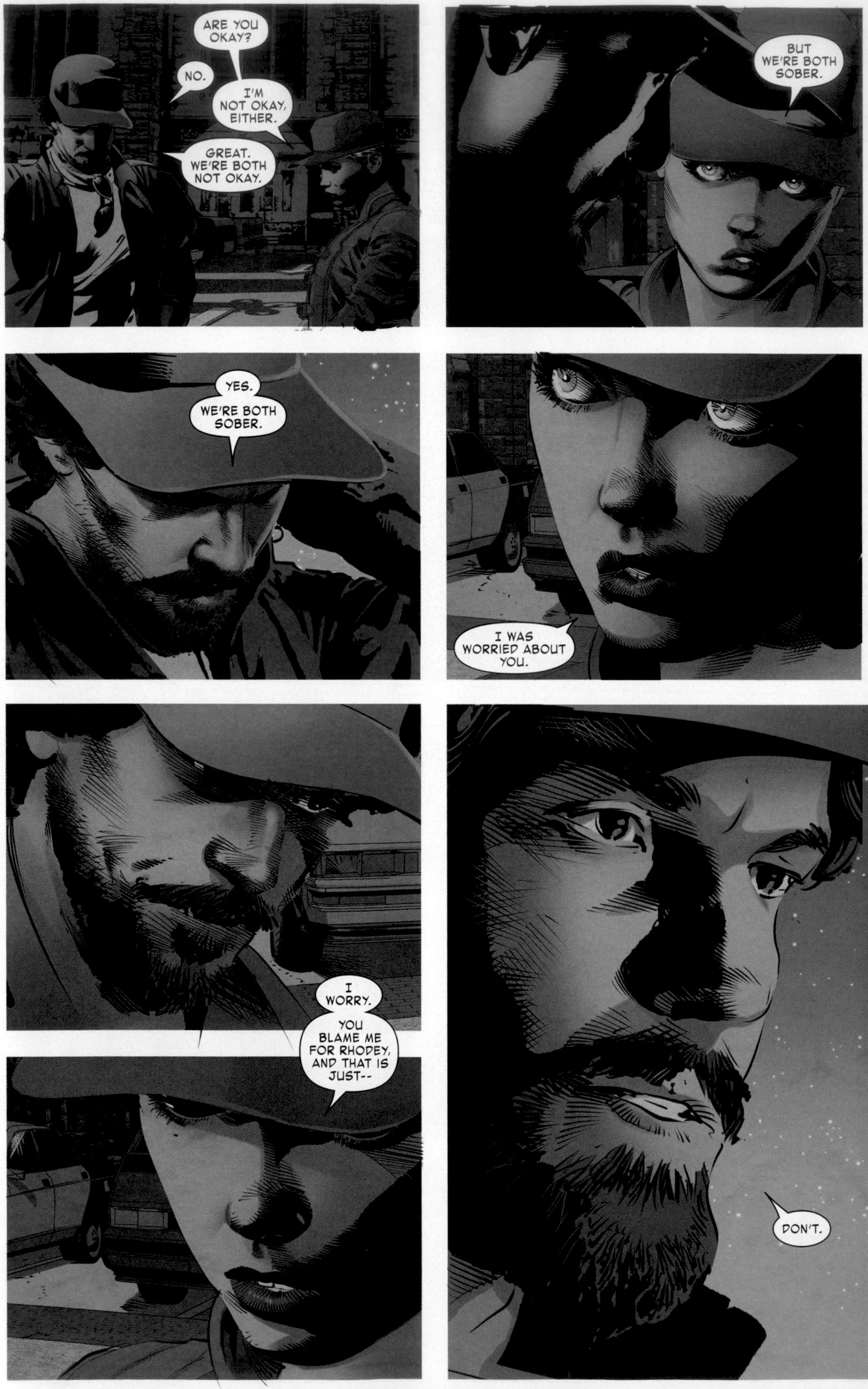
ARE YOU OKAY?
NO.
I'M NOT OKAY, EITHER.
GREAT. WE'RE BOTH NOT OKAY.
BUT WE'RE BOTH SOBER.
YES. WE'RE BOTH SOBER.
I WAS WORRIED ABOUT YOU.
I WORRY.
YOU BLAME ME FOR RHODEY, AND THAT IS JUST--
DON'T.

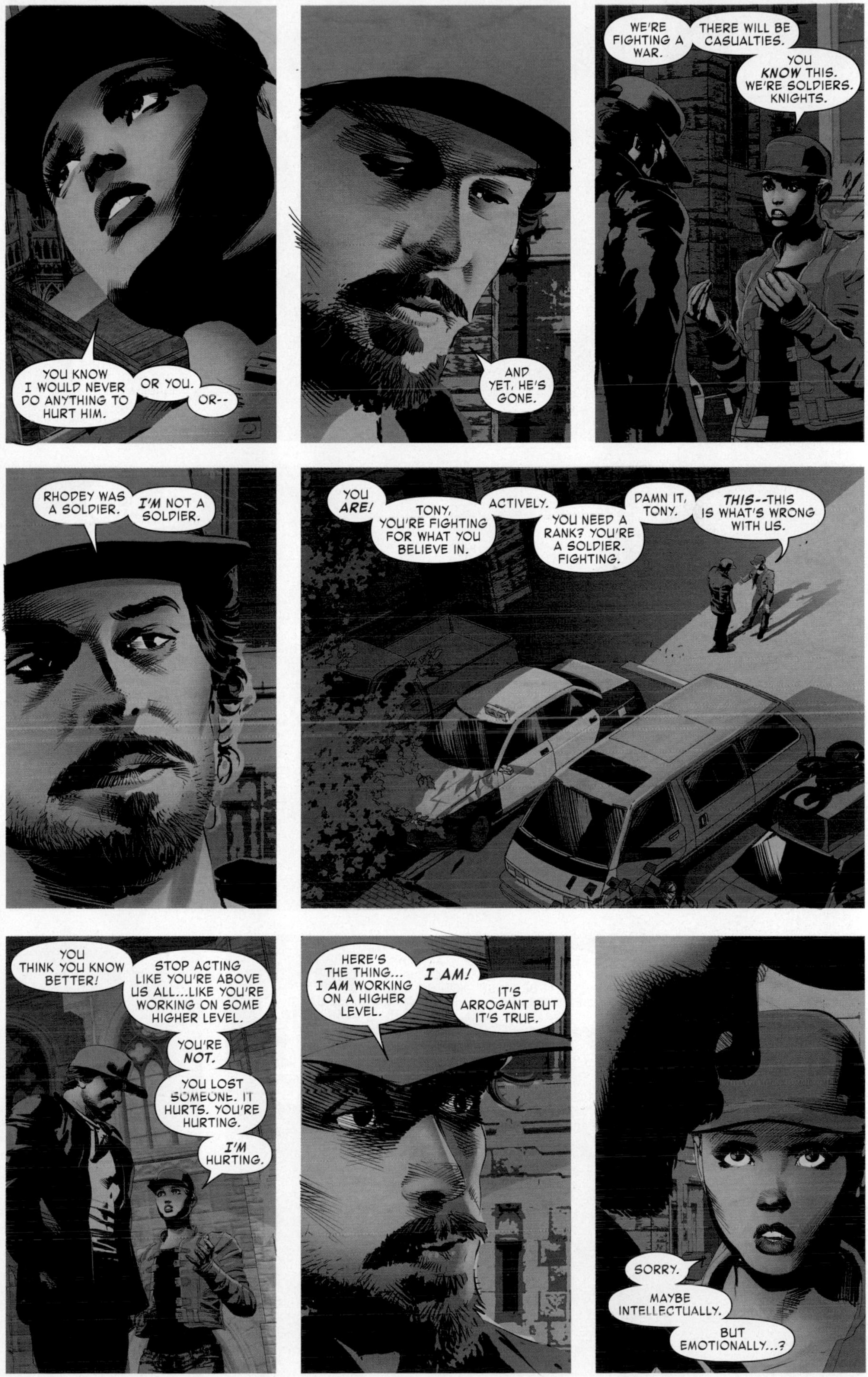
YOU KNOW I WOULD NEVER DO ANYTHING TO HURT HIM.
OR YOU.
OR--
AND YET, HE'S GONE.
WE'RE FIGHTING A WAR.
THERE WILL BE CASUALTIES.
YOU *KNOW* THIS. WE'RE SOLDIERS. KNIGHTS.
RHODEY WAS A SOLDIER.
I'M NOT A SOLDIER.
YOU *ARE!*
TONY, YOU'RE FIGHTING FOR WHAT YOU BELIEVE IN.
ACTIVELY.
YOU NEED A RANK? YOU'RE A SOLDIER. FIGHTING.
DAMN IT, TONY.
THIS--THIS IS WHAT'S WRONG WITH US.
YOU THINK YOU KNOW BETTER!
STOP ACTING LIKE YOU'RE ABOVE US ALL...LIKE YOU'RE WORKING ON SOME HIGHER LEVEL.
YOU'RE *NOT.*
YOU LOST SOMEONE. IT HURTS. YOU'RE HURTING.
I'M HURTING.
HERE'S THE THING... I *AM* WORKING ON A HIGHER LEVEL.
I AM!
IT'S ARROGANT BUT IT'S TRUE.
SORRY.
MAYBE INTELLECTUALLY.
BUT EMOTIONALLY...?

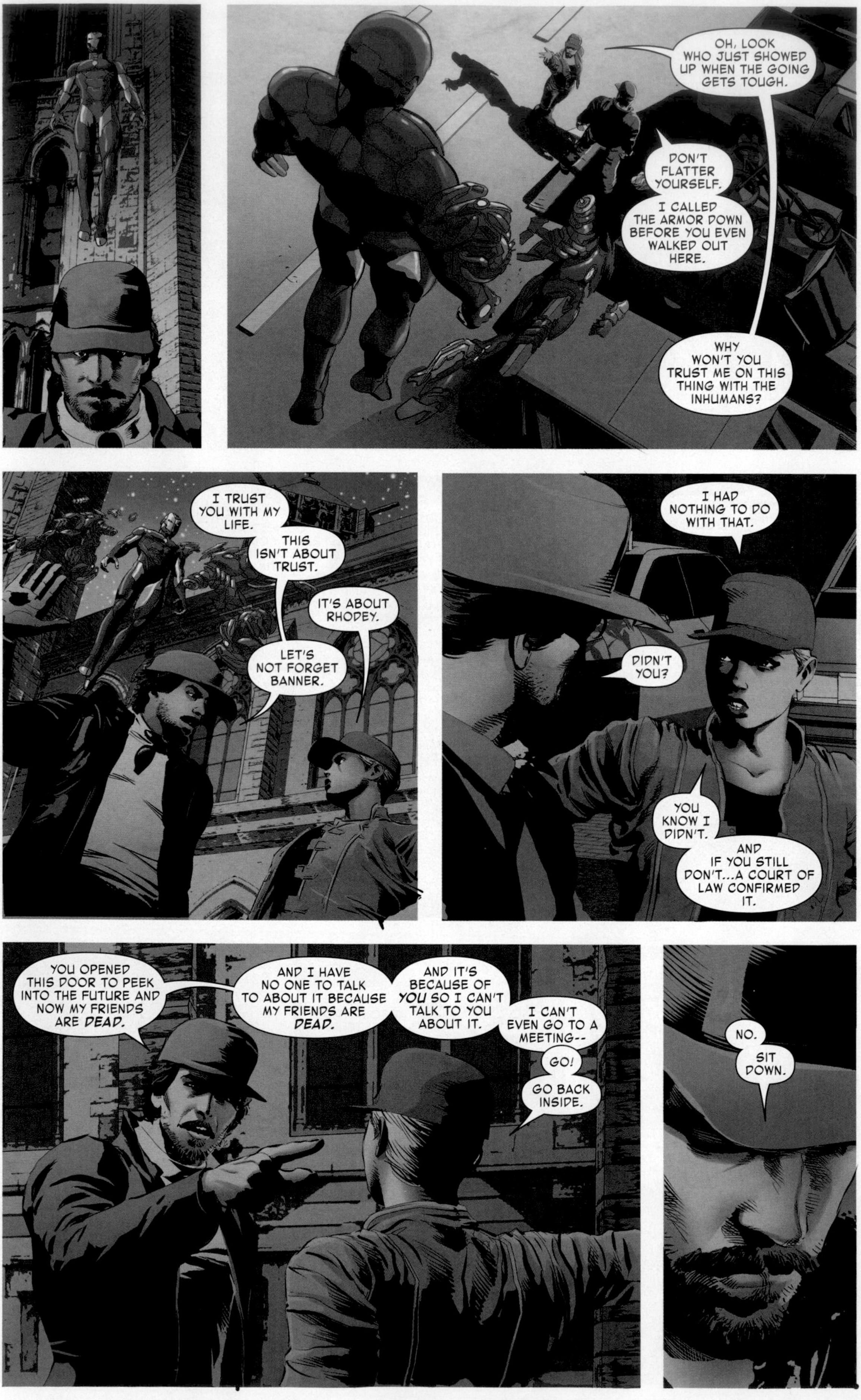
OH, LOOK WHO JUST SHOWED UP WHEN THE GOING GETS TOUGH.
DON'T FLATTER YOURSELF.
I CALLED THE ARMOR DOWN BEFORE YOU EVEN WALKED OUT HERE.
WHY WON'T YOU TRUST ME ON THIS THING WITH THE INHUMANS?
I TRUST YOU WITH MY LIFE.
THIS ISN'T ABOUT TRUST.
IT'S ABOUT RHODEY.
LET'S NOT FORGET BANNER.
I HAD NOTHING TO DO WITH THAT.
DIDN'T YOU?
YOU KNOW I DIDN'T.
AND IF YOU STILL DON'T...A COURT OF LAW CONFIRMED IT.
YOU OPENED THIS DOOR TO PEEK INTO THE FUTURE AND NOW MY FRIENDS ARE *DEAD.*
AND I HAVE NO ONE TO TALK TO ABOUT IT BECAUSE MY FRIENDS ARE *DEAD.*
AND IT'S BECAUSE OF *YOU* SO I CAN'T TALK TO YOU ABOUT IT.
I CAN'T EVEN GO TO A MEETING--
GO!
GO BACK INSIDE.
NO.
SIT DOWN.

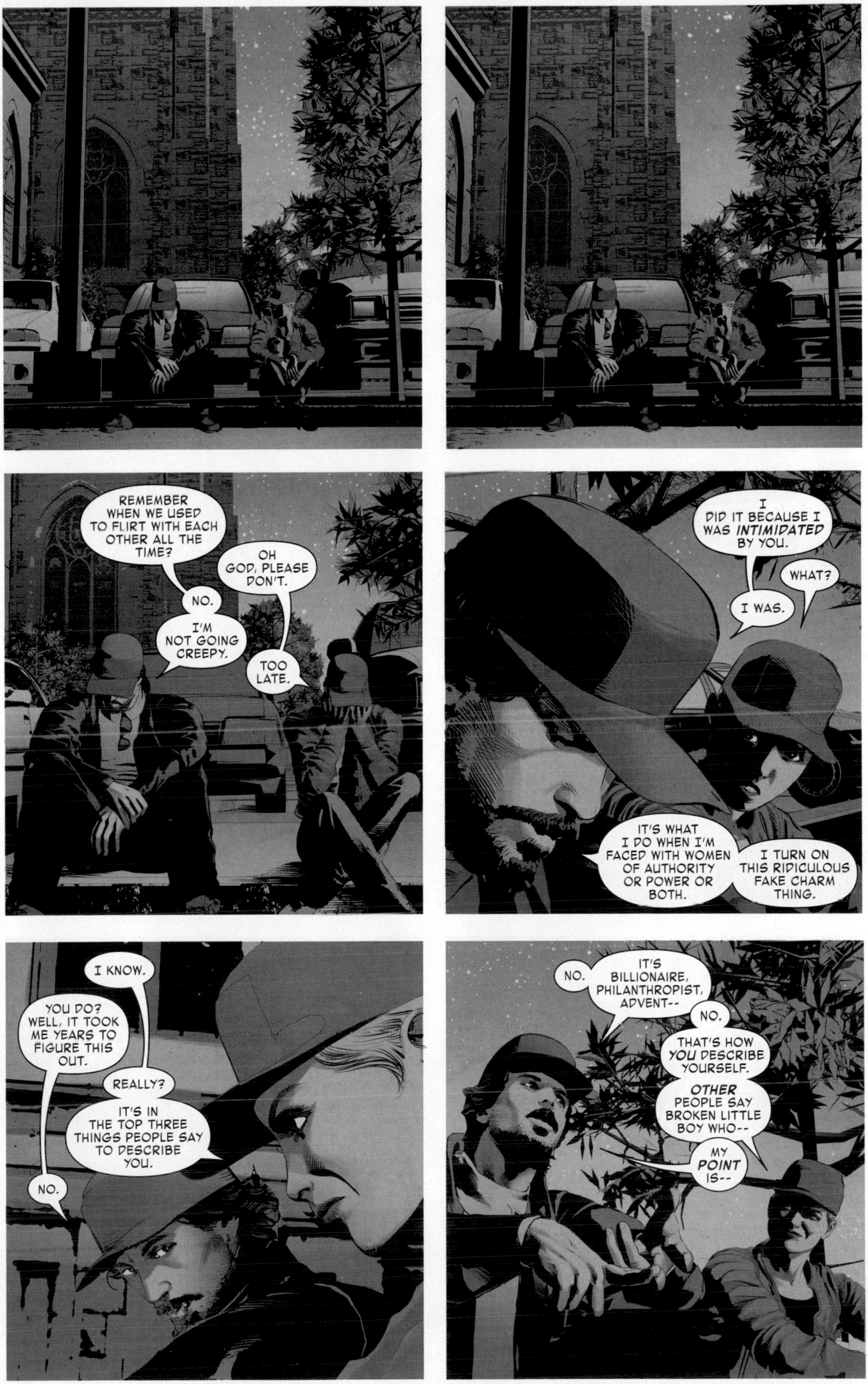
REMEMBER WHEN WE USED TO FLIRT WITH EACH OTHER ALL THE TIME?
NO.
I'M NOT GOING CREEPY.
OH GOD, PLEASE DON'T.
TOO LATE.
I DID IT BECAUSE I WAS INTIMIDATED BY YOU.
I WAS.
WHAT?
IT'S WHAT I DO WHEN I'M FACED WITH WOMEN OF AUTHORITY OR POWER OR BOTH.
I TURN ON THIS RIDICULOUS FAKE CHARM THING.
I KNOW.
YOU DO? WELL, IT TOOK ME YEARS TO FIGURE THIS OUT.
REALLY?
IT'S IN THE TOP THREE THINGS PEOPLE SAY TO DESCRIBE YOU.
NO.
NO.
IT'S BILLIONAIRE, PHILANTHROPIST, ADVENT--
NO.
THAT'S HOW YOU DESCRIBE YOURSELF.
OTHER PEOPLE SAY BROKEN LITTLE BOY WHO--
MY POINT IS--

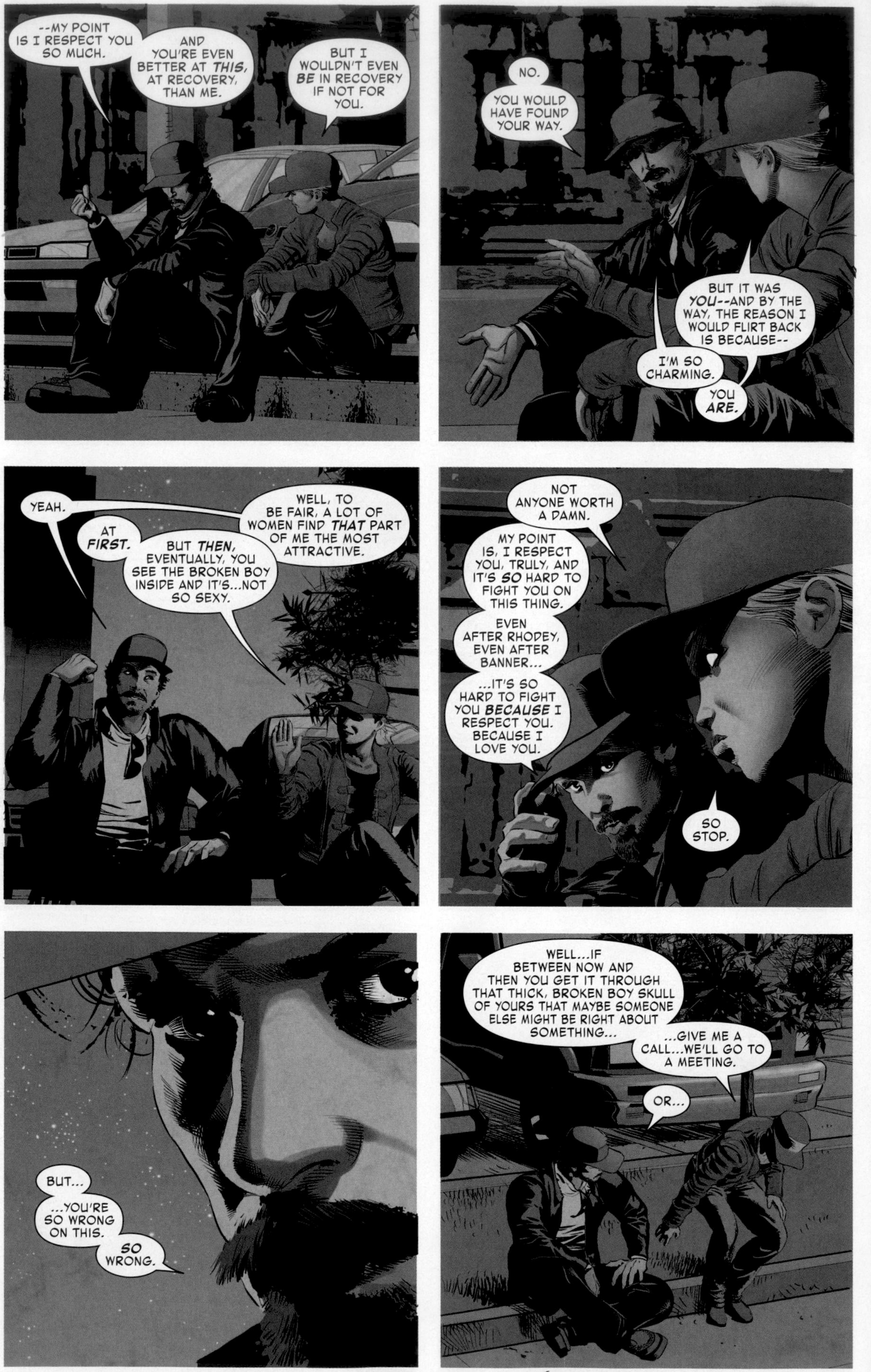
--MY POINT IS I RESPECT YOU SO MUCH.
AND YOU'RE EVEN BETTER AT *THIS,* AT RECOVERY, THAN ME.
BUT I WOULDN'T EVEN *BE* IN RECOVERY IF NOT FOR YOU.
NO.
YOU WOULD HAVE FOUND YOUR WAY.
BUT IT WAS *YOU*--AND BY THE WAY, THE REASON I WOULD FLIRT BACK IS BECAUSE--
I'M SO CHARMING.
YOU *ARE.*
WELL, TO BE FAIR, A LOT OF WOMEN FIND *THAT* PART OF ME THE MOST ATTRACTIVE.
YEAH.
AT *FIRST.*
BUT *THEN,* EVENTUALLY, YOU SEE THE BROKEN BOY INSIDE AND IT'S...NOT SO SEXY.
NOT ANYONE WORTH A DAMN.
MY POINT IS, I RESPECT YOU, TRULY, AND IT'S *SO* HARD TO FIGHT YOU ON THIS THING.
EVEN AFTER RHODEY, EVEN AFTER BANNER...
...IT'S SO HARD TO FIGHT YOU *BECAUSE* I RESPECT YOU. BECAUSE I LOVE YOU.
SO STOP.
BUT...
...YOU'RE SO WRONG ON THIS.
SO WRONG.
WELL...IF BETWEEN NOW AND THEN YOU GET IT THROUGH THAT THICK, BROKEN BOY SKULL OF YOURS THAT MAYBE SOMEONE ELSE MIGHT BE RIGHT ABOUT SOMETHING...
...GIVE ME A CALL...WE'LL GO TO A MEETING.
OR...

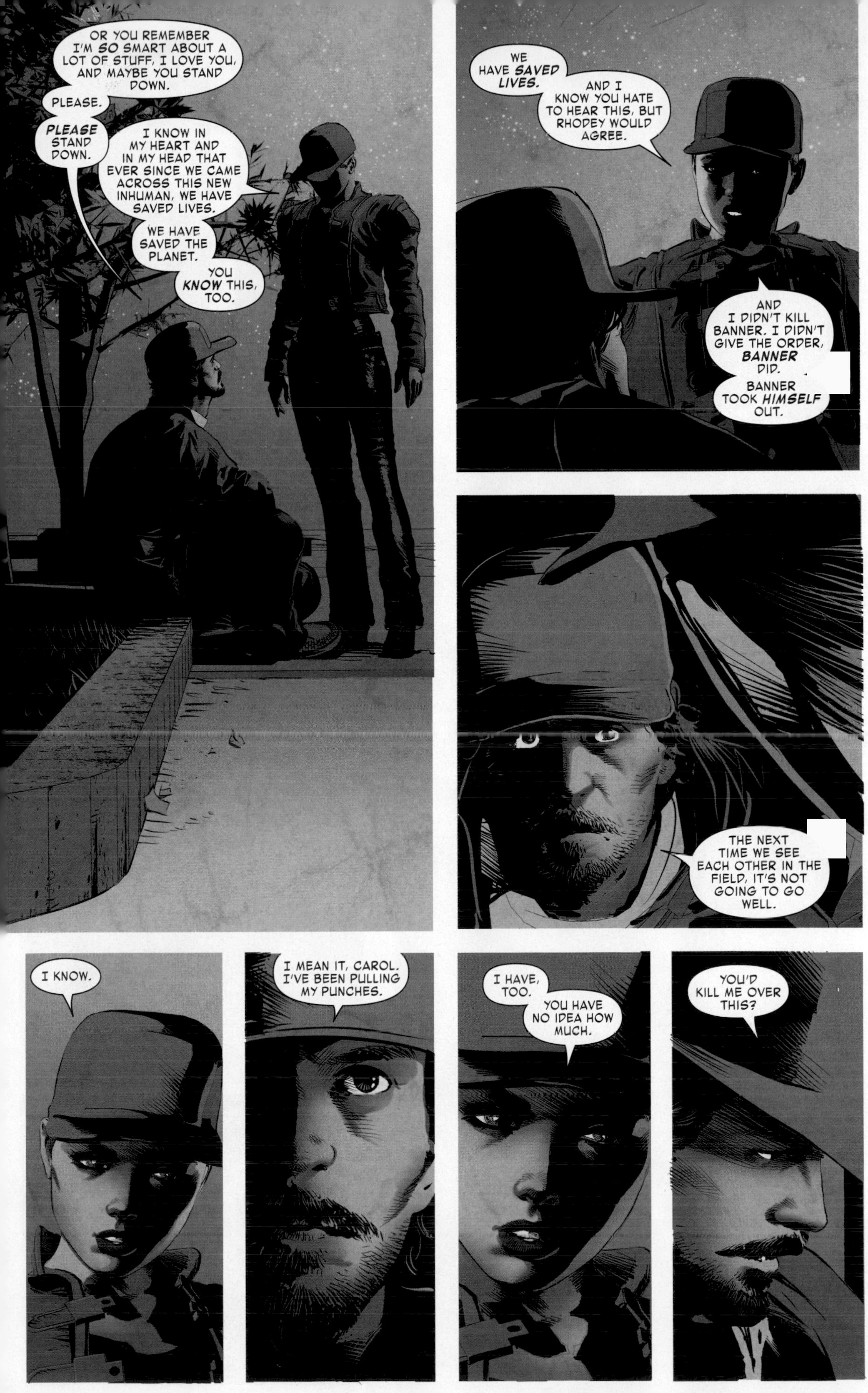
OR YOU REMEMBER I'M SO SMART ABOUT A LOT OF STUFF, I LOVE YOU, AND MAYBE YOU STAND DOWN.
PLEASE.
PLEASE STAND DOWN.
I KNOW IN MY HEART AND IN MY HEAD THAT EVER SINCE WE CAME ACROSS THIS NEW INHUMAN, WE HAVE SAVED LIVES.
WE HAVE SAVED THE PLANET.
YOU KNOW THIS, TOO.
WE HAVE SAVED LIVES.
AND I KNOW YOU HATE TO HEAR THIS, BUT RHODEY WOULD AGREE.
AND I DIDN'T KILL BANNER. I DIDN'T GIVE THE ORDER, BANNER DID.
BANNER TOOK HIMSELF OUT.
THE NEXT TIME WE SEE EACH OTHER IN THE FIELD, IT'S NOT GOING TO GO WELL.
I KNOW.
I MEAN IT, CAROL. I'VE BEEN PULLING MY PUNCHES.
I HAVE, TOO.
YOU HAVE NO IDEA HOW MUCH.
YOU'D KILL ME OVER THIS?

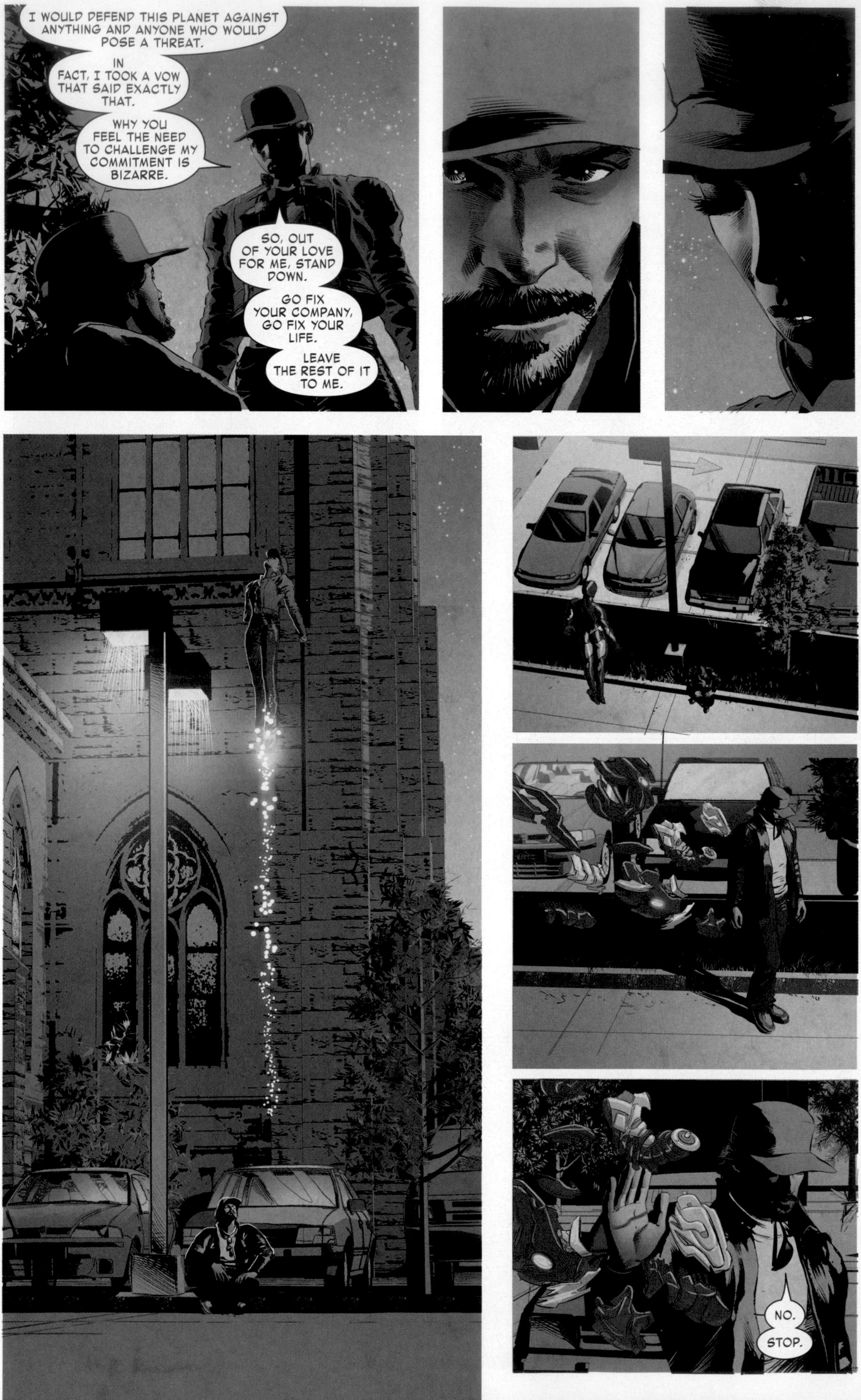
I WOULD DEFEND THIS PLANET AGAINST ANYTHING AND ANYONE WHO WOULD POSE A THREAT.
IN FACT, I TOOK A VOW THAT SAID EXACTLY THAT.
WHY YOU FEEL THE NEED TO CHALLENGE MY COMMITMENT IS BIZARRE.
SO, OUT OF YOUR LOVE FOR ME, STAND DOWN.
GO FIX YOUR COMPANY, GO FIX YOUR LIFE.
LEAVE THE REST OF IT TO ME.
NO.
STOP.

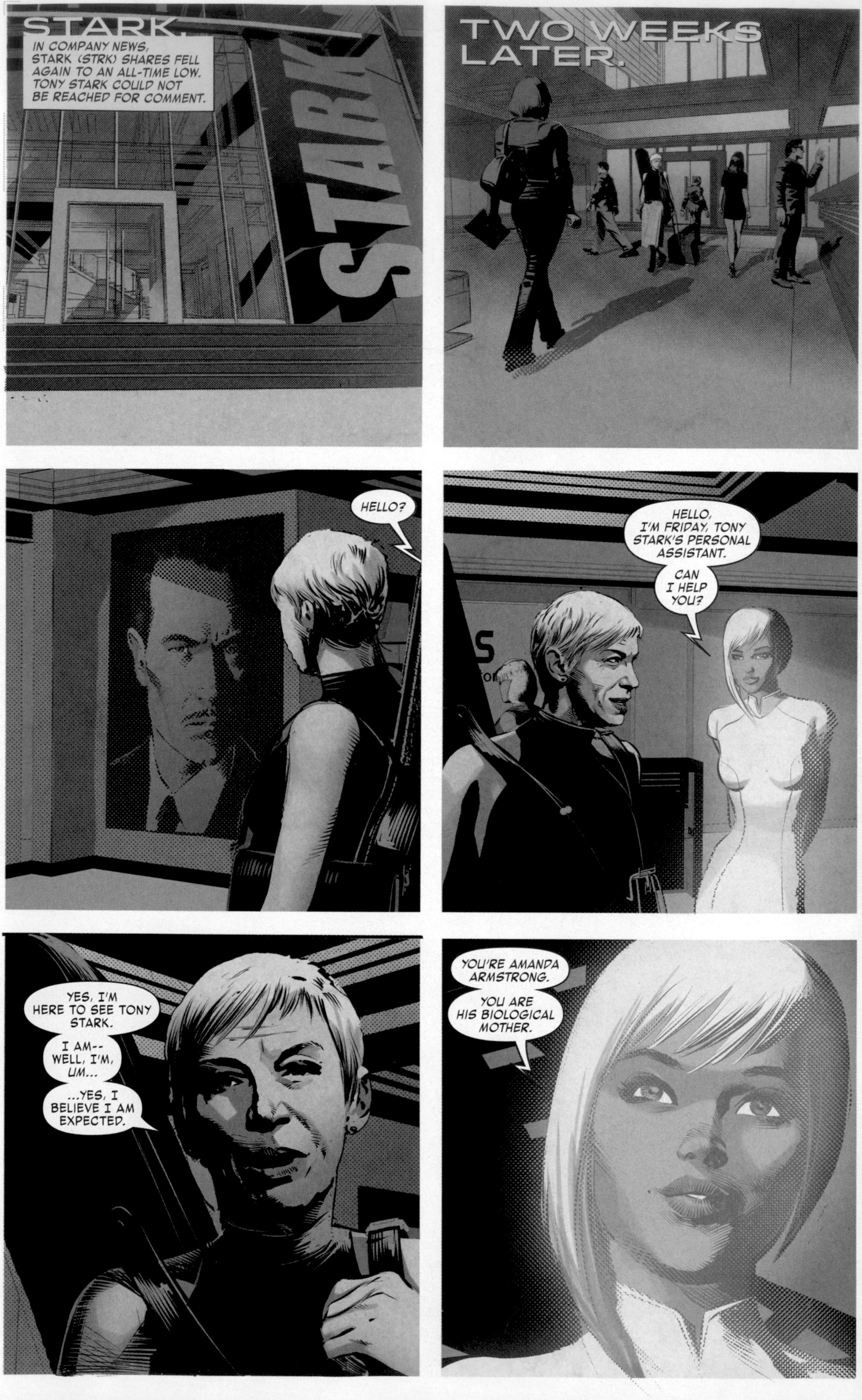
STARK.
IN COMPANY NEWS, STARK (STRK) SHARES FELL AGAIN TO AN ALL-TIME LOW. TONY STARK COULD NOT BE REACHED FOR COMMENT.
STARK
TWO WEEKS LATER.
HELLO?
HELLO, I'M FRIDAY, TONY STARK'S PERSONAL ASSISTANT.
CAN I HELP YOU?
YES, I'M HERE TO SEE TONY STARK.
I AM-- WELL, I'M, UM...
...YES, I BELIEVE I AM EXPECTED.
YOU'RE AMANDA ARMSTRONG.
YOU ARE HIS BIOLOGICAL MOTHER.

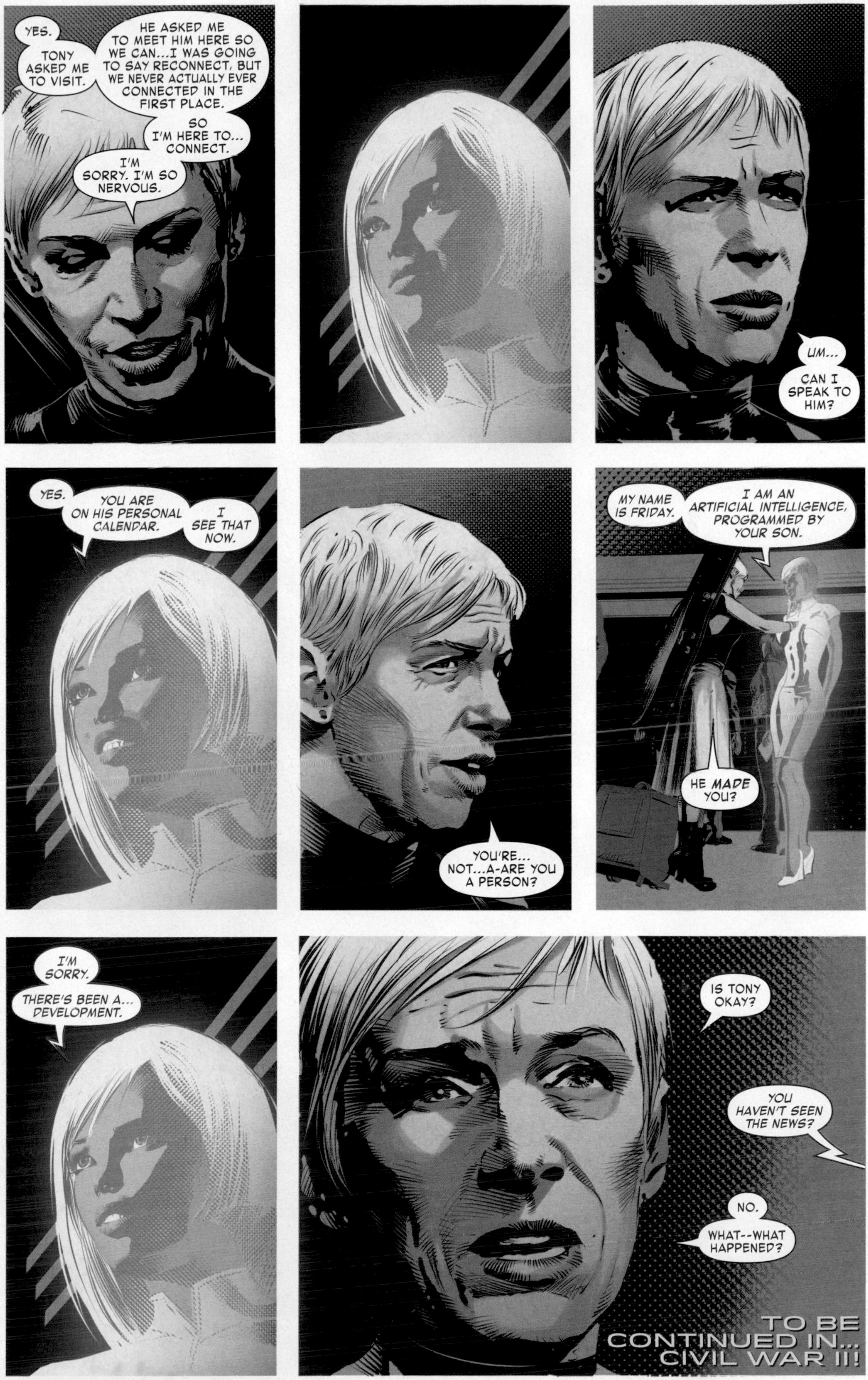
YES.
TONY ASKED ME TO VISIT.
HE ASKED ME TO MEET HIM HERE SO WE CAN...I WAS GOING TO SAY RECONNECT, BUT WE NEVER ACTUALLY EVER CONNECTED IN THE FIRST PLACE.
SO I'M HERE TO... CONNECT.
I'M SORRY. I'M SO NERVOUS.
UM...
CAN I SPEAK TO HIM?
YES.
YOU ARE ON HIS PERSONAL CALENDAR.
I SEE THAT NOW.
YOU'RE... NOT...A-ARE YOU A PERSON?
MY NAME IS FRIDAY.
I AM AN ARTIFICIAL INTELLIGENCE, PROGRAMMED BY YOUR SON.
HE MADE YOU?
I'M SORRY.
THERE'S BEEN A... DEVELOPMENT.
IS TONY OKAY?
YOU HAVEN'T SEEN THE NEWS?
NO.
WHAT--WHAT HAPPENED?
TO BE CONTINUED IN... CIVIL WAR II!

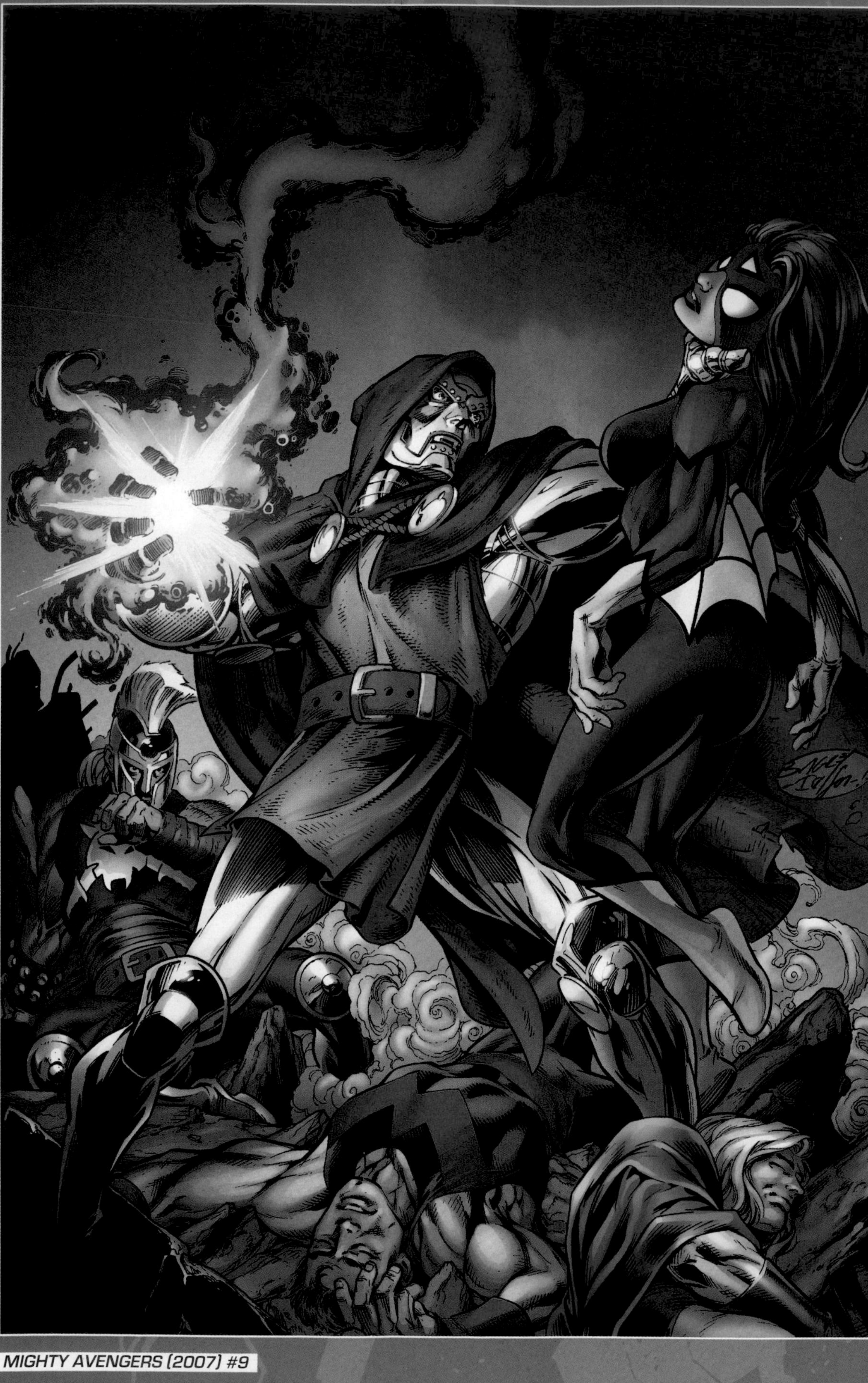

MIGHTY AVENGERS (2007) #9

AND THERE CAME A DAY, A DAY UNLIKE ANY OTHER, WHEN EARTH'S MIGHTIEST HEROES FOUND
THEMSELVES UNITED AGAINST A COMMON THREAT! ON THAT DAY, THE AVENGERS WERE BORN,
TO FIGHT THE FOES NO SINGLE SUPER HERO COULD WITHSTAND!

THE MIGHTY AVENGERS

PREVIOUSLY...

THE MIGHTY AVENGERS BATTLE THE ENTIRE POPULATION OF NEW YORK
CITY AS ITS CITIZENS ARE TRANSFORMED INTO SYMBIOTES AFTER A
MYSTERIOUS VIRUS DROPS FROM A SATELLITE IN ORBIT ABOVE THE
EARTH. WHEN IRON MAN INVESTIGATES THE SATELLITE'S ORIGIN, HE
DISCOVERS THAT IT BELONGS TO NONE OTHER THAN LATVERIAN
MONARCH VICTOR VON DOOM.

IRON MAN GATHERS THE AVENGERS AND HIS AGENTS OF S.H.I.E.L.D.
AND BRINGS THE FIGHT TO LATVERIA...

BRIAN MICHAEL BENDIS
WRITER

MARK BAGLEY
PENCILER

**DANNY MIKI & CRIME LAB STUDIOS'
ALLEN MARTINEZ & VICTOR OLAZABA**
INKERS

JUSTIN PONSOR
COLORIST

MARKO DJURDJEVIC
ARTIST, YEAR 1211

ARTMONKEYS' DAVE LANPHEAR
LETTERER

MARK BAGLEY
WITH **JOHN DELL** (#9), **DANNY MIKI** (#10-11) & **JASON KEITH** (#9-11)
COVER ART

MOLLY LAZER
ASSOCIATE EDITOR

TOM BREVOORT
EDITOR

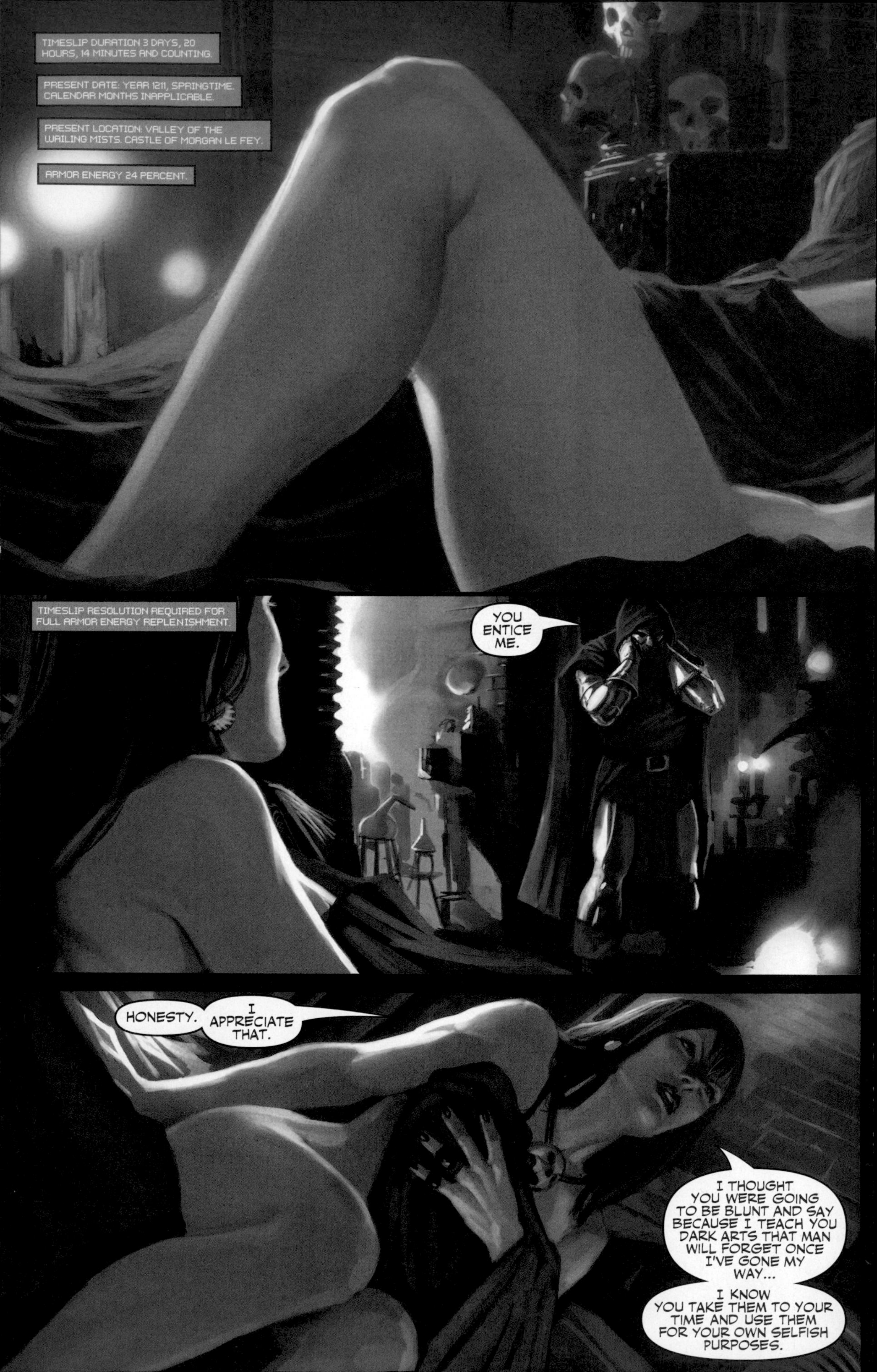
TIMESLIP DURATION 3 DAYS, 20 HOURS, 14 MINUTES AND COUNTING.
PRESENT DATE: YEAR 1211, SPRINGTIME. CALENDAR MONTHS INAPPLICABLE.
PRESENT LOCATION: VALLEY OF THE WAILING MISTS. CASTLE OF MORGAN LE FEY.
ARMOR ENERGY 24 PERCENT.
TIMESLIP RESOLUTION REQUIRED FOR FULL ARMOR ENERGY REPLENISHMENT.
YOU ENTICE ME.
HONESTY.
I APPRECIATE THAT.
I THOUGHT YOU WERE GOING TO BE BLUNT AND SAY BECAUSE I TEACH YOU DARK ARTS THAT MAN WILL FORGET ONCE I'VE GONE MY WAY...
I KNOW YOU TAKE THEM TO YOUR TIME AND USE THEM FOR YOUR OWN SELFISH PURPOSES.

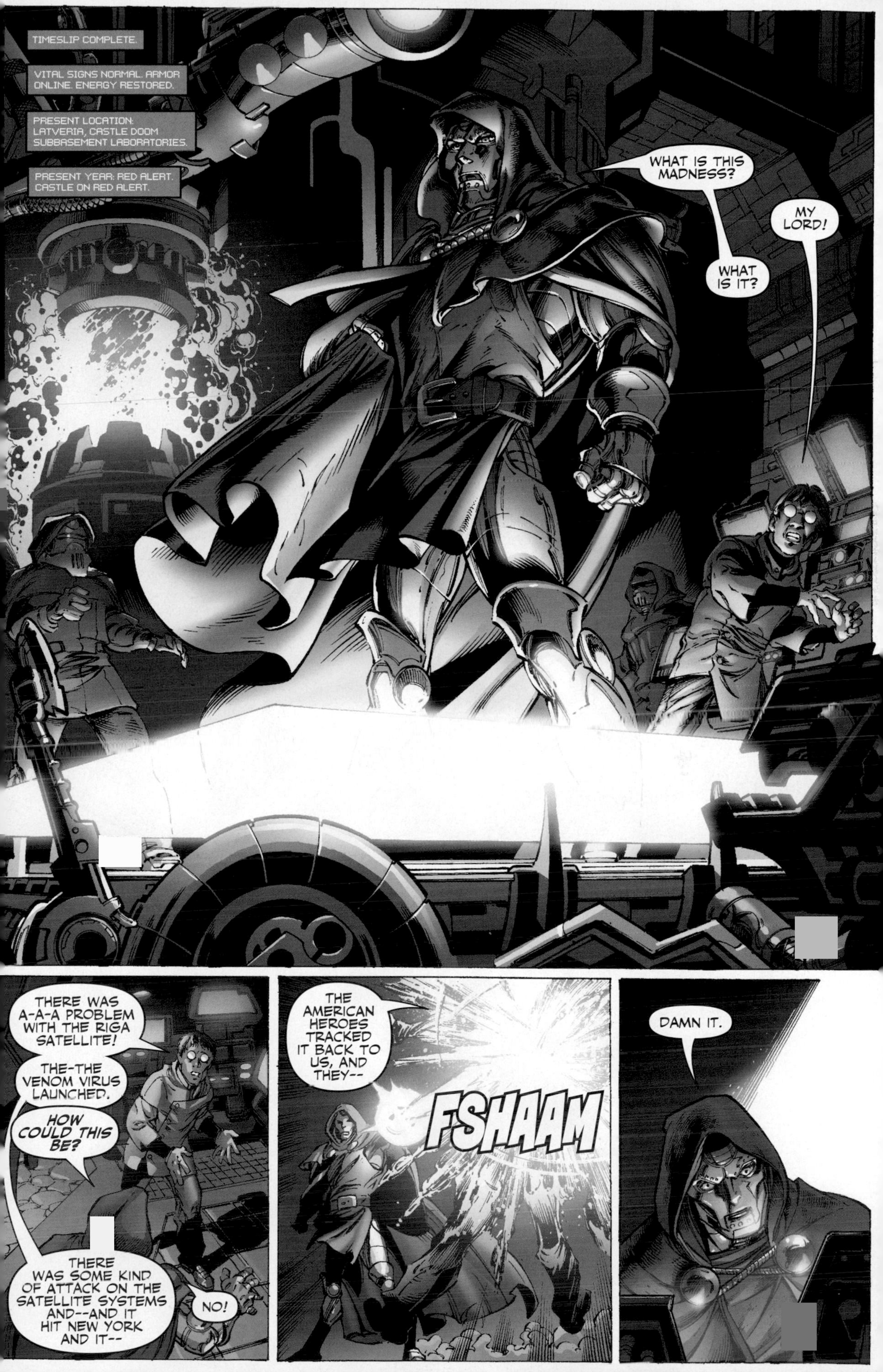
TIMESLIP COMPLETE.
VITAL SIGNS NORMAL. ARMOR ONLINE. ENERGY RESTORED.
PRESENT LOCATION: LATVERIA, CASTLE DOOM SUBBASEMENT LABORATORIES.
PRESENT YEAR: RED ALERT. CASTLE ON RED ALERT.
WHAT IS THIS MADNESS?
WHAT IS IT?
MY LORD!
THERE WAS A-A-A PROBLEM WITH THE RIGA SATELLITE!
THE-THE VENOM VIRUS LAUNCHED.
HOW COULD THIS BE?
THERE WAS SOME KIND OF ATTACK ON THE SATELLITE SYSTEMS AND--AND IT HIT NEW YORK AND IT--
NO!
THE AMERICAN HEROES TRACKED IT BACK TO US, AND THEY--
FSHAAM
DAMN IT.

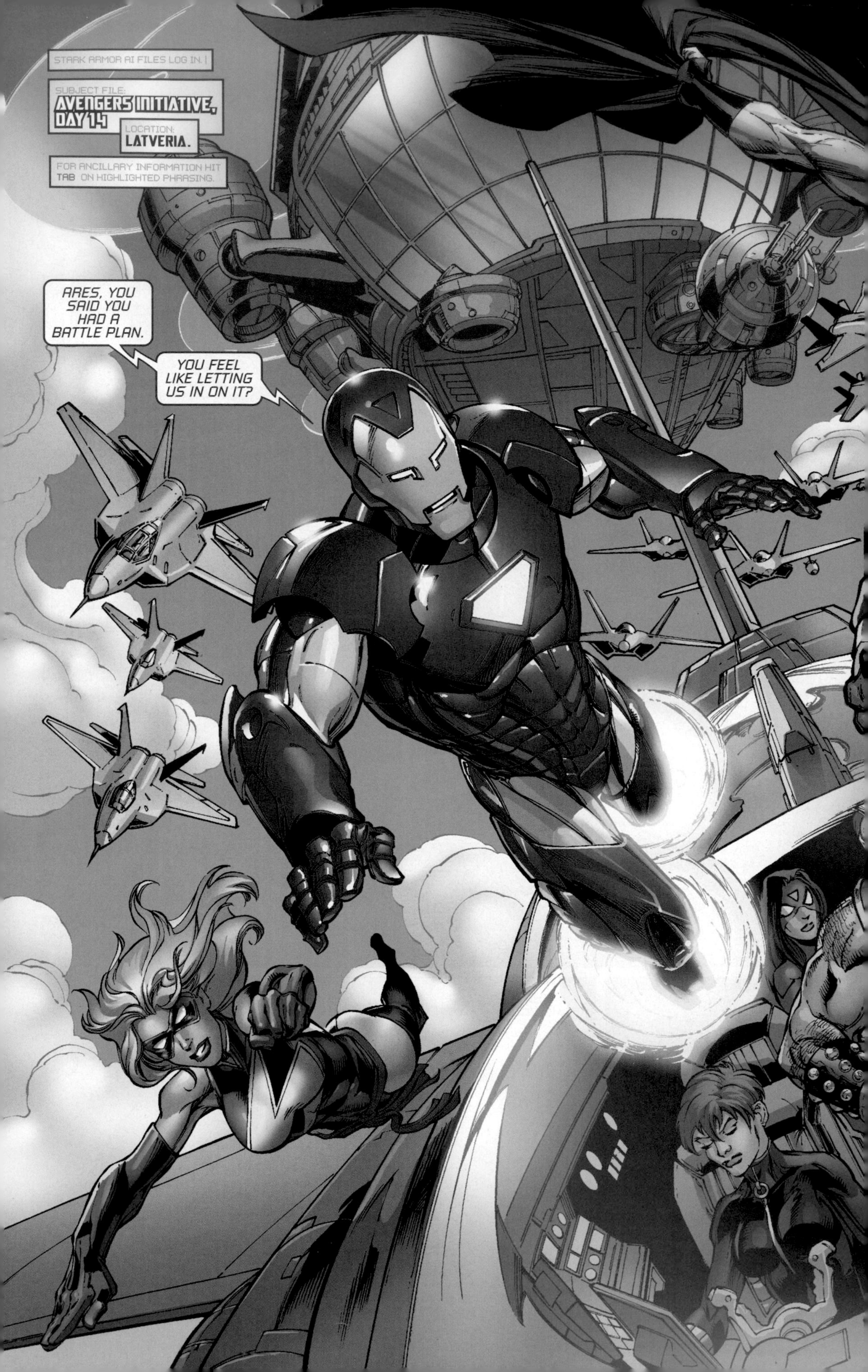
STARK ARMOR AI FILES LOG IN. |
SUBJECT FILE:
AVENGERS INITIATIVE, DAY 14
LOCATION:
LATVERIA.
FOR ANCILLARY INFORMATION HIT TAB ON HIGHLIGHTED PHRASING.
ARES, YOU SAID YOU HAD A BATTLE PLAN.
YOU FEEL LIKE LETTING US IN ON IT?

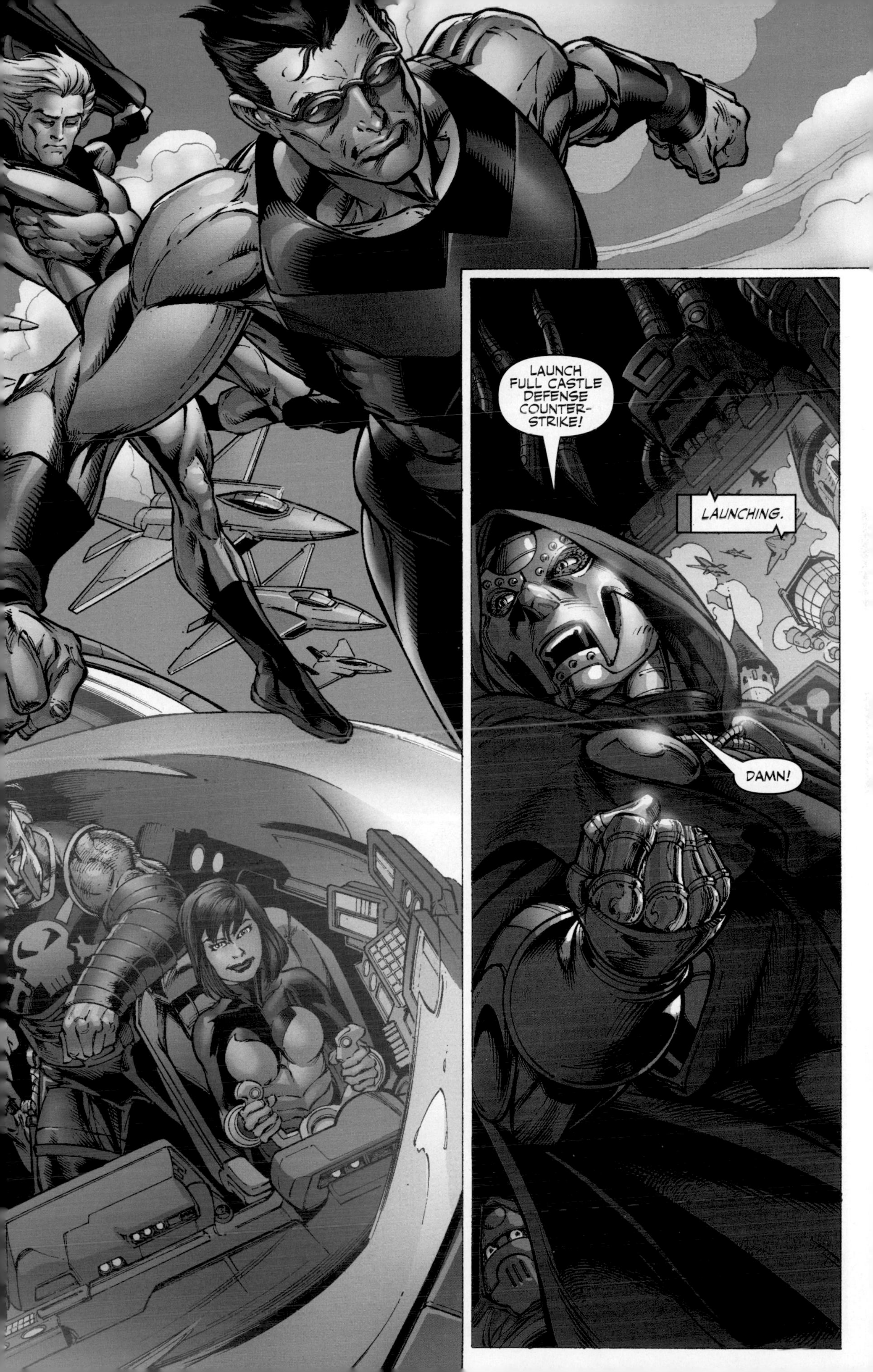
LAUNCH FULL CASTLE DEFENSE COUNTER-STRIKE!
LAUNCHING.
DAMN!

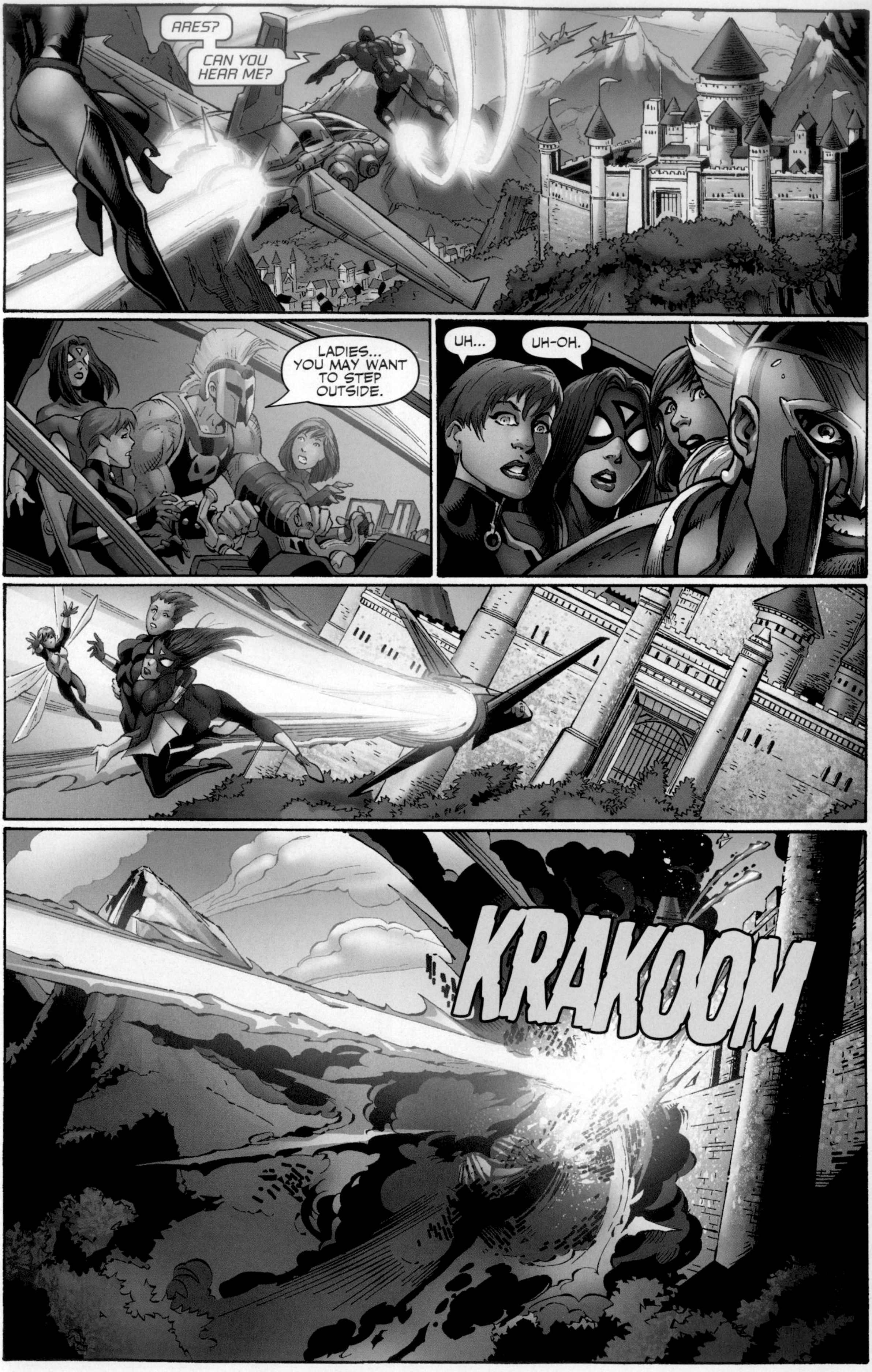
ARES?
CAN YOU HEAR ME?
LADIES... YOU MAY WANT TO STEP OUTSIDE.
UH...
UH-OH.
KRAKOOM

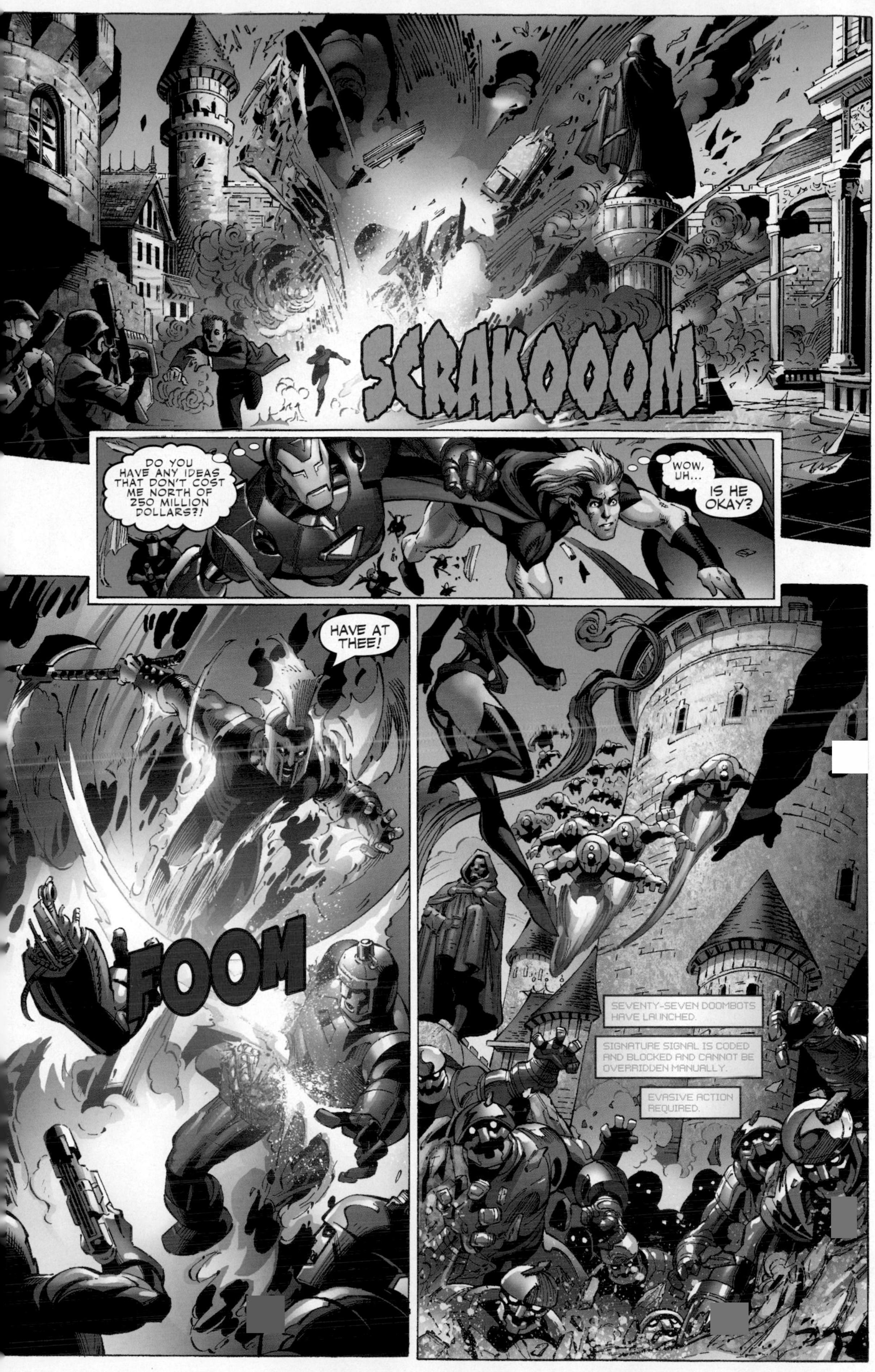
SCRAKOOOM
DO YOU HAVE ANY IDEAS THAT DON'T COST ME NORTH OF 250 MILLION DOLLARS?!
WOW, UH...
IS HE OKAY?
HAVE AT THEE!
FOOM
SEVENTY-SEVEN DOOMBOTS HAVE LAUNCHED.
SIGNATURE SIGNAL IS CODED AND BLOCKED AND CANNOT BE OVERRIDDEN MANUALLY.
EVASIVE ACTION REQUIRED.

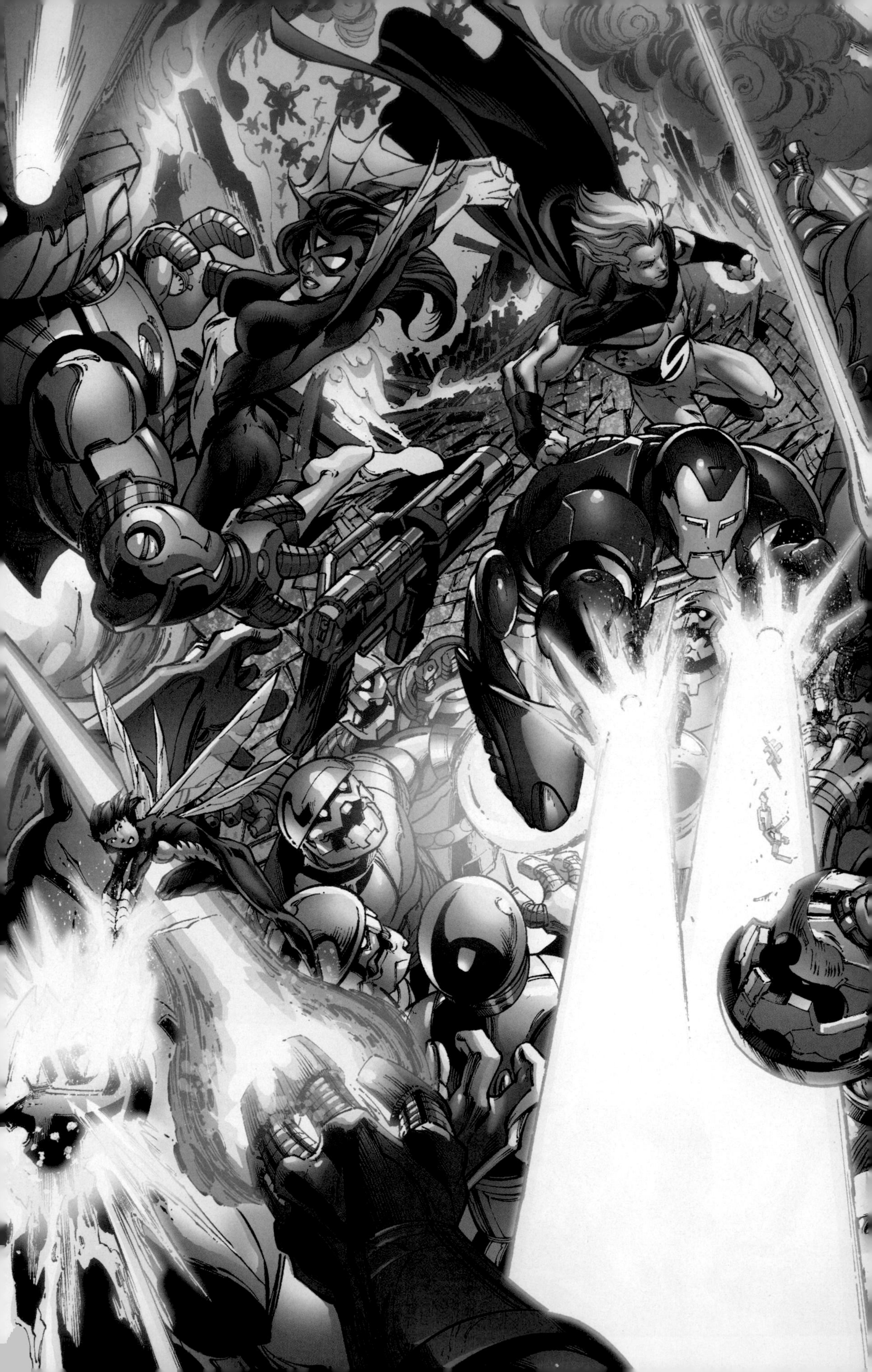

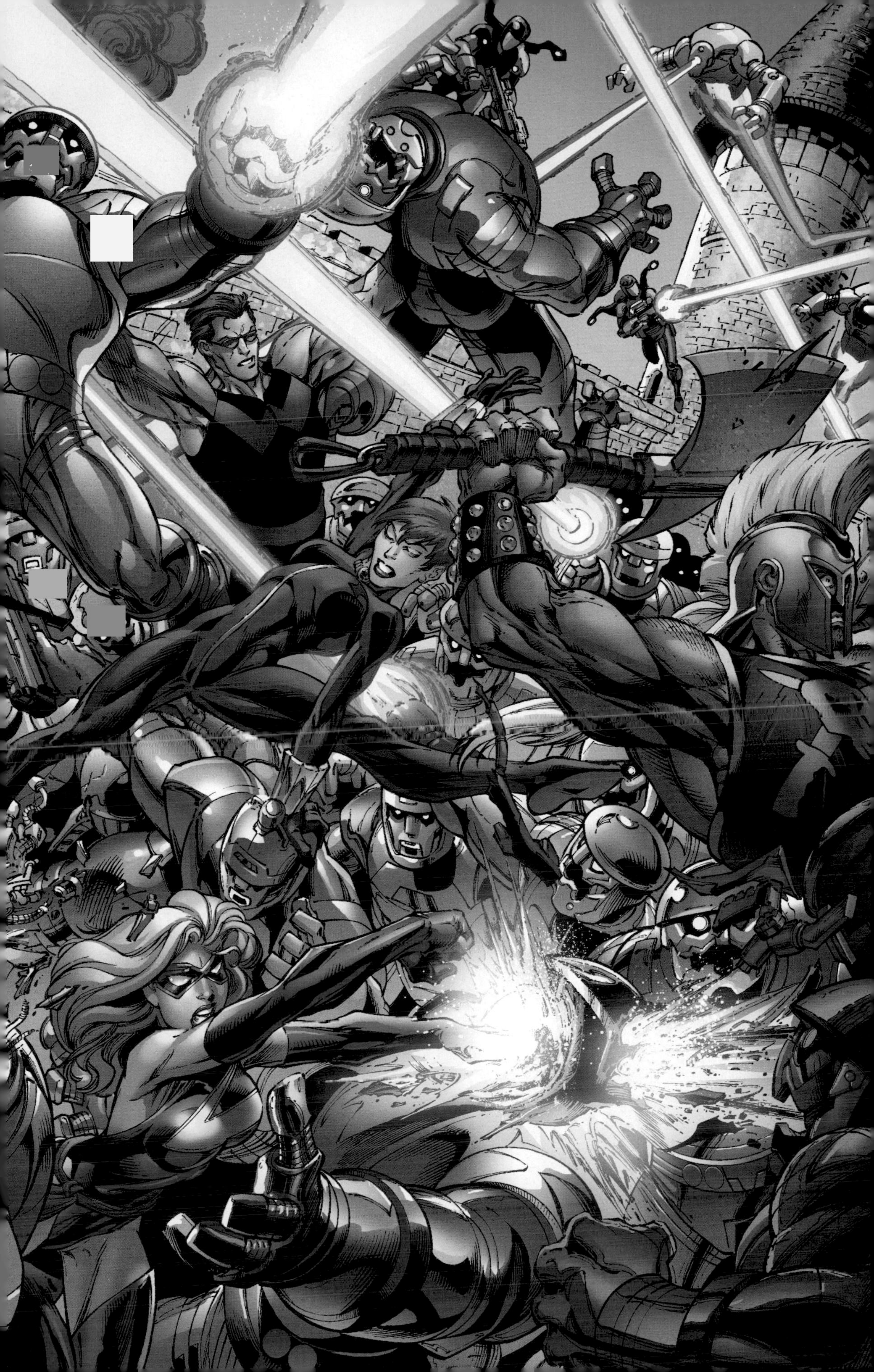

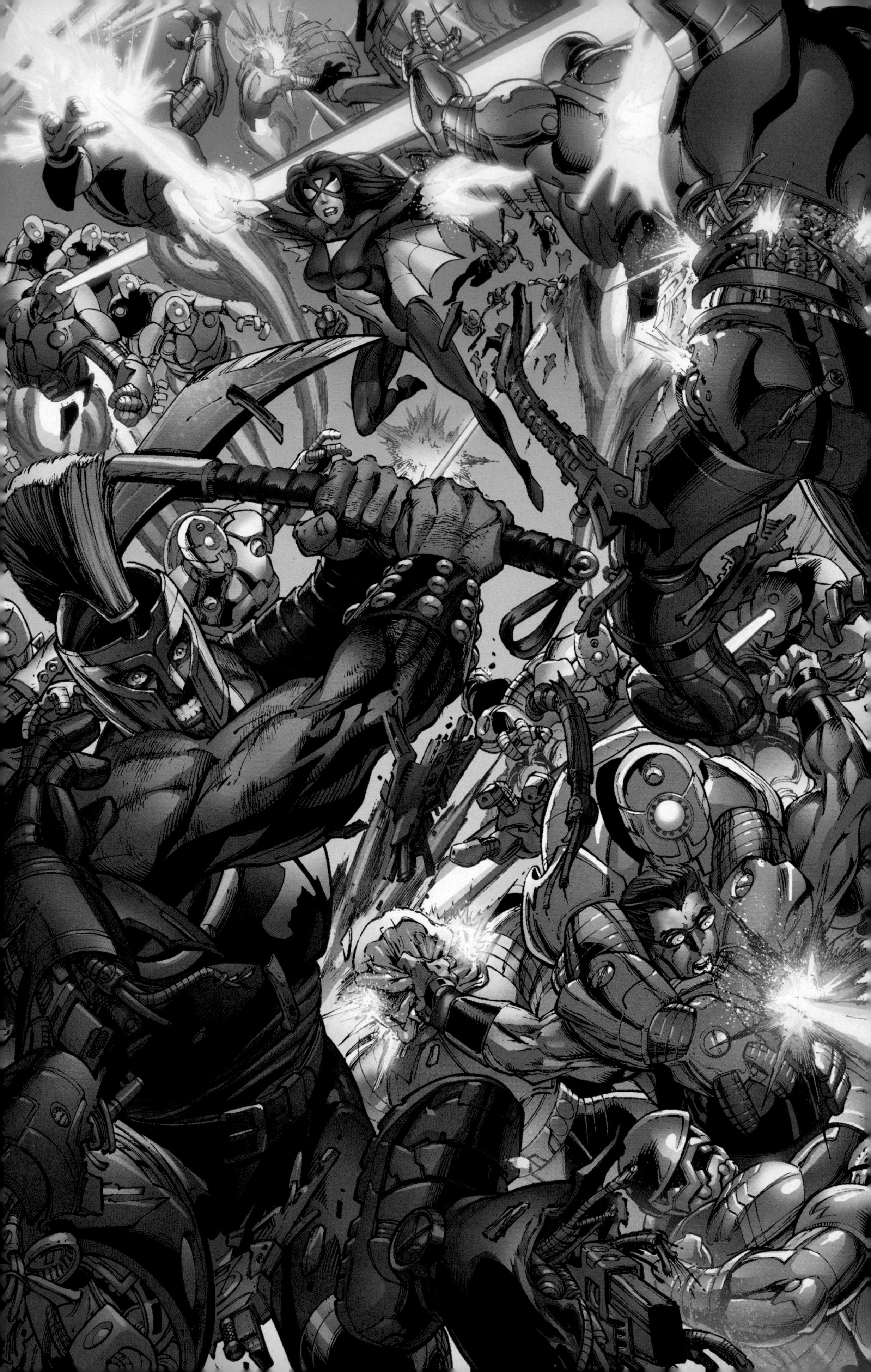

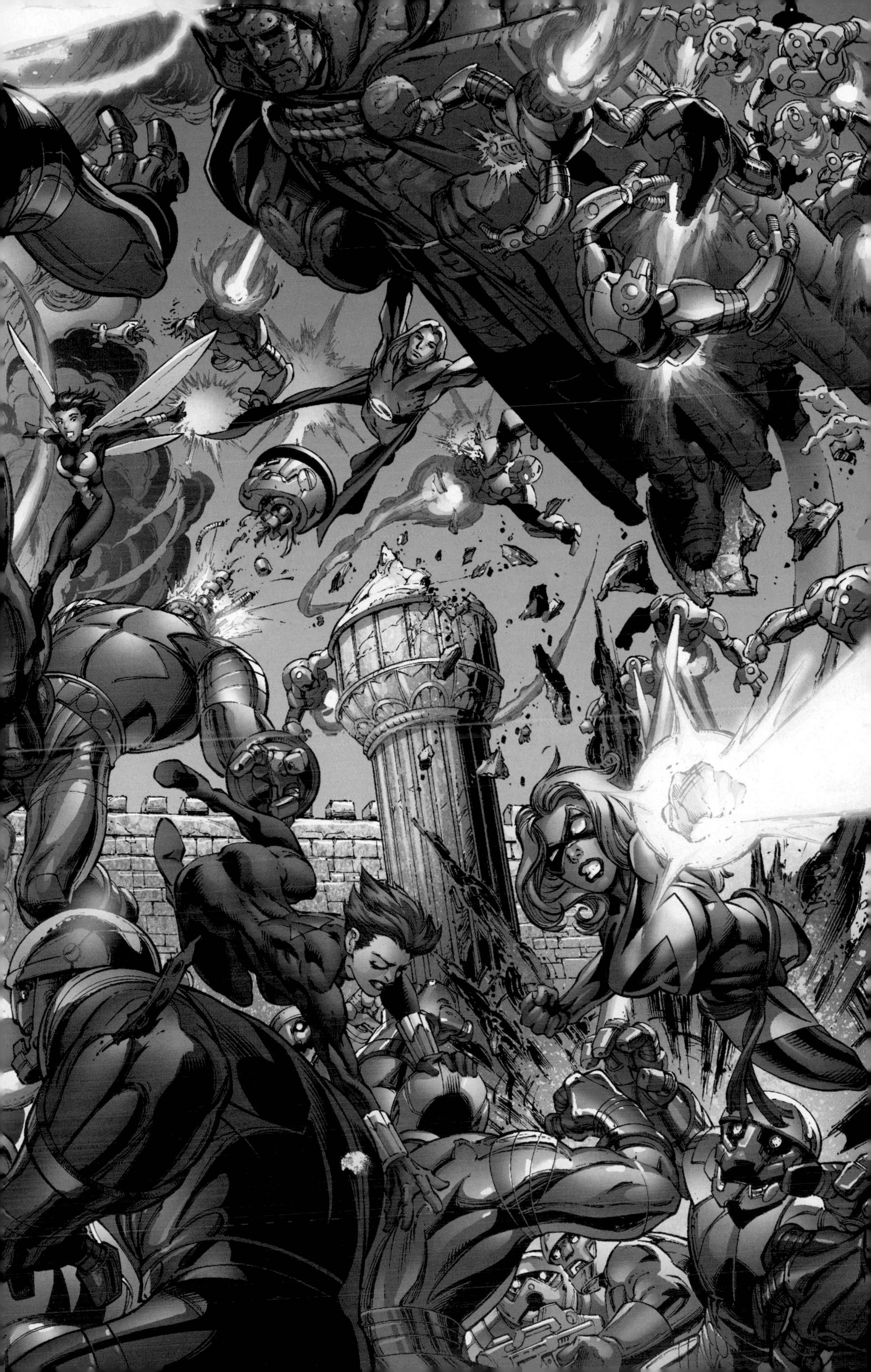

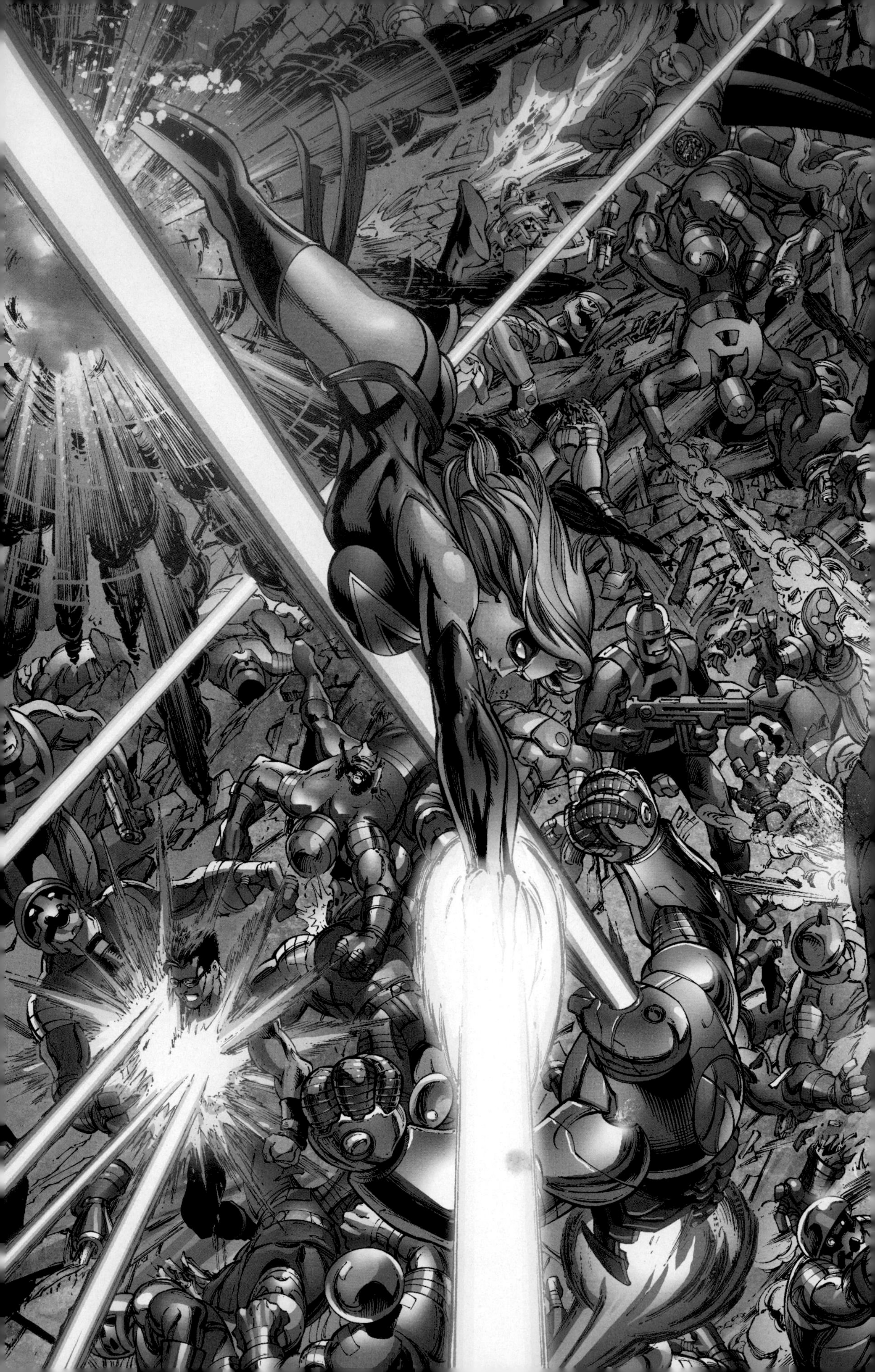

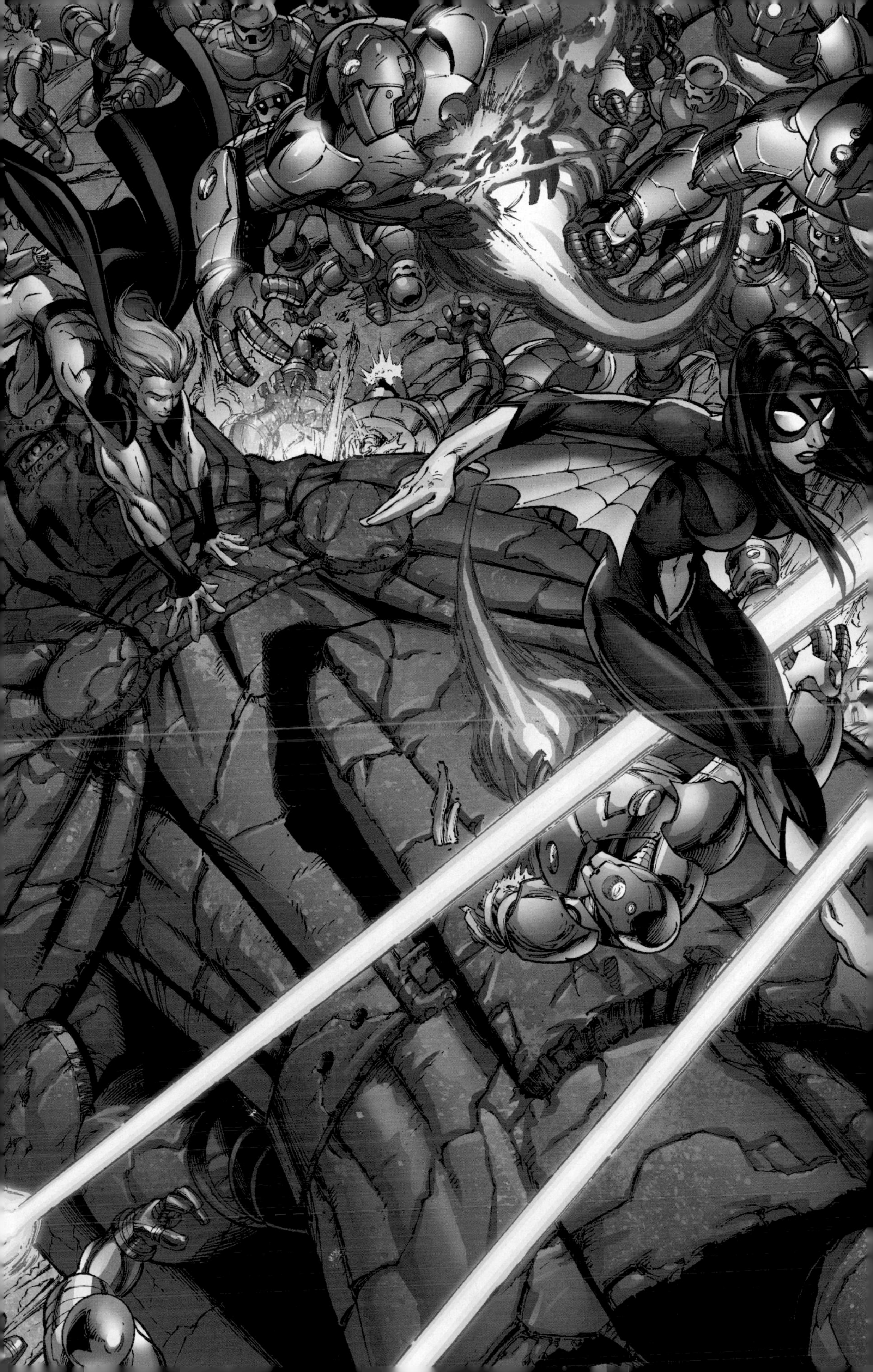

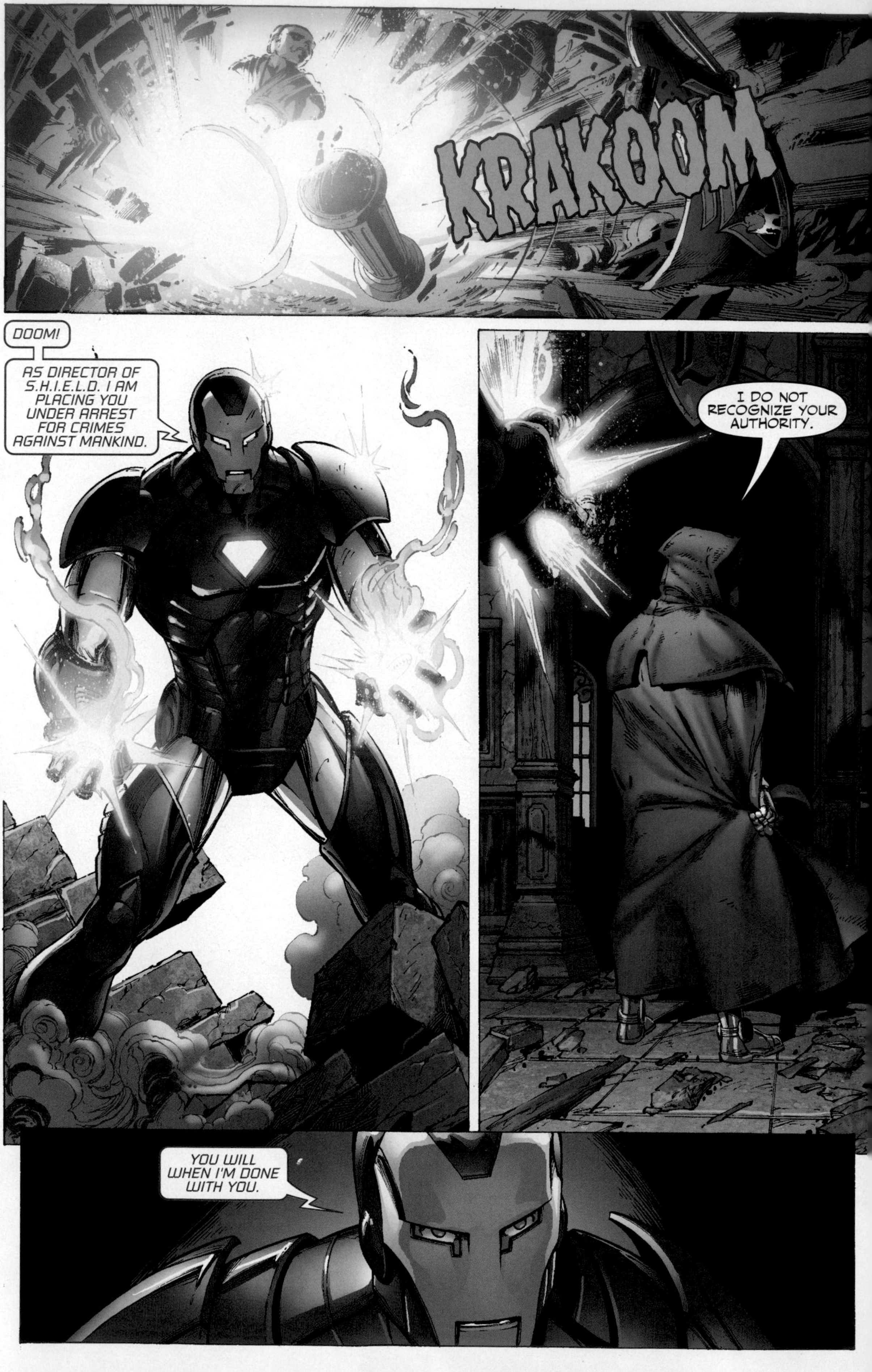

KRAKOOM
DOOM!
AS DIRECTOR OF S.H.I.E.L.D. I AM PLACING YOU UNDER ARREST FOR CRIMES AGAINST MANKIND.
I DO NOT RECOGNIZE YOUR AUTHORITY.
YOU WILL WHEN I'M DONE WITH YOU.

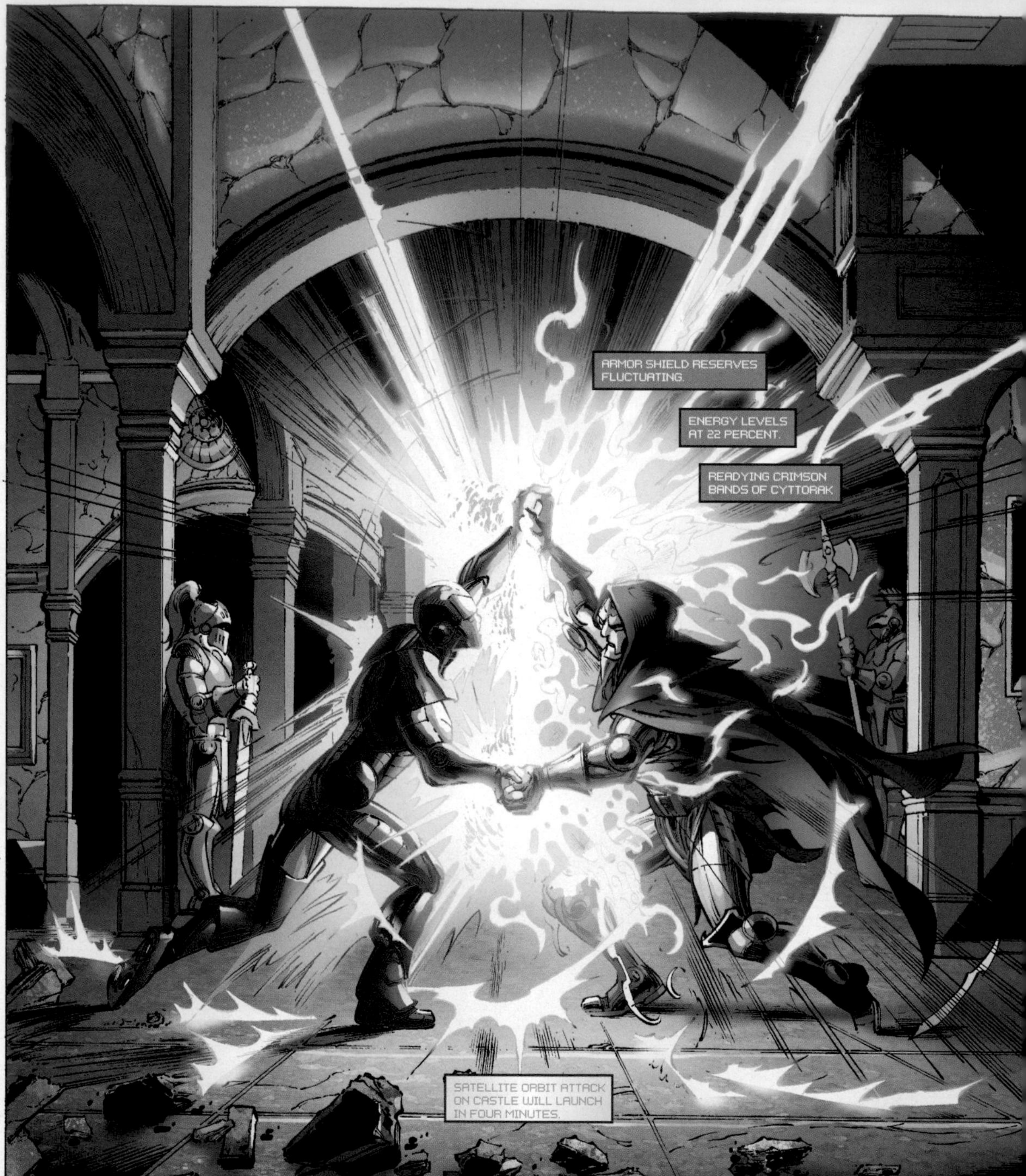
ARMOR SHIELD RESERVES FLUCTUATING.
ENERGY LEVELS AT 22 PERCENT.
READYING CRIMSON BANDS OF CYTTORAK
SATELLITE ORBIT ATTACK ON CASTLE WILL LAUNCH IN FOUR MINUTES.

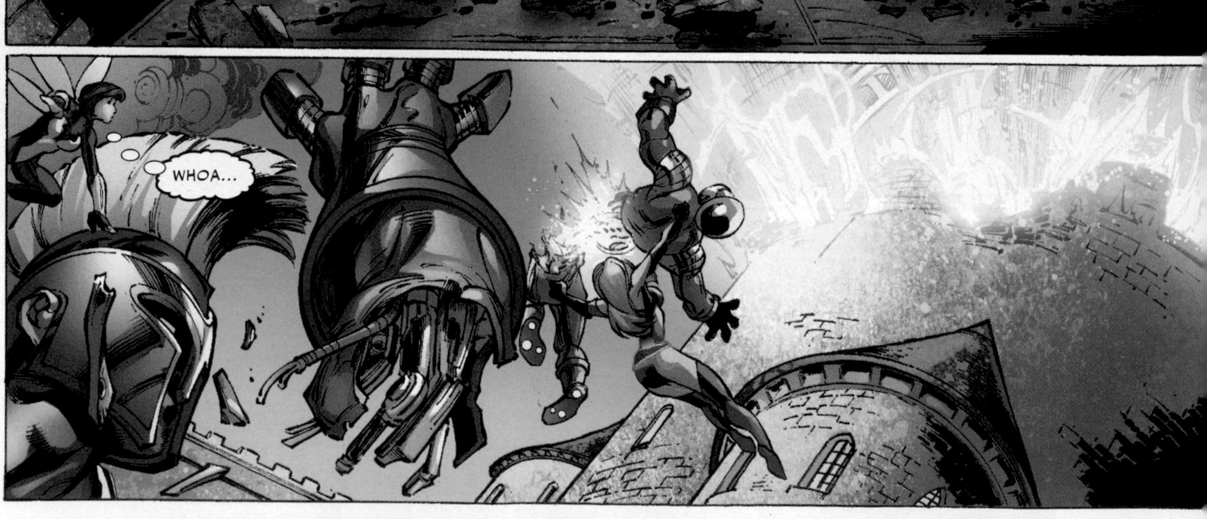
WHOA...

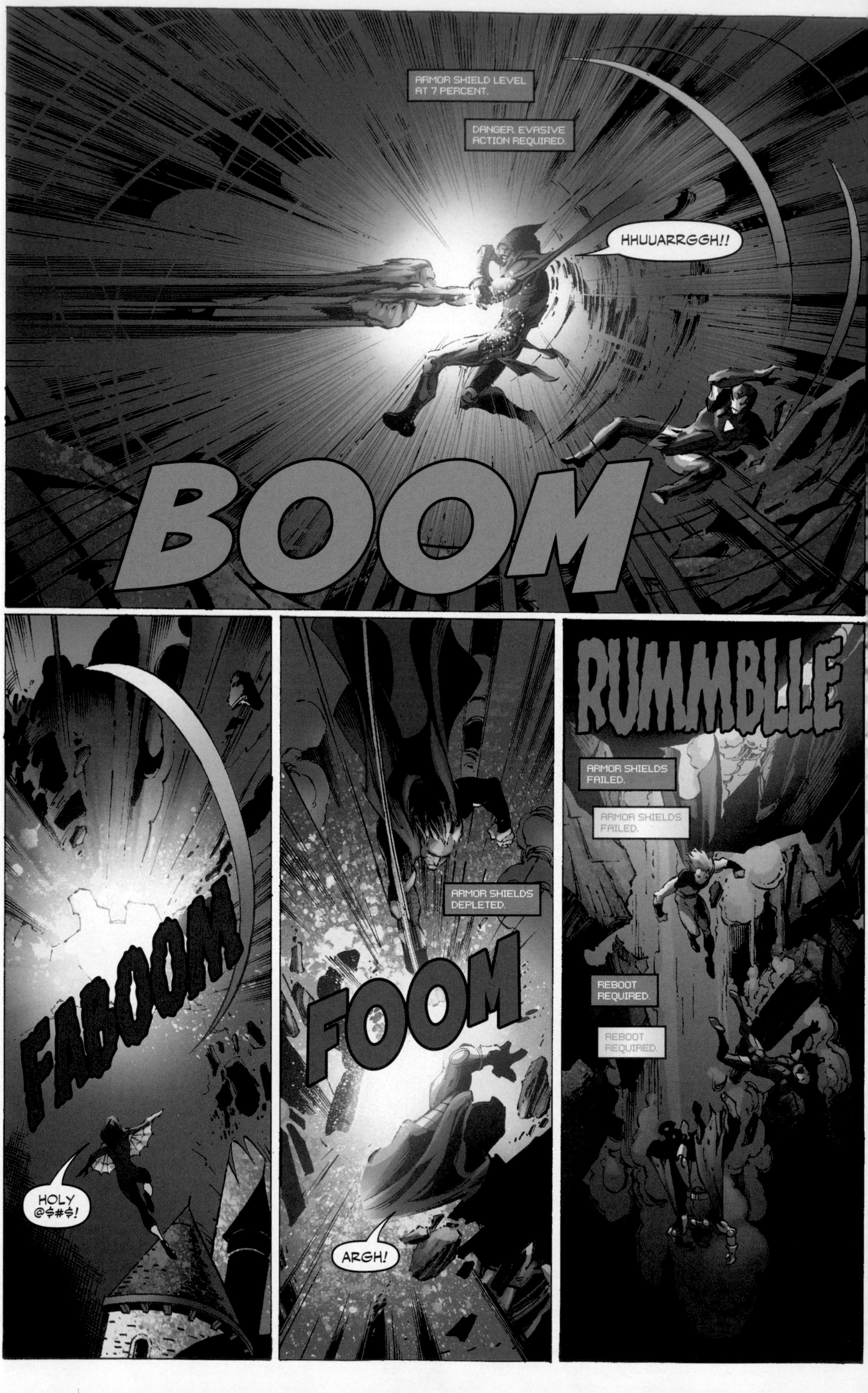

ARMOR SHIELD LEVEL AT 7 PERCENT.
DANGER. EVASIVE ACTION REQUIRED.
HHUUARRGGH!!
BOOM
FABOOM
HOLY @$#$!
ARMOR SHIELDS DEPLETED.
FOOM
ARGH!
RUMMBLLE
ARMOR SHIELDS FAILED.
ARMOR SHIELDS FAILED.
REBOOT REQUIRED.
REBOOT REQUIRED.

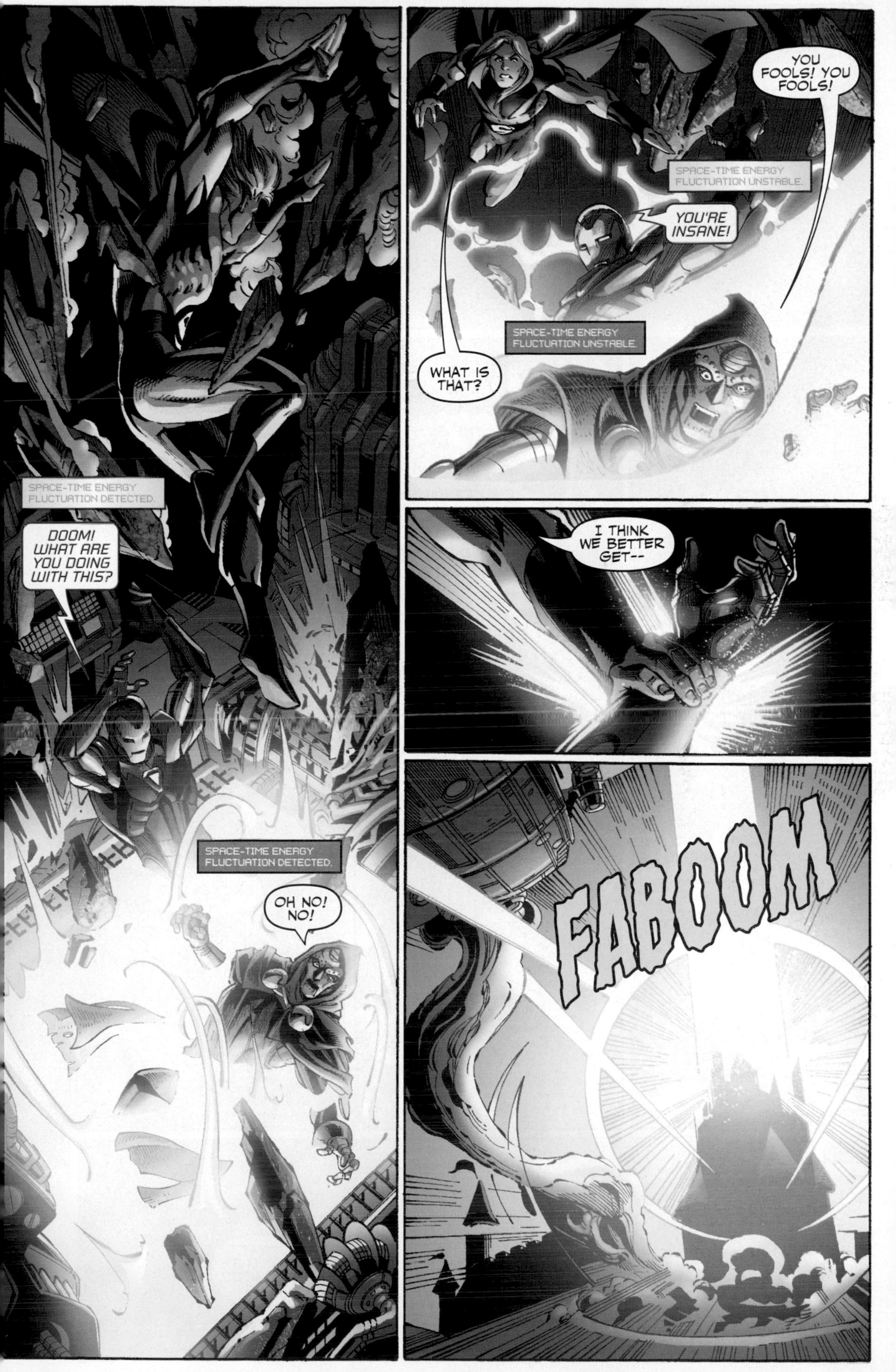
SPACE-TIME ENERGY FLUCTUATION DETECTED.
DOOM! WHAT ARE YOU DOING WITH THIS?
SPACE-TIME ENERGY FLUCTUATION DETECTED.
OH NO! NO!
YOU FOOLS! YOU FOOLS!
SPACE-TIME ENERGY FLUCTUATION UNSTABLE.
YOU'RE INSANE!
SPACE-TIME ENERGY FLUCTUATION UNSTABLE.
WHAT IS THAT?
I THINK WE BETTER GET--
FABOOM

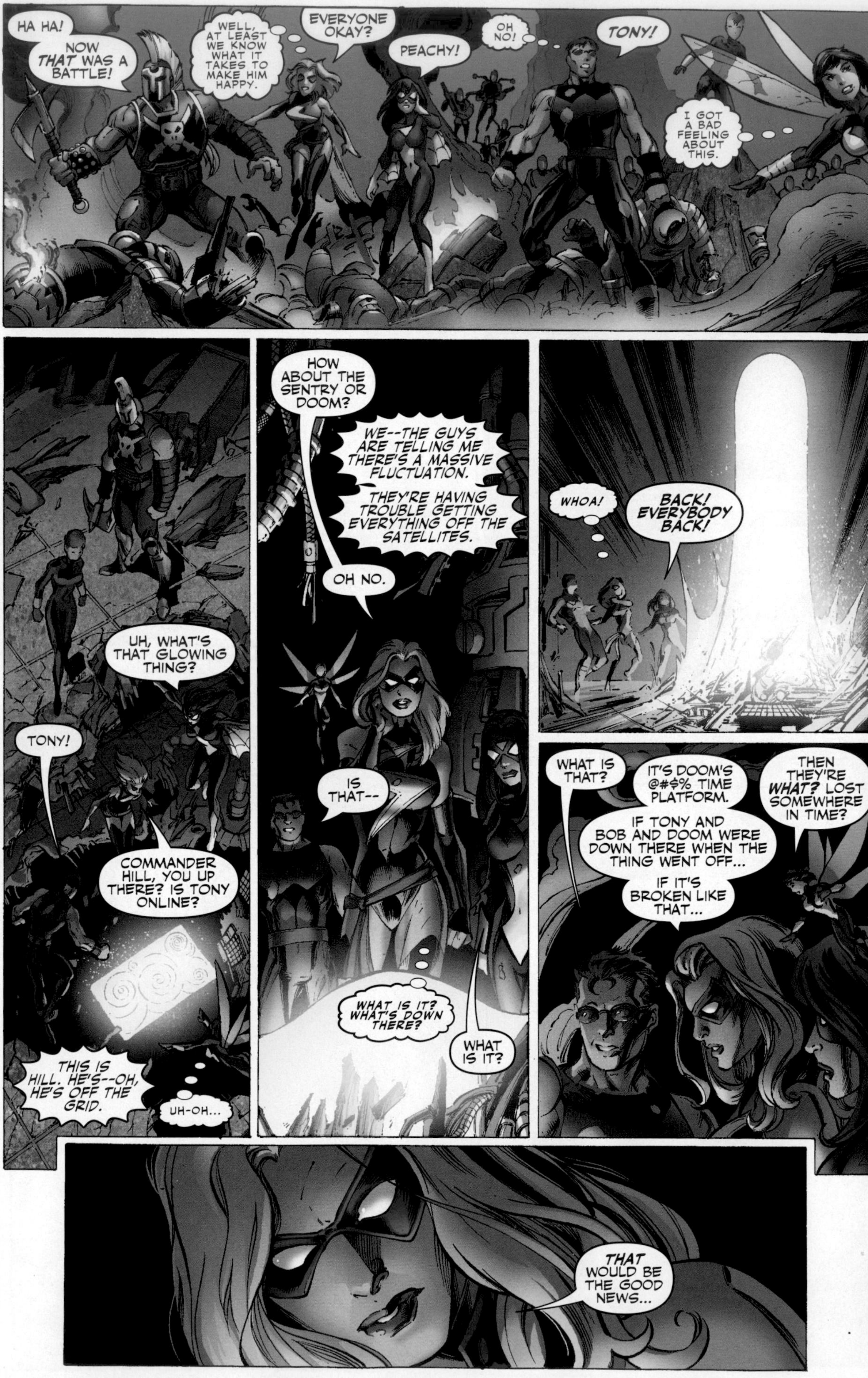
HA HA!
NOW THAT WAS A BATTLE!
WELL, AT LEAST WE KNOW WHAT IT TAKES TO MAKE HIM HAPPY.
EVERYONE OKAY?
PEACHY!
OH NO!
TONY!
I GOT A BAD FEELING ABOUT THIS.
UH, WHAT'S THAT GLOWING THING?
TONY!
COMMANDER HILL, YOU UP THERE? IS TONY ONLINE?
THIS IS HILL. HE'S--OH, HE'S OFF THE GRID.
UH-OH...
HOW ABOUT THE SENTRY OR DOOM?
WE--THE GUYS ARE TELLING ME THERE'S A MASSIVE FLUCTUATION.
THEY'RE HAVING TROUBLE GETTING EVERYTHING OFF THE SATELLITES.
OH NO.
IS THAT--
WHAT IS IT? WHAT'S DOWN THERE?
WHAT IS IT?
WHOA!
BACK! EVERYBODY BACK!
WHAT IS THAT?
IT'S DOOM'S @#$% TIME PLATFORM.
IF TONY AND BOB AND DOOM WERE DOWN THERE WHEN THE THING WENT OFF...
IF IT'S BROKEN LIKE THAT...
THEN THEY'RE WHAT? LOST SOMEWHERE IN TIME?
THAT WOULD BE THE GOOD NEWS...

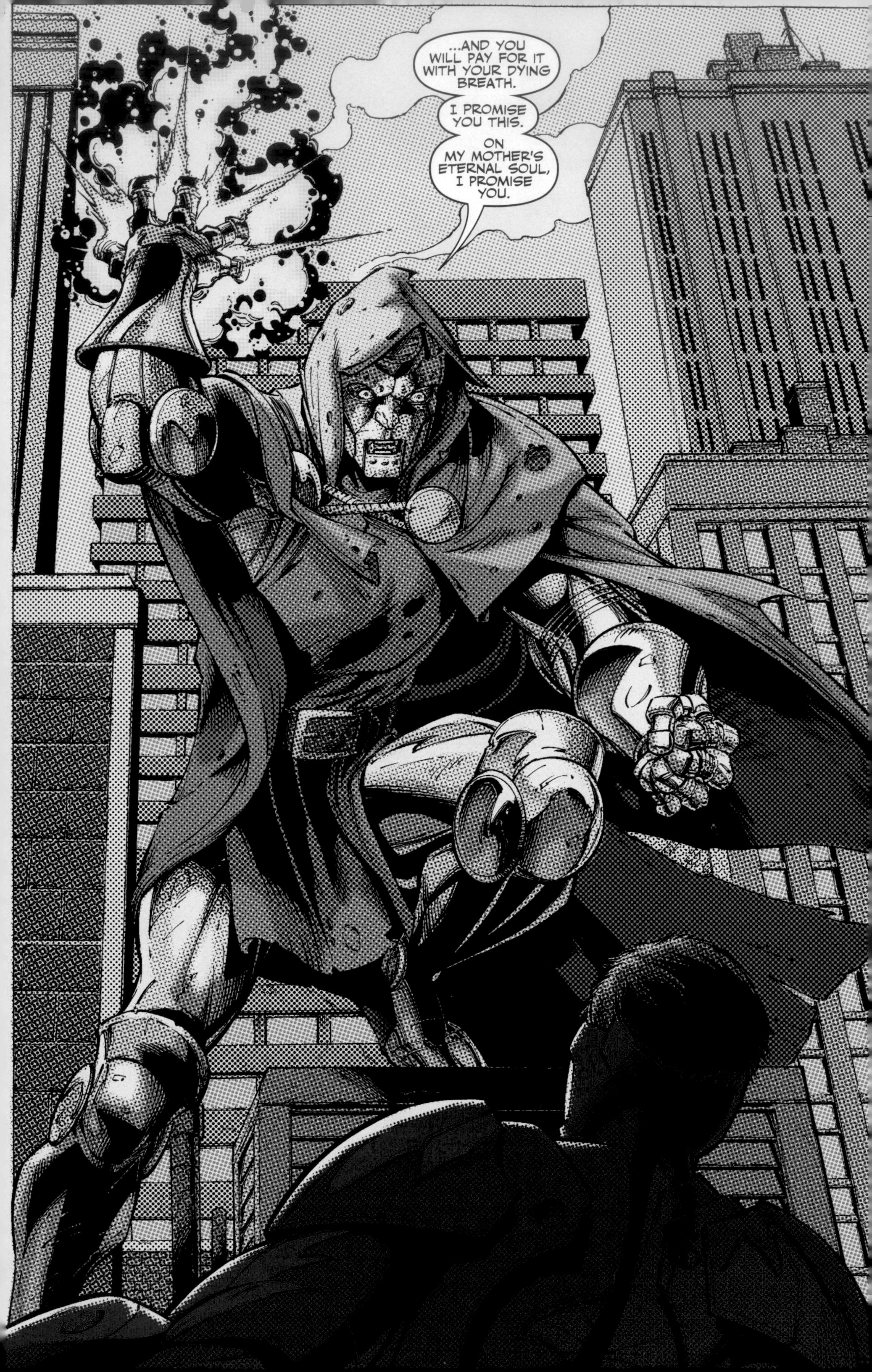
...AND YOU WILL PAY FOR IT WITH YOUR DYING BREATH.
I PROMISE YOU THIS.
ON MY MOTHER'S ETERNAL SOUL, I PROMISE YOU.

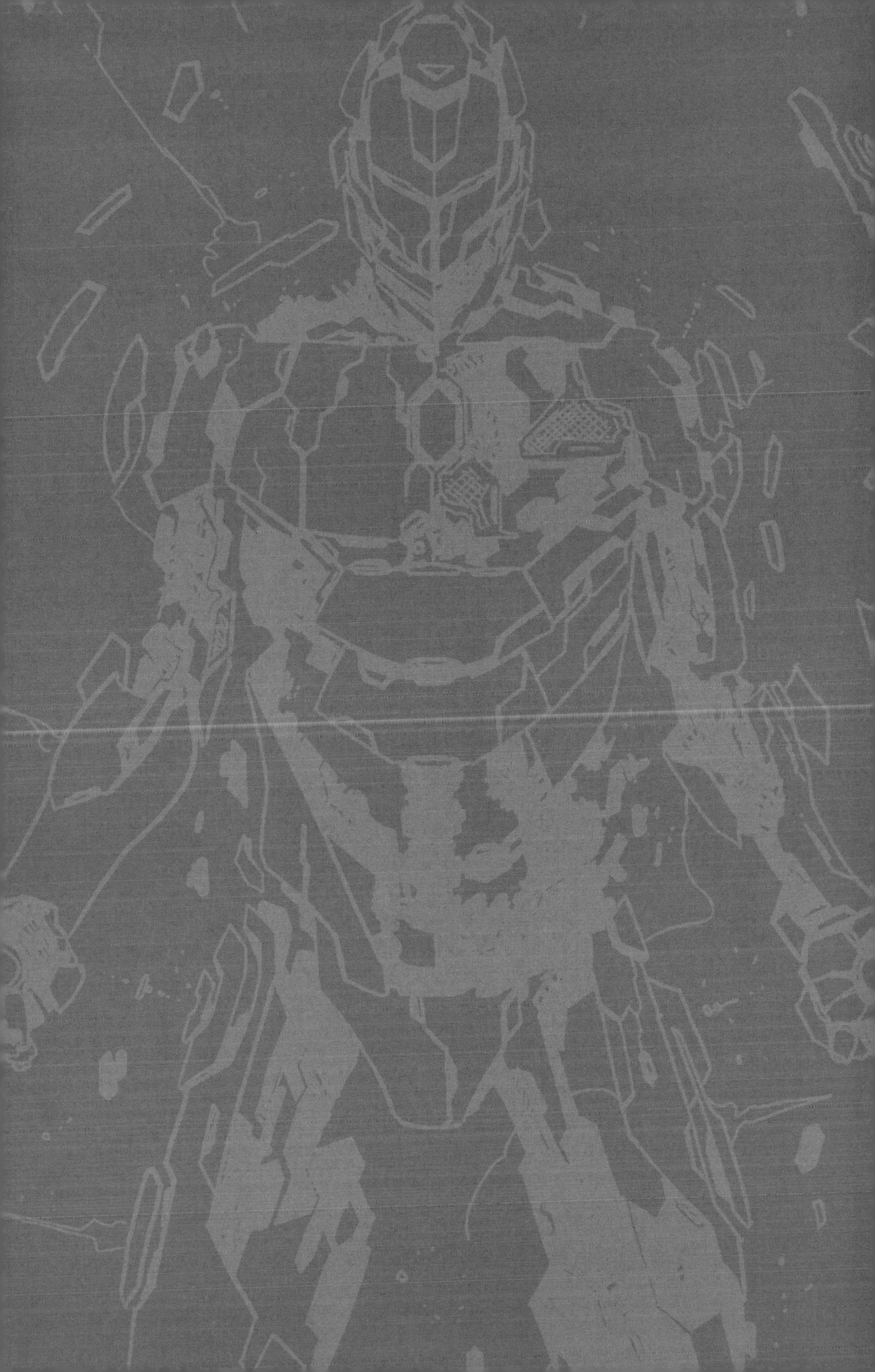

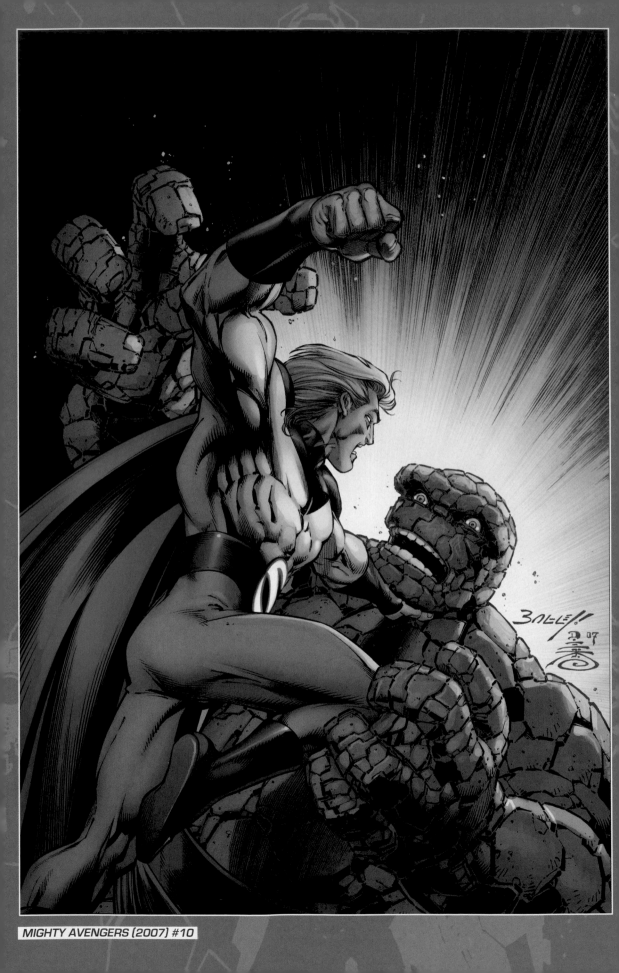

MIGHTY AVENGERS (2007) #10

And there came a *day*, a day unlike any *other*, when *Earth's mightiest heroes and heroines* found themselves *united* against a common threat. On that day, the *Avengers* were born — to fight the foes no *single* super hero could withstand! Through the years, their roster has *prospered*, changing *many times*, but their *glory* has never been denied! Heed the *call*, then — for now, the *Avengers Assemble!*

THE MIGHTY AVENGERS! ™

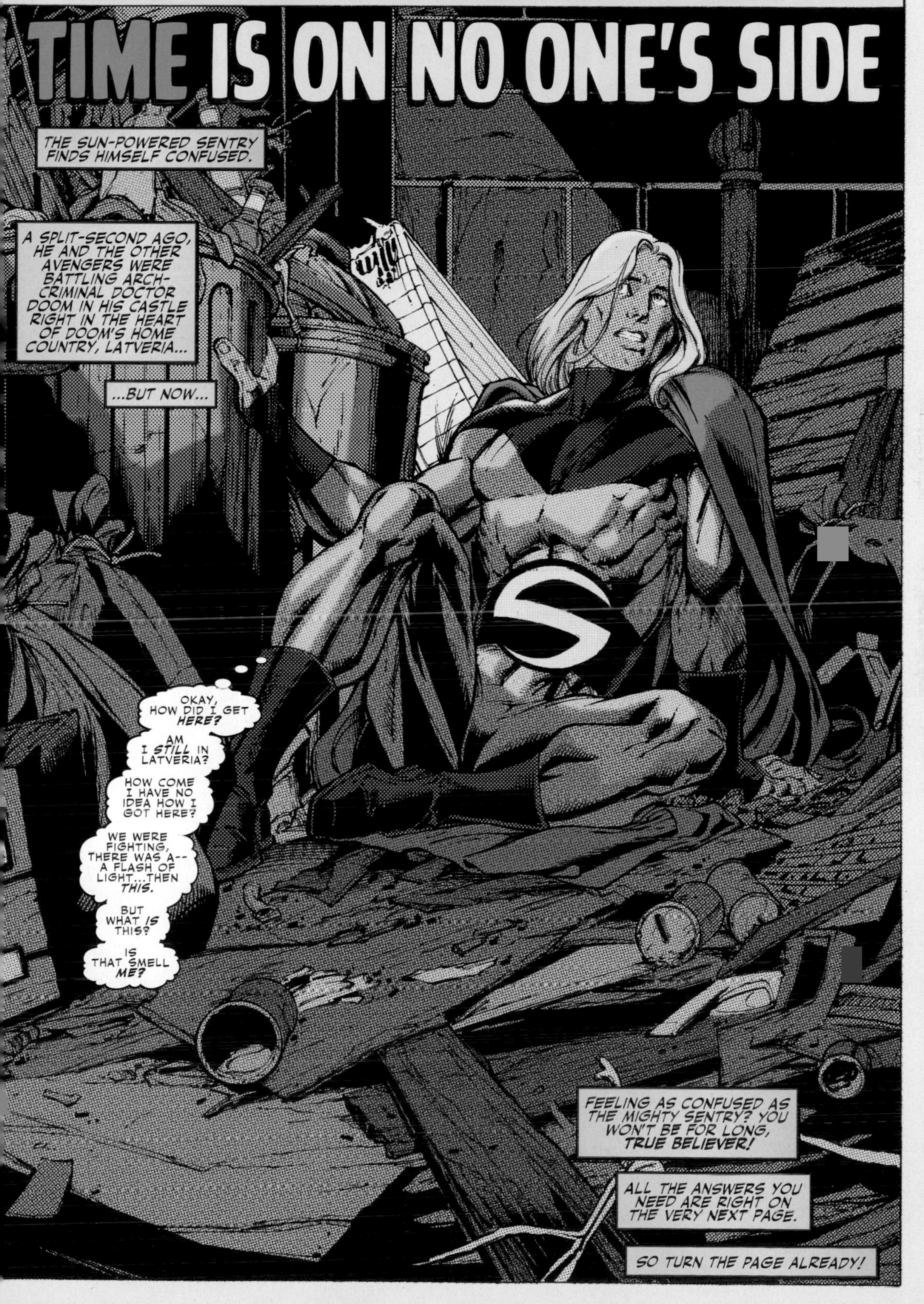
TIME IS ON NO ONE'S SIDE
THE SUN-POWERED SENTRY FINDS HIMSELF CONFUSED.
A SPLIT-SECOND AGO, HE AND THE OTHER AVENGERS WERE BATTLING ARCH-CRIMINAL DOCTOR DOOM IN HIS CASTLE RIGHT IN THE HEART OF DOOM'S HOME COUNTRY, LATVERIA...
...BUT NOW...
OKAY, HOW DID I GET HERE?
AM I STILL IN LATVERIA?
HOW COME I HAVE NO IDEA HOW I GOT HERE?
WE WERE FIGHTING, THERE WAS A-- A FLASH OF LIGHT...THEN THIS.
BUT WHAT IS THIS?
IS THAT SMELL ME?
FEELING AS CONFUSED AS THE MIGHTY SENTRY? YOU WON'T BE FOR LONG, TRUE BELIEVER!
ALL THE ANSWERS YOU NEED ARE RIGHT ON THE VERY NEXT PAGE.
SO TURN THE PAGE ALREADY!

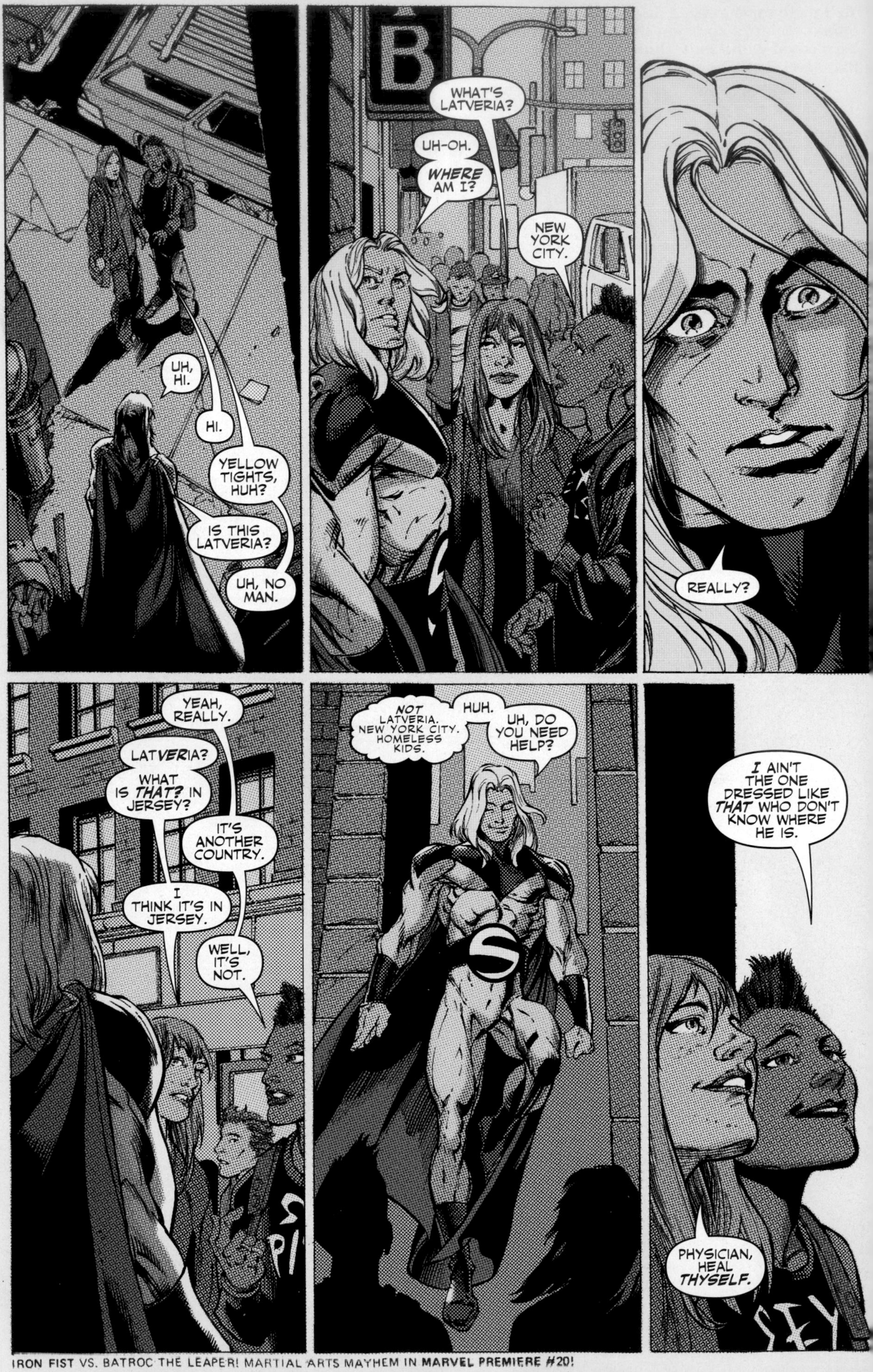
UH, HI.
HI.
YELLOW TIGHTS, HUH?
IS THIS LATVERIA?
UH, NO MAN.
WHAT'S LATVERIA?
UH-OH. *WHERE* AM I?
NEW YORK CITY.
REALLY?
YEAH, REALLY.
LAT*VER*IA?
WHAT IS *THAT?* IN JERSEY?
IT'S ANOTHER COUNTRY.
I THINK IT'S IN JERSEY.
WELL, IT'S NOT.
NOT LATVERIA. NEW YORK CITY. HOMELESS KIDS.
HUH.
UH, DO YOU NEED HELP?
I AIN'T THE ONE DRESSED LIKE *THAT* WHO DON'T KNOW WHERE HE IS.
PHYSICIAN, HEAL *THYSELF.*

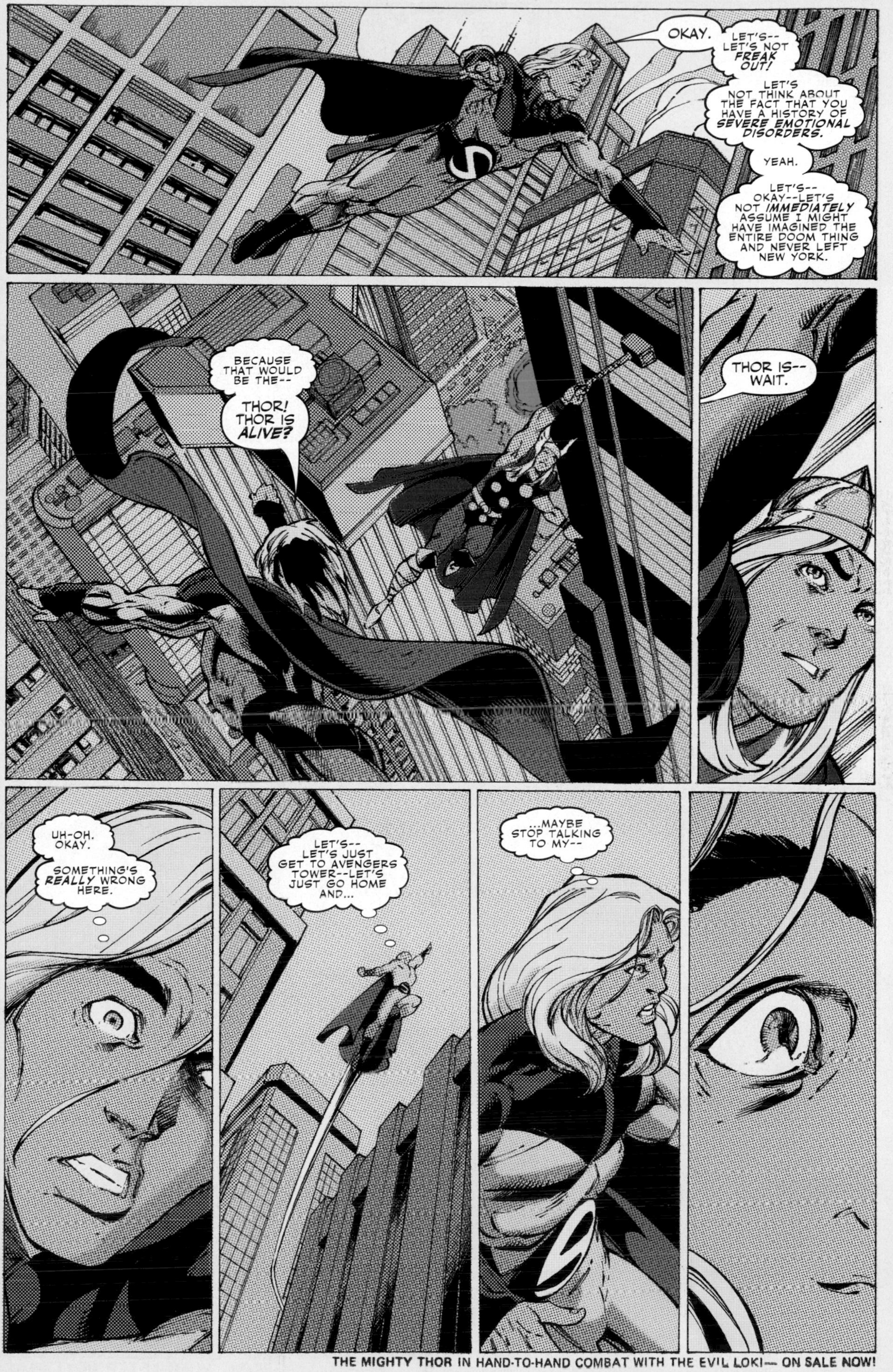
OKAY.
LET'S-- LET'S NOT FREAK OUT!
LET'S NOT THINK ABOUT THE FACT THAT YOU HAVE A HISTORY OF SEVERE EMOTIONAL DISORDERS.
YEAH.
LET'S-- OKAY--LET'S NOT IMMEDIATELY ASSUME I MIGHT HAVE IMAGINED THE ENTIRE DOOM THING AND NEVER LEFT NEW YORK.
BECAUSE THAT WOULD BE THE--
THOR! THOR IS ALIVE?
THOR IS-- WAIT.
UH-OH. OKAY.
SOMETHING'S REALLY WRONG HERE.
LET'S-- LET'S JUST GET TO AVENGERS TOWER--LET'S JUST GO HOME AND...
...MAYBE STOP TALKING TO MY--

CONTINUED AFTER NEXT PAGE

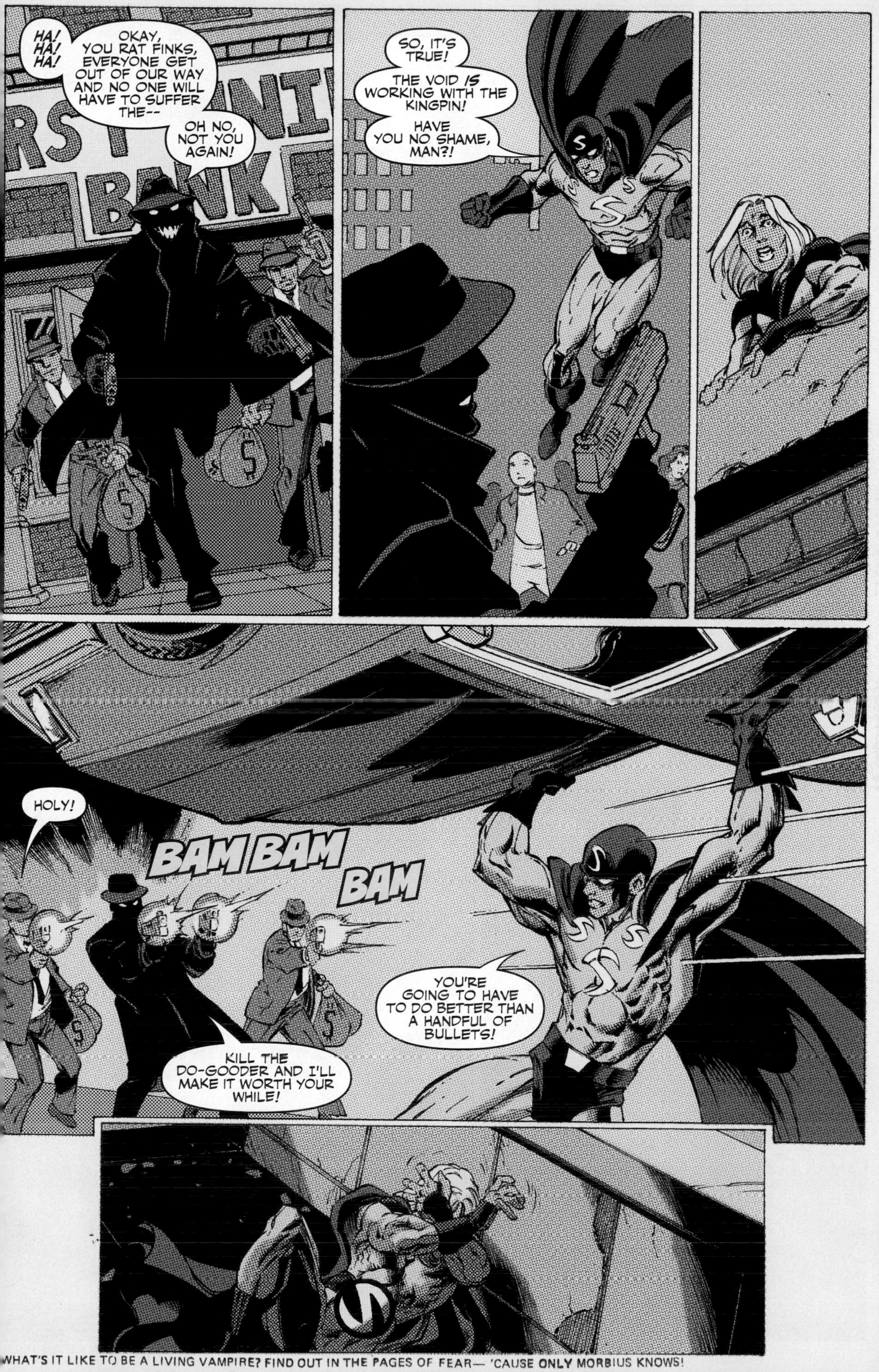
HA! HA! HA!
OKAY, YOU RAT FINKS, EVERYONE GET OUT OF OUR WAY AND NO ONE WILL HAVE TO SUFFER THE--
OH NO, NOT YOU AGAIN!
SO, IT'S TRUE!
THE VOID *IS* WORKING WITH THE KINGPIN!
HAVE YOU NO SHAME, MAN?!
HOLY!
BAM BAM BAM
YOU'RE GOING TO HAVE TO DO BETTER THAN A HANDFUL OF BULLETS!
KILL THE DO-GOODER AND I'LL MAKE IT WORTH YOUR WHILE!

NOW! THE BATTLE YOU'VE BEEN WAITING FOR—GHOST RIDER VS. THE HULK

CONTINUED AFTER NEXT PAGE

CONTINUED AFTER NEXT PAGE

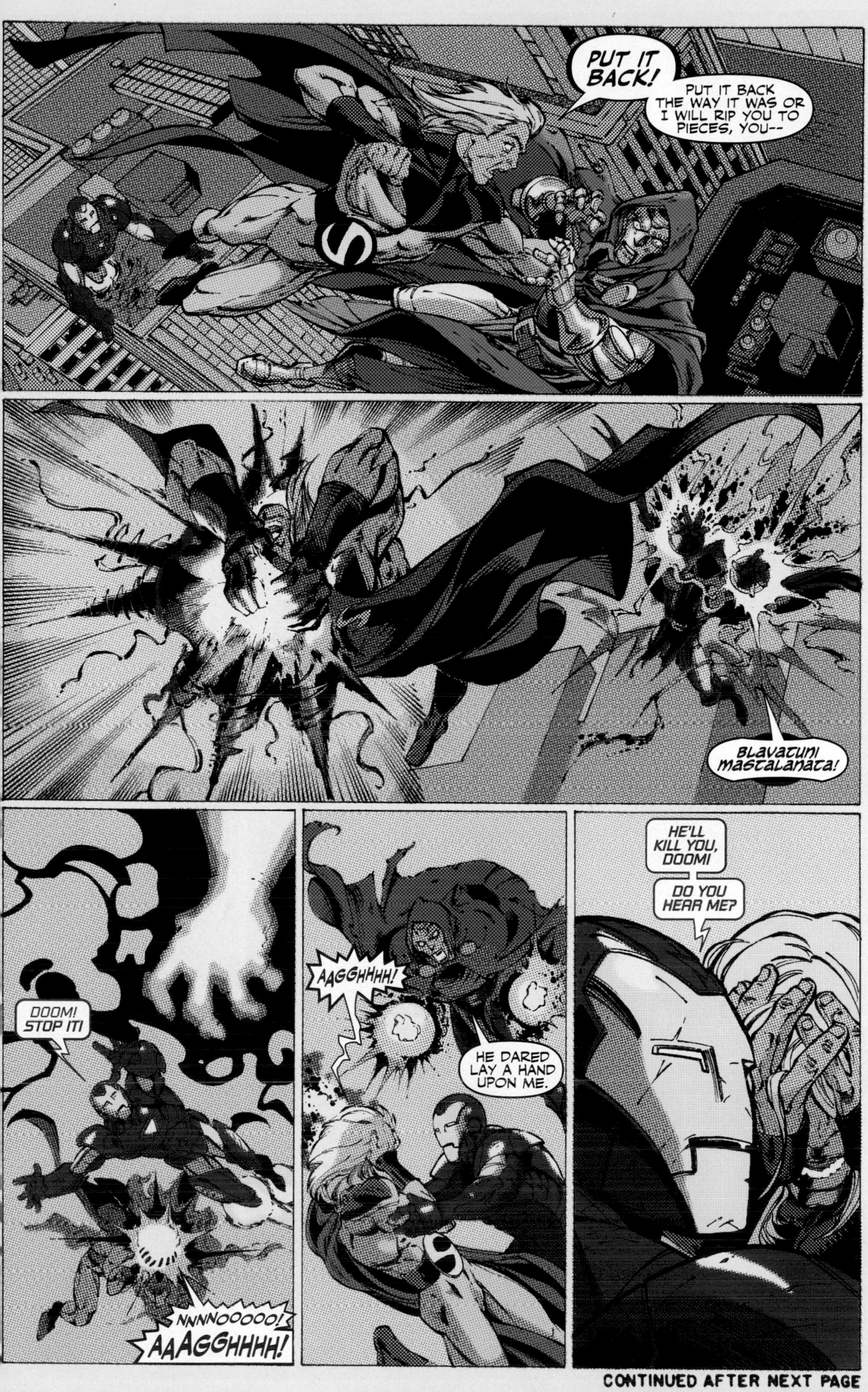
PUT IT BACK!
PUT IT BACK THE WAY IT WAS OR I WILL RIP YOU TO PIECES, YOU--
BLAVATUNI MASTALANATA!
DOOM! STOP IT!
NNNNOOOOO! AAAGGHHHH!
AAGGHHHH!
HE DARED LAY A HAND UPON ME.
HE'LL KILL YOU, DOOM!
DO YOU HEAR ME?

CONTINUED AFTER NEXT PAGE

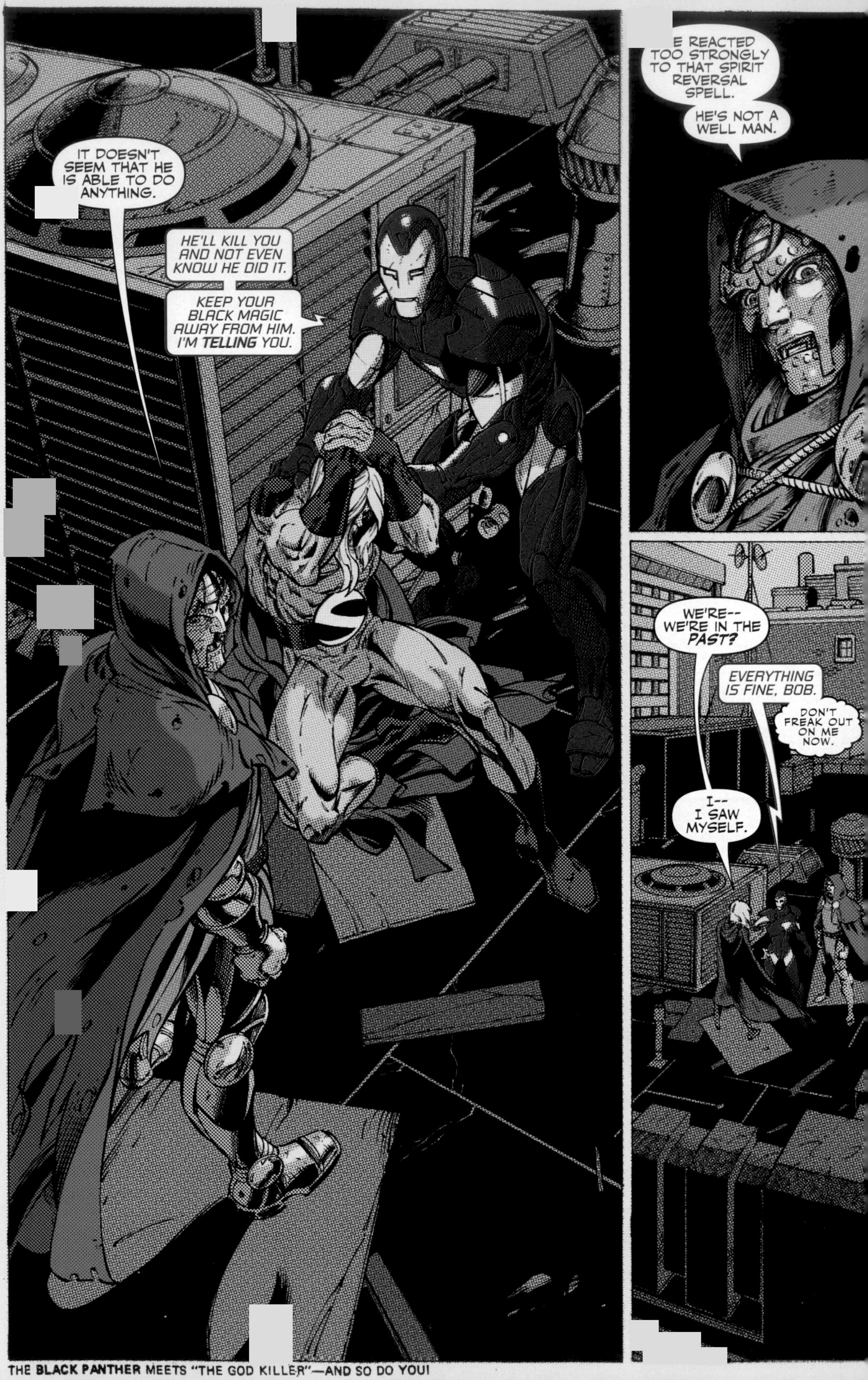
IT DOESN'T SEEM THAT HE IS ABLE TO DO ANYTHING.
HE'LL KILL YOU AND NOT EVEN KNOW HE DID IT.
KEEP YOUR BLACK MAGIC AWAY FROM HIM. I'M *TELLING* YOU.
E REACTED TOO STRONGLY TO THAT SPIRIT REVERSAL SPELL.
HE'S NOT A WELL MAN.
WE'RE-- WE'RE IN THE *PAST?*
EVERYTHING IS FINE, BOB.
DON'T FREAK OUT ON ME NOW.
I-- I SAW MYSELF.

THE **BLACK PANTHER** MEETS "THE GOD KILLER"—AND SO DO YOU!

OH, YEAH. BECAUSE OF THAT THING WITH THE PIRATES.

REGARDLESS. IT'S IN THERE.

LET'S GO. I WANT TO GET OUT OF HERE!

WE CAN'T JUST GO IN.

HE'S YOUR FRIEND. YOU COULD GET IN.

I COULD.

BUT THEN REED WOULD KNOW I WAS HERE AND THE POINT OF ALL THIS IS THAT WE DON'T WANT THEM KNOWING WE'RE HERE BECAUSE IT'LL CHANGE THE COURSE OF HUMAN HISTORY.

REED RICHARDS HAS ONE?

YES.

HOW DO YOU KNOW?

HE TOOK IT FROM ME.

IT'S THE BAXTER BUILDING. IT'S AS FORTIFIED AND SECURE AS ANYTHING ANYWHERE IN THE WORLD IS FORTIFIED AND SECURE.

ONE WOULD ARGUE THAT A MAN LIKE REED RICHARDS, LIKE YOU, LIKE MYSELF, HAS SEEN AND DONE SO MUCH...

...THAT A TIME-SPACE EVENT LIKE THIS WOULDN'T MATTER AS IT WOULD TO A COMMON PERSON WHO HAS HAD NO EXPERIENCE IN SUCH THINGS.

MAYBE.

BUT THAT'S AN AWFUL BIG GAMBLE.

I'D HATE TO BE WRONG AND WE GET BACK HOME AND THE APES HAVE TAKEN OVER BECAUSE OF SOMETHING WE SAID OR DID HERE.

I DON'T DISAGREE.

DOCTOR DOOM HAS SEEN "PLANET OF THE APES." THAT IS HARD TO PICTURE.

I-- I WANT TO GO HOME.

CONTINUED AFTER NEXT PAGE

CONTINUED AFTER NEXT PAGE

THE LIVING MUMMY VS. THE ELEMENTALS! THE WAR STARTS IN SUPERNATURAL THRILLERS "12!

IN GIANT-SIZE DEFENDERS #4: ENTER YELLOWJACKET... AND THE SQUADRON SINISTER MUST FOLLOW!

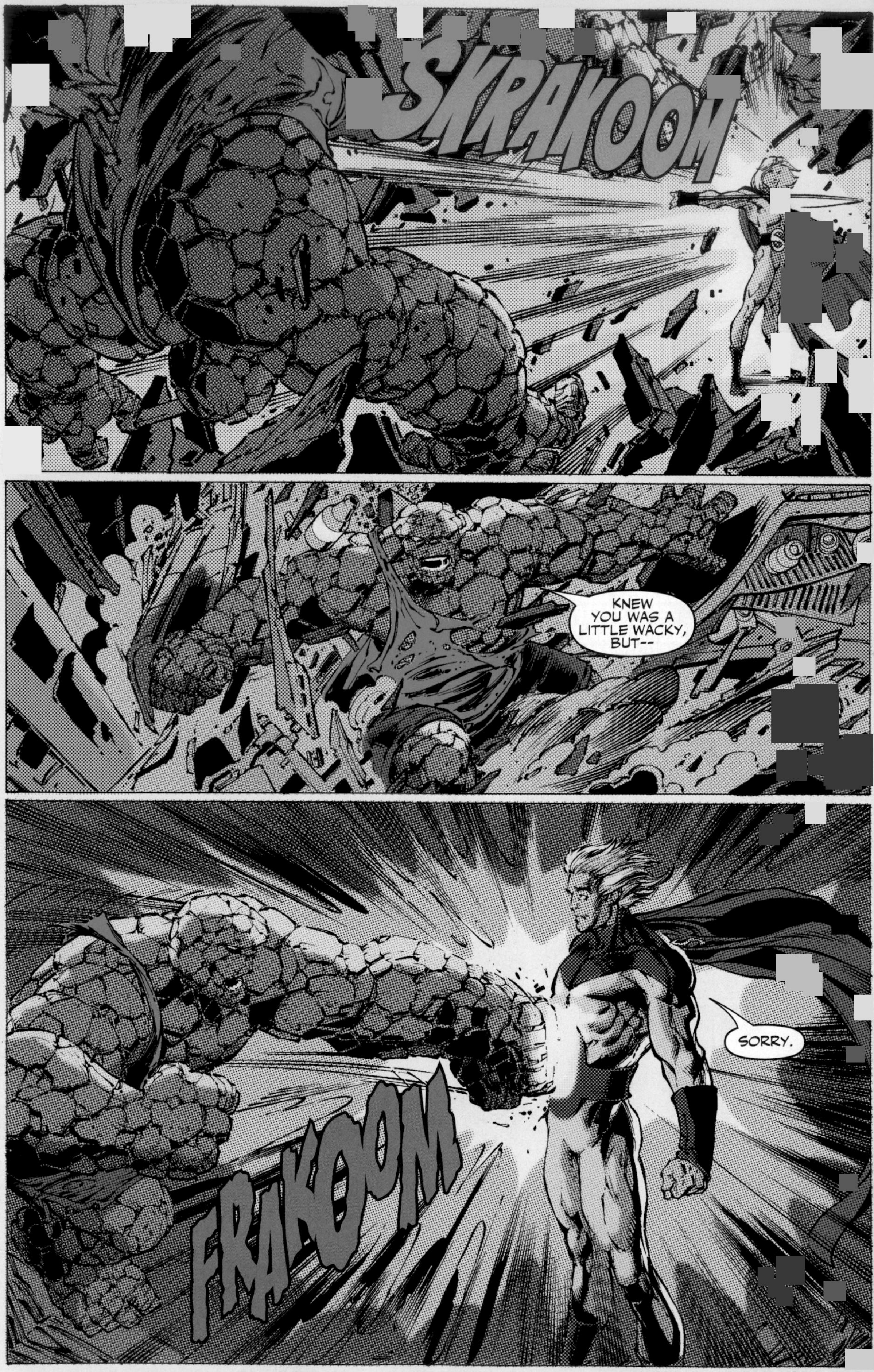
SKRAKOOM
KNEW YOU WAS A LITTLE WACKY, BUT--
SORRY.
FRAKOOM

CONTINUED AFTER NEXT PAGE

CONTINUED AFTER NEXT PAGE

THE SERPENT SQUAD STRIKES—IN CAPTAIN AMERICA #181!

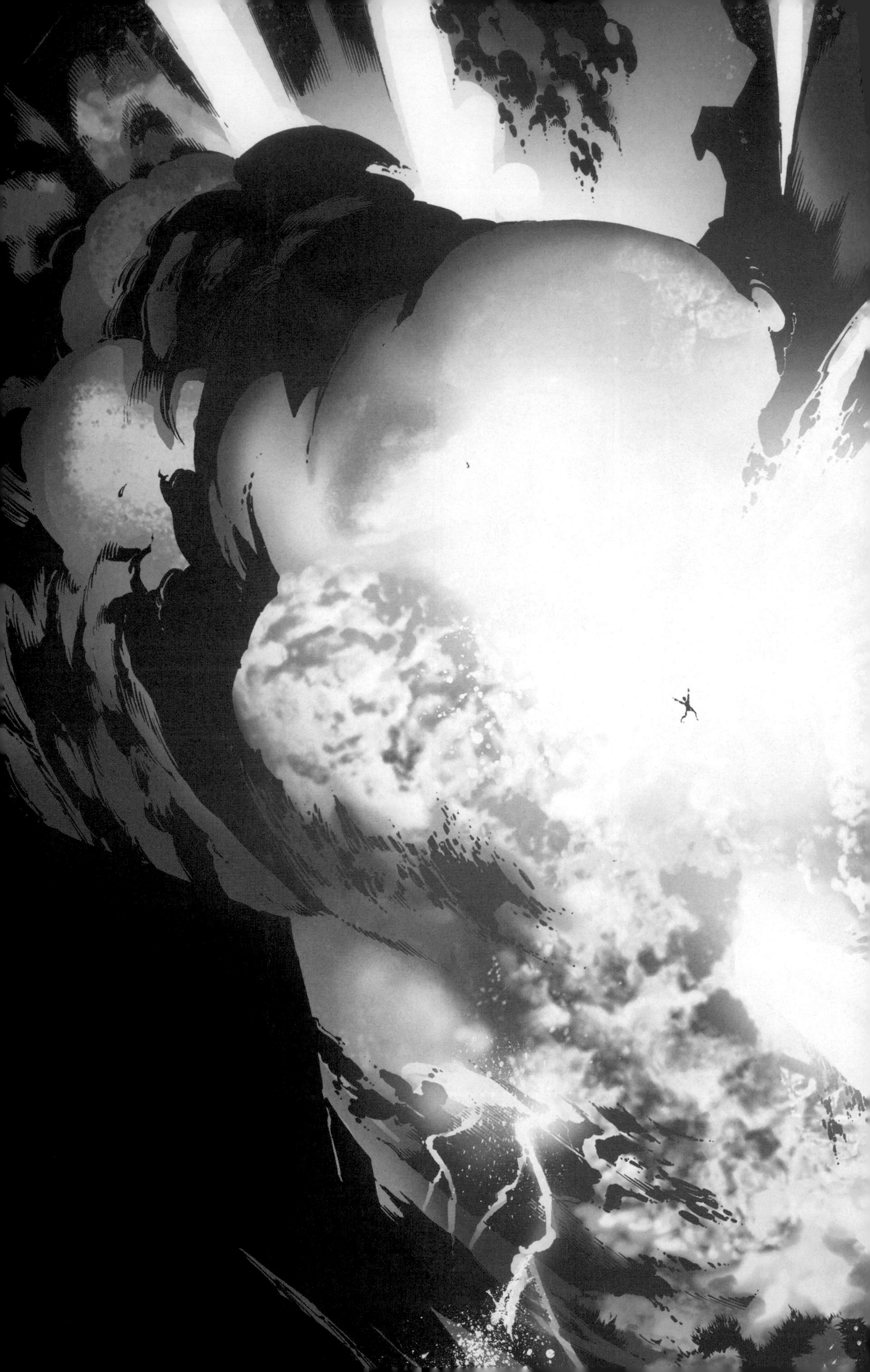

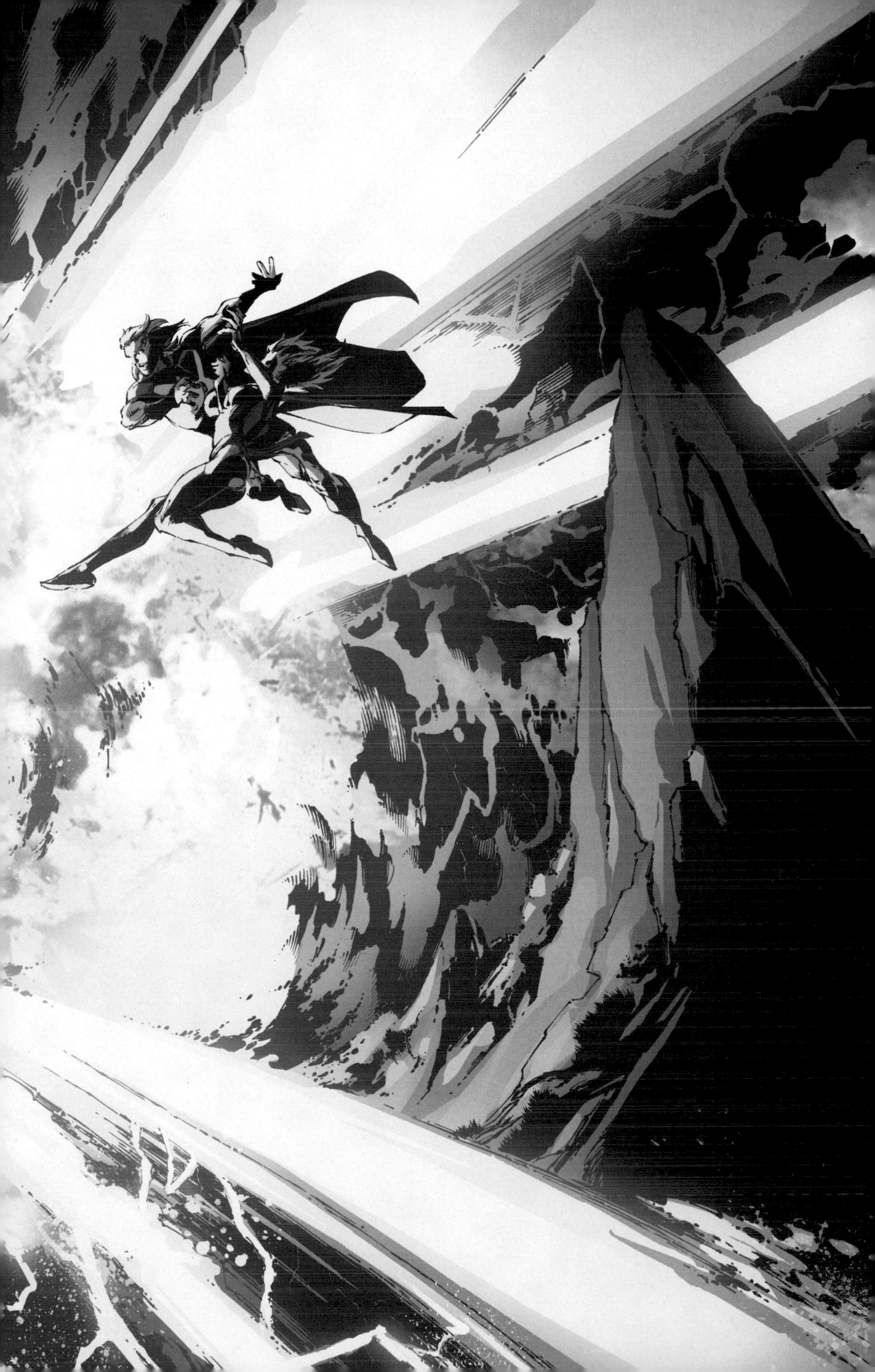

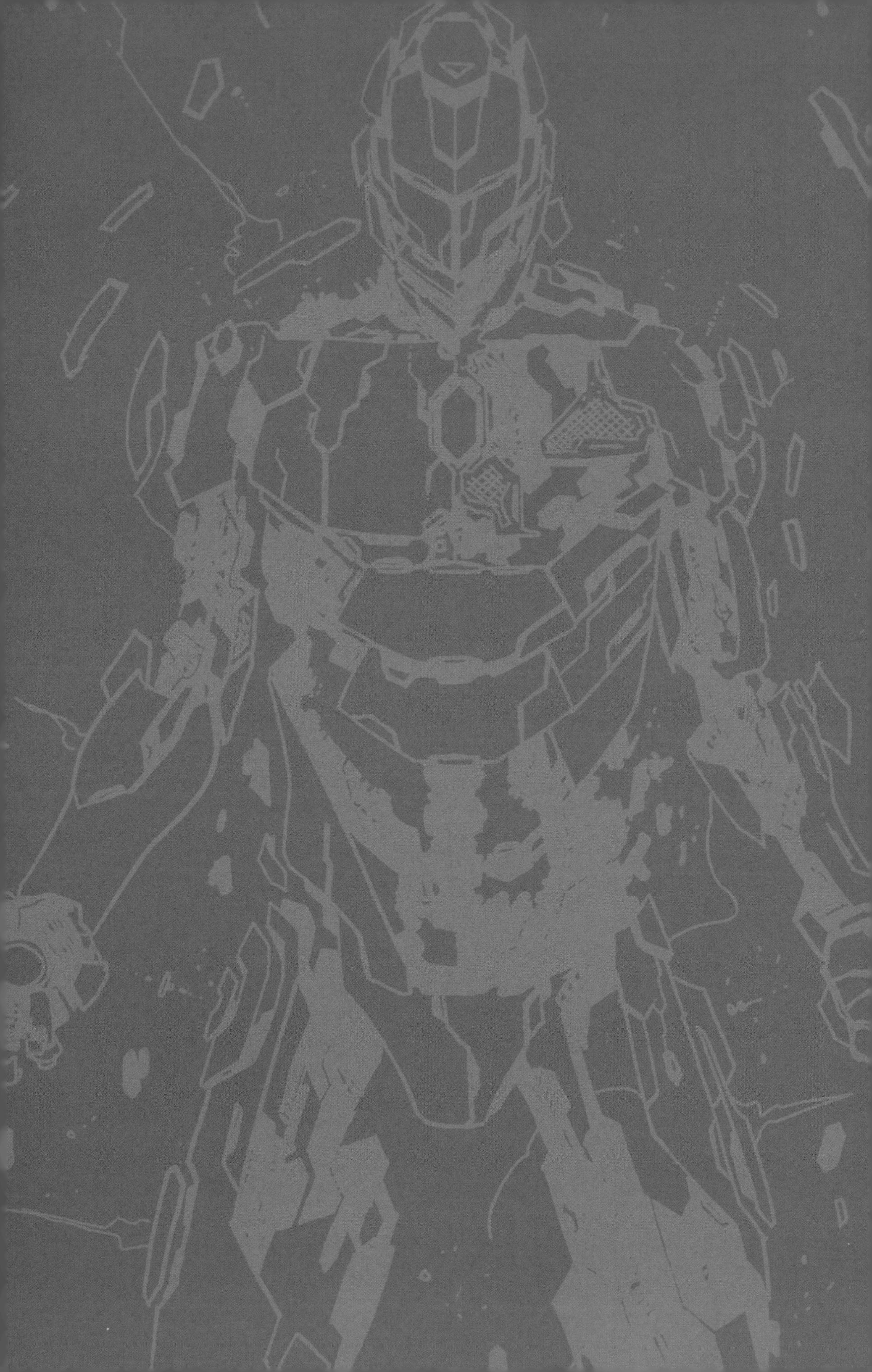

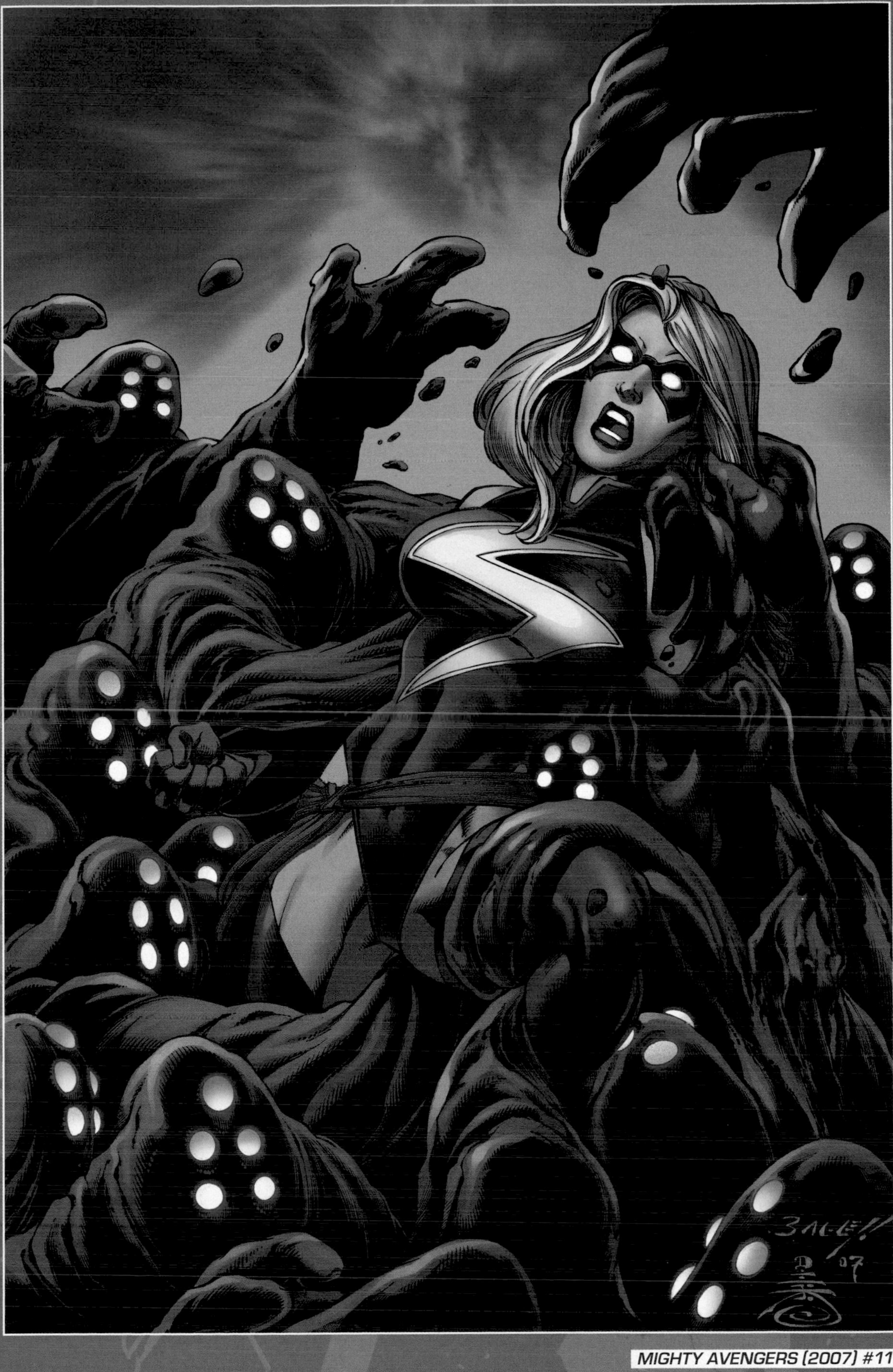
BALE!! '07

MIGHTY AVENGERS (2007) #11

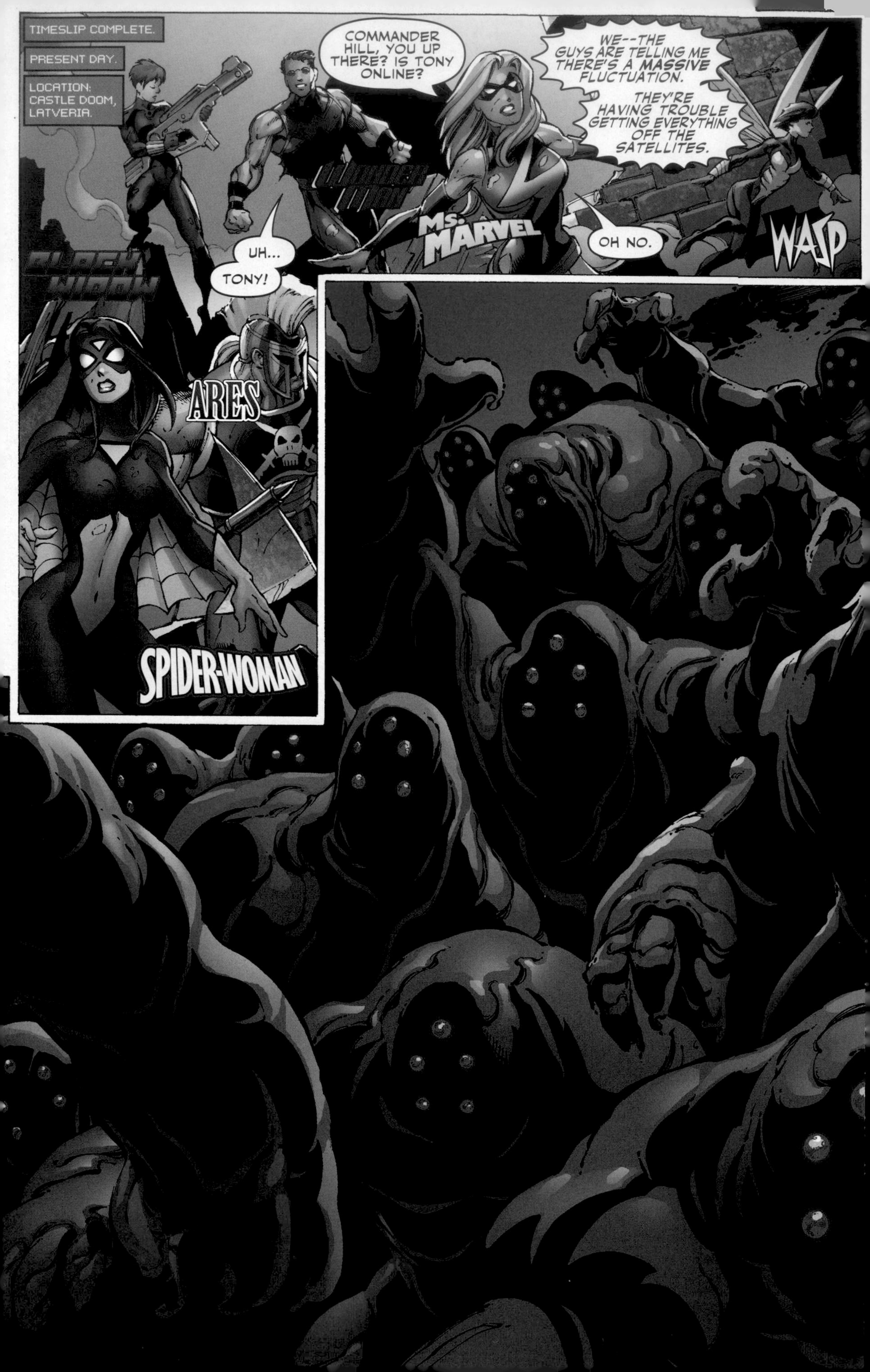
TIMESLIP COMPLETE.
PRESENT DAY.
LOCATION: CASTLE DOOM, LATVERIA.
COMMANDER HILL, YOU UP THERE? IS TONY ONLINE?
WE--THE GUYS ARE TELLING ME THERE'S A MASSIVE FLUCTUATION.
THEY'RE HAVING TROUBLE GETTING EVERYTHING OFF THE SATELLITES.
MS. MARVEL
WASP
UH...
TONY!
OH NO.
ARES
SPIDER-WOMAN

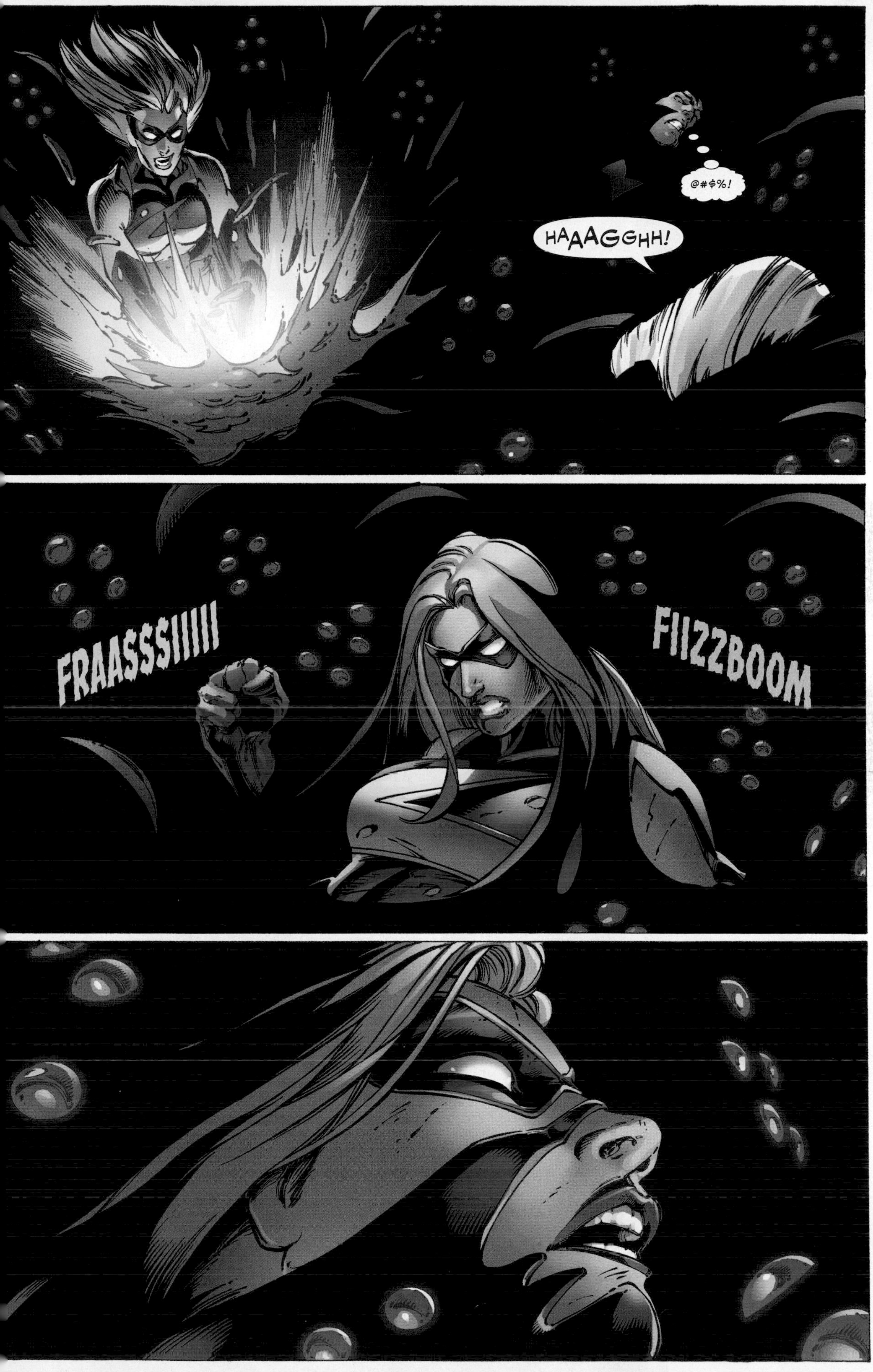
@#$%!
HAAAGGHH!
FRAASSSIIIIII
FIIZZBOOM

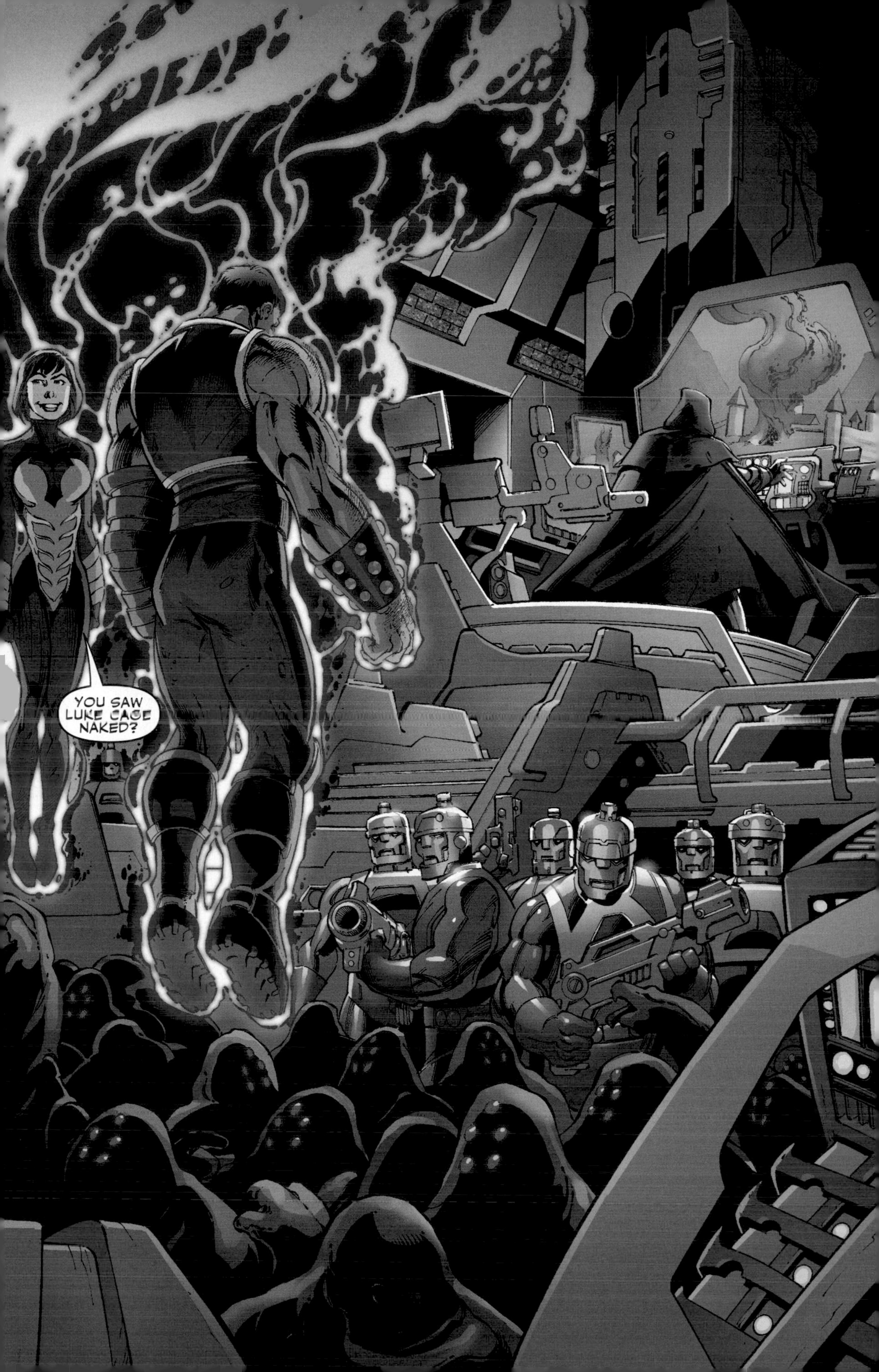
YOU SAW LUKE CAGE NAKED?

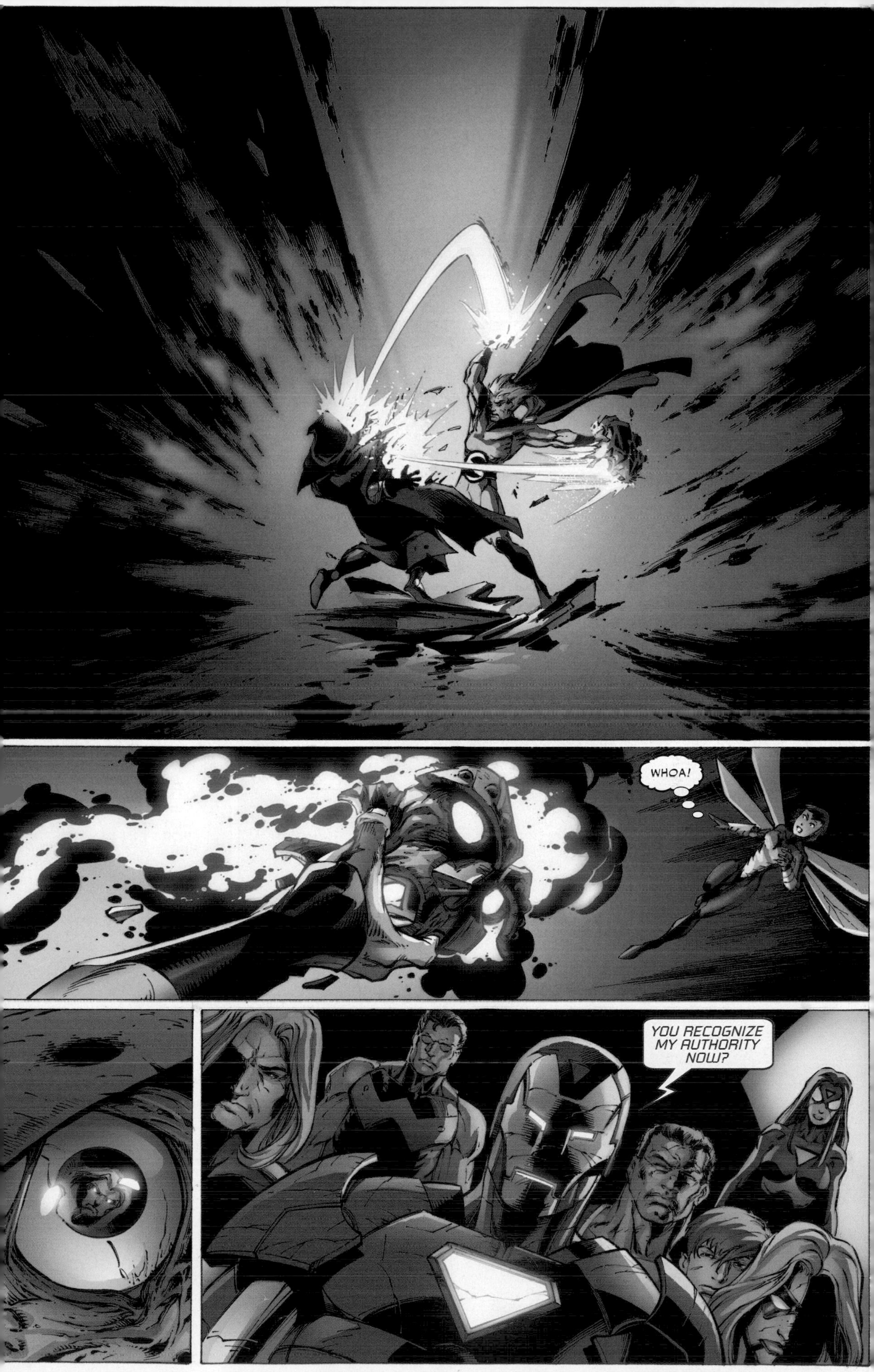
WHOA!
YOU RECOGNIZE MY AUTHORITY NOW?

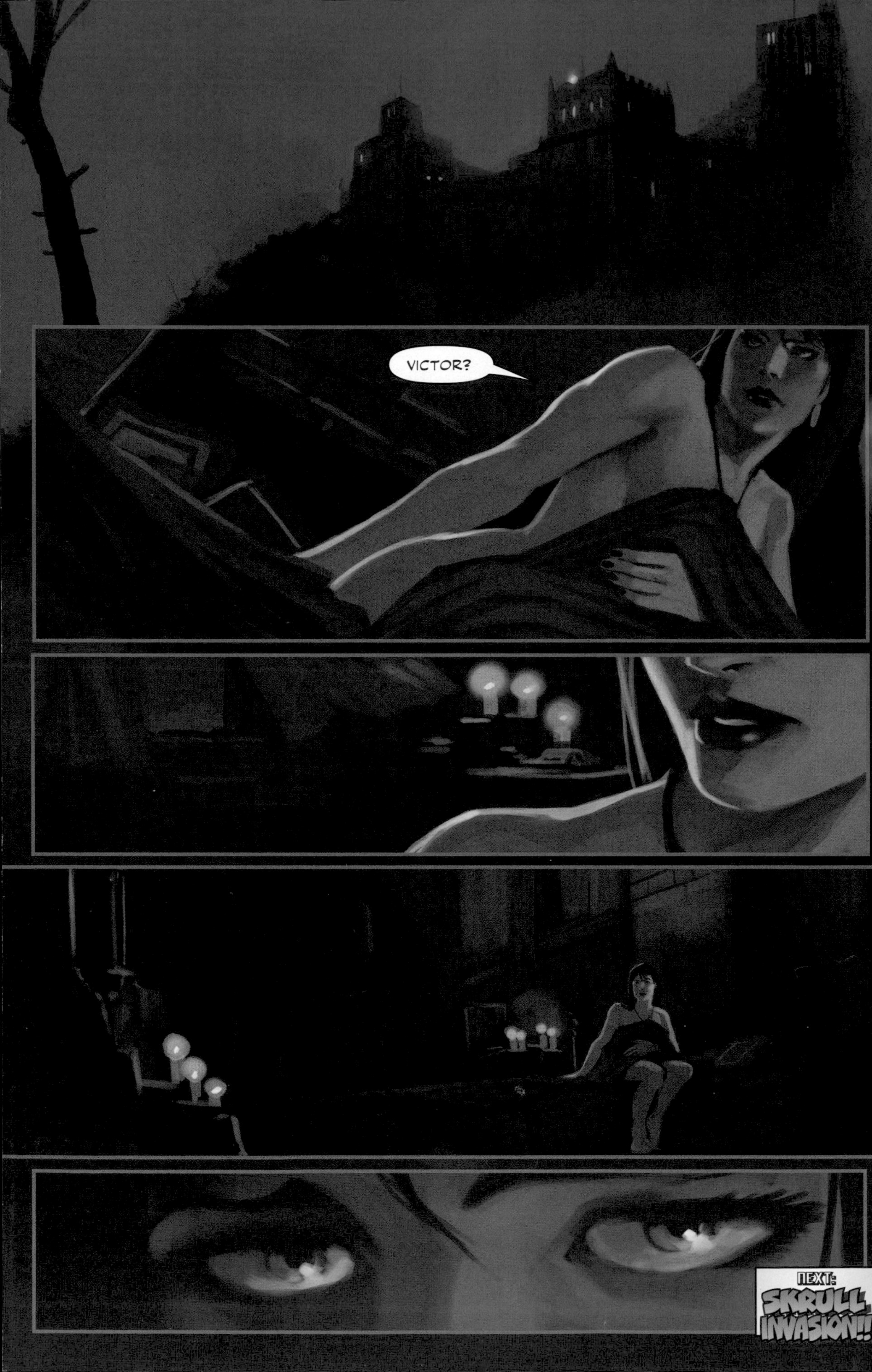
VICTOR?
NEXT:
SKRULL INVASION!!

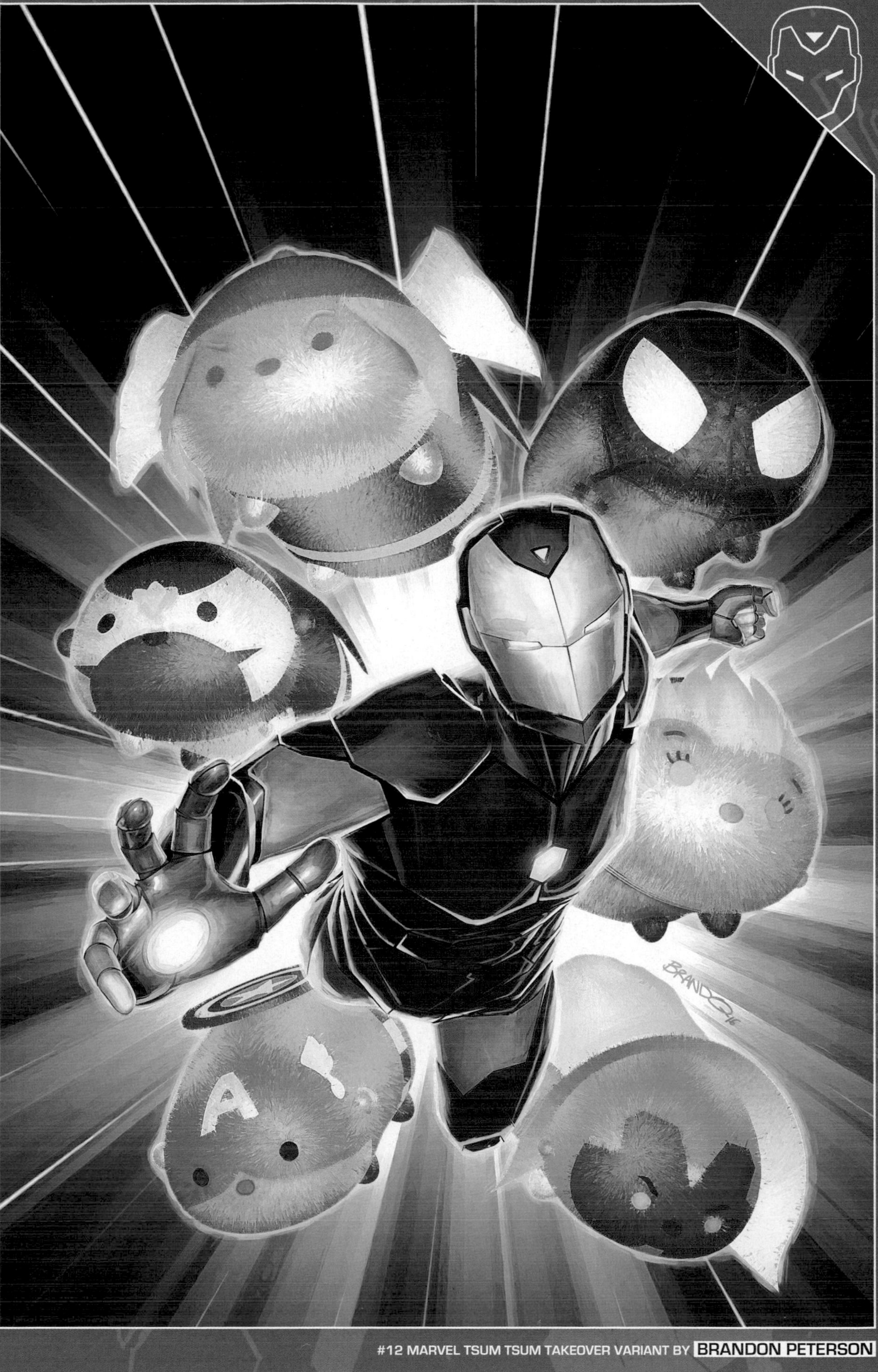
BRANDO '16

#12 MARVEL TSUM TSUM TAKEOVER VARIANT BY BRANDON PETERSON

FREE
DIGITAL COPY

TO REDEEM YOUR CODE FOR A FREE DIGITAL COPY:

1 GO TO MARVEL.COM/REDEEM. OFFER EXPIRES ON 2/8/19.

2 FOLLOW THE ON-SCREEN INSTRUCTIONS TO REDEEM YOUR DIGITAL COPY.

3 LAUNCH THE MARVEL COMICS APP TO READ YOUR COMIC NOW.

4 YOUR DIGITAL COPY WILL BE FOUND UNDER THE 'MY COMICS' TAB.

5 READ AND ENJOY.

YOUR FREE DIGITAL COPY WILL BE AVAILABLE ON:

MARVEL COMICS APP FOR APPLE IOS® DEVICES

MARVEL COMICS APP FOR ANDROID™ DEVICES

TMA3IBW2CB75